∽ · ∽ · ∽

"Occupational licensure as an interference in free markets gets less attention than its importance for both good and ill warrants. Morris Kleiner is our foremost expert on this important topic, and this book shares what he has learned. Whatever your policy instincts, this book provides important new insights. It is a great and valuable accomplishment."

—*Lawrence Summers, Charles W. Eliot University Professor at Harvard University*

"Morris Kleiner is the leading expert in the nation, and perhaps the world, on the causes and effects of occupational licensing. His book *Stages of Occupational Regulation* presents five case studies of occupations—interior designers, mortgage brokers, preschool teachers, electricians and plumbers, and dentists and hygienists—that are at different stages of government regulation, and then uses these case studies to provide new insights as to how regulation affects practitioners, consumers, and the public at large. His focus throughout is on the efficiency and equity impacts of regulation, and this very interesting, carefully researched, and well-written book will provide readers with a new appreciation of the importance of occupational regulation in American society."

—*Ronald G. Ehrenberg, Irving M. Ives Professor of Industrial and Labor Relations and Economics, Cornell University*

"*Stages of Occupational Regulation: Analysis of Case Studies* makes a great companion to Kleiner's previous book, *Licensing Occupations: Ensuring Quality or Restricting Competition?* In addition to providing an excellent summary of the literature, the book presents original research examining a broad range of effects of occupational licensing regulations—effects on wages, entry into the occupation, and adverse outcomes both for consumers and for licensed professionals. The book delves into how these effects differ among occupations that are licensed in only a handful of states, those that are universally licensed, and those with licensing regimes lying somewhere in between, describing the details of the economics and public policy issues at play. *Stages of Occupational Regulation* also contains a wealth of ideas for future research."

—*Bradley Larsen, Department of Economics, Stanford University*

∽ · ∽ · ∽

———— ∽ · ∽ · ∽ ————

"*Stages of Occupational Regulation* blends detailed institutional knowledge, historical perspective, and economic analysis to present the costs and benefits of the growing rate of occupational licensing in the U.S. economy. Kleiner is a clear and engaging narrator, using occupations at various stages of licensing requirements, from mortgage brokers to dental hygienists, to illustrate the political economy of heightened regulation and to clarify who wins and who loses from the process. This book, with its wealth of real-world detail, is a welcome companion to Kleiner's earlier statistical studies on occupational licensing and cements his place as the foremost expert on this important labor market institution."

—*Leah Boustan, Department of Economics, University of California at Los Angeles*

"*Stages of Occupational Regulation* asks searching questions concerning the use of occupational regulation as a policy lever. Where it is necessary, we are invited to consider the appropriate form that should be employed, and Professor Kleiner helpfully continues an important conversation about this oft-neglected topic."

—*Adam Parfitt, Executive Director, Council on Licensure, Enforcement, and Regulation (CLEAR)*

"Supported by cogent and persuasive historical, institutional, and quantitative analyses, *Stages of Occupational Regulation: Analysis of Case Studies* provides new insights into the evolution and impacts of occupational regulation on the U.S. economy."

—*Adriana D. Kugler, Vice-Provost for Faculty and Professor of Public Policy, Georgetown University*

"To paraphrase Tolstoy, all unlicensed professions are alike; each licensed profession is licensed in its own way. Morris Kleiner has shined a light on this increasingly pervasive labor market regulation with a variety of informative case studies, each of which helps us understand why professions are licensed, who is affected, and why it matters."

—*Charles Wheelan, Harris School of Public Policy, University of Chicago*

———— ∽ · ∽ · ∽ ————

Stages of Occupational Regulation

Stages of Occupational Regulation

Analysis of Case Studies

Morris M. Kleiner

2013

W.E. Upjohn Institute for Employment Research
Kalamazoo, Michigan

Library of Congress Cataloging-in-Publication Data

Kleiner, Morris M.
  Stages of occupational regulation : analysis of case studies / Morris M. Kleiner.
    pages cm
  Includes bibliographical references and index.
  ISBN 978-0-88099-459-0 (pbk. : alk. paper) — ISBN 0-88099-459-2 (pbk. : alk.
paper) — ISBN 978-0-88099-460-6 (hardcover : alk. paper) — ISBN 0-88099-460-6
(hardcover : alk. paper)
  1. Occupations—Licenses—United States. 2. Professions—Licenses—United
States. 3. Trade regulation—United States. 4. Labor market—United States. I. Title.
  HD3630.U7K5753 2013
  331.7'10973—dc23
                                    2013031945

The facts presented in this study and the observations and viewpoints expressed are
the sole responsibility of the author. They do not necessarily represent positions of
the W.E. Upjohn Institute for Employment Research.

Cover design by Alcorn Publication Design.
Index prepared by Diane Worden.
Printed in the United States of America.
Printed on recycled paper.

Contents

Figures

Tables

Boxes

Preface

I was left wanting more . . . I liken it to the cliffhanger in a work of fiction; it has made me eager for the next installment.

—Alice Ramey (2010), Bureau of Labor Statistics economist, in her review of *Licensing Occupations: Ensuring Quality or Restricting Competition?*

As this epigraph attests, I am reasonably certain that at least one reader was on the edge of her seat while turning the pages of my last book, *Licensing Occupations: Ensuring Quality or Restricting Competition?*, published by the W.E. Upjohn Institute for Employment Research in 2006. Occupational licensing is not a topic that often gets mentioned with the same sense of anticipation as a Robert Ludlum spellbinder or a Sherlock Holmes mystery, but I will take modest praise wherever I can find it. Therefore, to satisfy the wishes of Alice Ramey and any other readers for a follow-up work, I have written this current book.

The goal of this book is to provide new insights into how occupational regulation influences practitioners, consumers, and the public. To accomplish this goal, I provide detailed case studies of occupations at various stages of governmental regulation. The occupations selected are those of interior designers, mortgage brokers, preschool teachers, electricians and plumbers, and dentists and hygienists. Although the groups examined were not randomly selected, they reflect large occupational groups that have important economic and labor market effects.

Each chapter presents the evolution and anatomy of each profession. It asks why the occupation sought licensing or other forms of governmental regulation. Furthermore, it seeks to explain to what extent regulation has changed over time and whether there is a convergence of state regulations to a national standard. What qualitative changes have occurred within the occupation? Have individuals that have attained an occupational license gained higher wages as a consequence? Have other nonmonetary outcomes within the occupation been influenced by regulation? Have consumers been affected by regulations through changes in prices and the quality of the service? To what extent do the duration and intensity of governmental regulations influence the members of the profession?

By analyzing these questions, I have attempted to focus on the relevance of each issue with as much economic and statistical rigor as possible. Furthermore, I have attempted to examine the equity and efficiency trade-offs as these occupations become more highly regulated over time. Specifically, to what extent is access to the regulated service reduced for those whose incomes are low? In contrast, do higher-income individuals gain by having more good-quality service providers with higher levels of training and experience? George Shultz, the astute academic and later premier statesman, opined that lags occur with general public policy issues, but that politicians are impatient (Shultz 1995). Occupational licensing generally fits this model, since it is an institution whose effects are not immediately apparent, but rather reveal their efficacy over some time. Specifically, occupational licensing usually does not regulate current practitioners, implements new exams, and develops educational and location-specific requirements so that implementing these policies takes many years. Consequently, the labor market or consumer outcomes are not immediately apparent. Understanding this institution requires a longer-run perspective before wage, price, quality, and distributional effects can be fully realized. An approach that evaluates the various stages of occupational regulation can help capture and illuminate the role that this institution has in labor and service markets.

To correspond with my initial lengthy examination of the topic, readers should bring some knowledge of economics and statistics to this work in order to fully understand the material. General readers without this background, however, should have little difficulty comprehending the major portions of the book and will be able to understand its key elements. Even when the material becomes more specialized, readers without a technical background may judiciously push on, since the essential arguments and evidence explained in the book are easily understood.

—Morris M. Kleiner

Acknowledgments

I am most grateful to a large number of individuals and institutions for their assistance in researching and writing this book. For their most valuable assistance I thank Hwikwon Ham, Matthew Hendricks, Grant Hoheisel, Kwon Won Park, and Evgeny Vorotnikov. The staff at the Herman Reference Room of the Center for Human Resources and Industrial Relations at the University of Minnesota, the library staff at the Federal Reserve Bank of Minneapolis, and the librarians at the W.E. Upjohn Institute for Employment Research all provided valued assistance. The staff and especially Jim Poterba at the National Bureau of Economic Research were most helpful in their administrative efforts to see the project to fruition. Elaine Pioske at the Humphrey School of Public Affairs provided much-appreciated administrative support.

Helpful comments for several parts of the book were provided by many of my colleagues. I am particularly indebted to Richard Todd for his earlier work with me on Chapter 3. Also, I am grateful to Kevin Hallock and Samuel Kleiner for their comments on various sections of the book. Participants in seminars at the University of Minnesota, Harvard University, Princeton University, Cornell University, the London School of Economics, the National Bureau of Economic Research, the Bureau of Labor Statistics, the Federal Trade Commission, the Allied Social Science Associations, and the International Congress on Professional and Occupational Regulation provided helpful suggestions.

The economists at the Federal Reserve Bank of Minneapolis provided useful discussions that informed my analysis. I particularly want to thank Arthur Rolnick for his support of my research program during his tenure as director of research. I also want to thank Narayana Kocherlakota and Kei-Mu Yi for their continued support of my work on occupational regulation and the labor market. The staff at the Federal Reserve Bank of Minneapolis was most supportive, and I especially want to thank Joan Gieseke, who provided outstanding editorial assistance, and Barbara Drucker, who ably assisted with much-appreciated administrative support.

I was most fortunate to spend the better part of four summers working in the productive and enjoyable work environment of the Upjohn Institute as a visiting scholar. I was most fortunate to have the counsel and encouragement of the director, Randall Eberts, who also served as the monitor of the research project. I am especially grateful to Benjamin Jones, who read and commented on the entire manuscript. Jing Cai provided excellent research assistance for many of the chapters. Richard Wyrwa gave me useful feedback on the manuscript. Furthermore, the anonymous reviewers of the initial manuscript provided exceptionally useful comments for all the chapters in the book. The intellectual environment provided by the economists at the Upjohn Institute was exceptional.

The Center for Construction Research and Training financially supported and provided advice for the chapter on licensing in the construction industry. The cooperation of the Bureau of Labor Statistics was most beneficial, especially that of Brooks Pierce and Anthony Barkume, who worked patiently with me to explain the use of the proprietary data on construction occupational health and safety. I would like to thank Bari Elias, Yoav Elias, Yifat Kleiner, Anat Szendro, Keith Vargo, and Ellen Weinstein for their assistance with the cover for the book.

During my stays at the Upjohn Institute, largely spent working on this book, Jim and Sheryl Siegel and their family were the best hosts a visitor to Michigan could have asked for, and their friendship and stimulating conversations during my many stays in Michigan were delights. My immediate and extended family was most understanding while I worked on the book. Finally and most importantly, I want to thank Sally Mosow Kleiner for her encouragement, technical knowledge, and support. I dedicate this book to her.

—M.M.K.

1
Introduction and Overview

A dominant perspective on the development of policies for the regulation of occupational labor markets is that these workers should be regulated to ensure quality providers and high levels of service. In only some narrow areas should competitive labor markets alone be dominant. Others argue that occupational labor markets should be free of government regulation because they have little need for licensing through government rules, except in those cases where the health and safety of society are seriously threatened. Since World War II, the market for occupational oversight by government has grown to such an extent that by 2008 almost 40 percent of the U.S. labor market had, or was required to eventually obtain, either a license or certification from some form of local, state, or federal government (Kleiner and Krueger 2013).[1] Since governmental occupational regulation varies greatly depending on the occupation that is licensed, the purpose of this book is to examine a variety of occupations that are at different stages of regulation and determine to what extent regulation has influenced the individuals in the occupation, consumers, or other closely related occupational practitioners. Since governments at the local, state, and national levels are confronted with the interests of the members of the occupations—and in rare cases with the interests of consumers of the services seeking more regulation—the goal of this book is to provide new analysis and evidence on how these labor markets work in the face of new and continuing government regulations.

The book adds further background and new analysis to the issue in the law-versus-economics debate, which asks whether litigation or regulation is better for society (Kessler 2011). If regulation is efficient, then ubiquitous regulation, which is found in most advanced nations, adds greater impetus for economic development (Shleifer 2011). On the other hand, the general theme of law-and-economics research suggests that contracts and the courts are a substitute for regulation (Coase 1960). They argue that if potential externalities can be contracted around, no regulation is necessary. However, the growth of regulation through occupational licensing suggests that some manner of efficient regulation may be gaining as the dominant form of public policy. An additional issue that emerges with more regulation is that as occupational licensing becomes more prevalent, there is more room for litigation. This is because licensing develops more rules, which require legal interpretation. That results in further complaints adjudicated through the courts. The implications for economic growth are therefore unclear.

The common threads throughout the book include showing the growth of regulation and its variations over time. Each subsequent chapter shows an occupation that has a higher level of regulation. In this way, the successive chapters demonstrate the influence of increased regulation on the wages of the occupations and, where data were available, its effects on employment. A unique aspect of the book is that it portrays outcomes both for consumers in the case of regulation of mortgage brokers and for young children's educational attainment in the case of licensing of preschool teachers and their assistants. Another unique aspect of the analysis is the examination of occupations such as those of dentists and hygienists, who battle with regulators over who is permitted to do what type of work in dental offices. A further innovation is the examination of how regulations may influence the number of workplace injuries and deaths suffered by plumbers and electricians in the construction industry, which is the most hazardous industry, based on total numbers of workplace accidents in the United States. Overall, there are common aspects of the volume, yet each chapter delves into the unique historical or institutional aspects of a particular occupation and how it is regulated by government using data and analysis.

The evolution of occupational regulation has a long and distinguished intellectual history. Adam Smith, in his 1776 work *The Wealth of Nations*, notes that trades conspired to reduce the availability of "skilled craftsmen" in order to raise wages. Smith goes on to say that "to hinder him from employing this strength and dexterity in what manner he thinks proper without injury to his neighbor, is a plain violation of this most sacred property. It is a manifest encroachment upon the just liberty both of the workman, and of those who might be imposed to employ him" (Smith 1937).

In the United States, a structural shift in the economy has developed. The country has moved from a manufacturing-based economy, where unions and collective bargaining contracts previously were prominent, toward a service-oriented economy; the transformation has created a demand for a "web of rules" governing the workplace that has made licensing part of this evolution (Dunlop 1958). Although the number of union members has declined, occupational licensing has grown over the past 50 years (Kleiner 2006).

Occupational regulation in the United States generally takes three forms. The least restrictive form is registration, in which individuals file their names, addresses, and qualifications with a government agency before practicing their occupation. The registration process may include posting the equivalent of a surety bond or filing a fee. In contrast, certification permits any person to perform the relevant tasks, but the government—or sometimes a private, nonprofit agency—administers an examination and certifies those who have achieved the level of skill and knowledge for certification. For example, chartered financial analysts and car mechanics are generally certified but not licensed. The toughest form of regulation is licensure; this form of regulation is often referred to as "the right to practice." Under licensure laws, working in an occupation for compensation without first meeting government standards is illegal. In 2003, the Council of State Governments estimated that more than 800 occupations were licensed in at least one state, and more than 1,100 occupations were licensed, certified, or registered (Council on Licensure, Enforcement, and Regulation [CLEAR] 2004).

A simple view, or the perspective of a bureaucratic functionary, on occupational licensing by government suggests that administrative procedures regulate the supply of labor in the market. The regulators screen entrants to the profession and bar those whose skills or character traits suggest a tendency toward low-quality output. The regulators further monitor incumbents and discipline those whose performance is below the standards, with punishments that may include revocation of the license needed to practice. Assuming that entry and ongoing performance are controlled in these ways, one would expect the quality of service in the profession to be raised by occupational licensing but the supply to diminish.

In contrast, Milton Friedman questioned the assumption of unbiased gatekeepers and enforcers. Instead, he viewed licensing's entry restrictions as creating undesirable monopoly rents or incomes. Members of the occupation worked in their own self-interest to restrict supply, increase demand, and maximize "profits" for the members of the occupation. Friedman (1962) gives an example of doctors who expect to make a certain income or they will diagnose bogus ailments for which they will prescribe unnecessary treatments in order to achieve their expected income.

An expanded and segmented way of thinking about the issue of who gains from regulation was suggested by Carl Shapiro, who stated that both the average quality and the average prices or earnings from the services within the regulated occupation will rise as licensing requirements are implemented or tightened. The consequences are benefits for those who want higher quality, but at a cost to those who are in lower-quality service markets. Demand for the services of licensed workers could increase because of higher perceived quality and lower risk, but demand might also decrease for some segments of the occupation if some consumers demand lower-quality services that are precluded by the licensing procedures. An outward shift in demand could accentuate the increase in the price of services resulting from diminished supply and further boost provider incomes. Models of licensing assume that consumers can choose among three markets: 1) a market for mature producers known to sell high-quality services, 2) a market for mature producers known to produce low-quality services, and 3) a market for young producers whose quality of service (low or high) is not known by the consumer at the time of purchase (Shapiro 1986). The result is that seekers of high-quality services gain by regulation, and those who seek low-quality services are worse off because prices are higher and choices more limited. There is somewhat of a reverse Robin Hood effect, with the lower-income individuals losing and those with higher incomes gaining from occupational regulation.

Consumers and citizens often value the reduction in downside risk more than they value the benefits of a positive outcome. This preference by consumers for the status quo or for reducing the risk of a highly negative outcome has been called "loss aversion" by Kahneman and Tversky (1979). If the perception of licensing is that it leads to a reduction in the most serious losses, such as the spread of disease or the lack of structural integrity of a building, then this form of regulation can have public backing and support. These are the potential benefits against which the costs—which are most often the subject of analysis—are measured.

Unlike unions, which can engage in concerted activities such as strikes or work slowdowns, licensed workers neither sign collective agreements with their employers nor engage in strikes against employers to raise wages. Nonunion workers, who are covered by collective bargaining agreements but are not dues-paying members, usually receive most of the benefits of workers who are in the union. Occupational licensing can affect pay and employment through three main channels. First, licensing may increase perceived quality by imposing initial education, testing, continuing training requirements, internship requirements, or fees. These requirements are likely to diminish the number of less qualified or unmotivated individuals who could enter the occupation, and thereby they serve to drive up the average quality of human capital in workers in an occupation, as typically measured. A consequence is higher-quality outcomes for those who are able to obtain the service, but fewer practitioners and less access to the service.

Second, by using the state to monitor and prevent the potential work effort of unlicensed workers, competition by unlicensed individuals is virtually eliminated through the use of the state's enforcement powers. For example, the work of hair braiders, which is unlicensed, could be brought under the control of the cosmetology board and limited to only licensed cosmetologists or barbers (*Anderson v. Minnesota Board of Barber and Cosmetology Examiners* 2005). Furthermore, when demand fluctuates for traditional tasks, the board has the ability to expand the regulated work through establishing administrative rules and limiting the work of unregulated workers.

Third, the regulatory board, through its administrative procedures of establishing large entry barriers and moral suasion, can reduce the number of openings in schools that prepare individuals for licensed positions. In addition, by adjusting the pass rate on the licensing exam, the board can change the number of new entrants from in-state or the number of migrants from other states or nations (Tenn 2001; Pagliero 2010).

Some evidence suggests that licensing does restrict the supply of workers in regulated occupations. One application focuses on the comparison of occupations that are licensed in some states and not in others. The occupations examined were librarians (licensed in 19 states), respiratory therapists (licensed in 35 states), and dietitians and nutritionists (licensed in 36 states) from 1990 to 2000 using census data (Kleiner

2006). Using controls for state characteristics, the multivariate estimates show that in the states where the occupations were unlicensed,
the growth rate in employment was 20 percent faster than in states that
did license these occupations. Another study finds that the imposition of
greater licensing requirements by a state, such as requiring all students
studying to become funeral directors to take embalming classes, is associated with fewer women holding jobs as funeral directors relative to
men, by a range of between 18 and 24 percent (Cathles, Harrington, and
Krynski 2010).[2]

Studies of the effects of licensing on wages have, in many ways,
paralleled the research methods used to study the effects of unions on
wages (Lewis 1986). These approaches include cross-section estimates,
switchers from regulated to unregulated and vice versa over time, and
cross-sectional results from within-occupation comparisons (Gittleman
and Kleiner 2013). The general estimates of cross-sectional studies
using census data of state licensing's influence on wages with standard
labor market controls show a range from 10 to 18 percent for wage
increase associated with being covered or attaining an occupational
license. However, within-occupation wage variations, both for service
occupations and for individuals in jobs that repair things, suggest a wide
range of wage changes, from 0 to 40 percent, associated with regulation
within an occupation.

Although these results suggest that licensing—the toughest form
of regulation—matters for wage determination, the results do not use
national estimates, do not examine the levels of government that may
matter, and do not consider the influence of the requirements to become
licensed, such as education, testing, or internships, which may further
enhance wages. When these national estimates are developed, they
show that occupational licensing can raise earnings of individuals in
the occupations between 15 and 18 percent (Kleiner and Krueger 2010,
2013). I plan to examine in detail several occupations to learn when
these national trends apply to specific cases as occupations achieve
varying levels of regulation over time.

FURTHER COMPARISONS OF UNIONS AND
OCCUPATIONAL LICENSING

As I point out in an ealier volume (*Licensing Occupations: Ensuring Quality or Restricting Competition?*, Kleiner 2006), unions and licensing membership are moving in different directions (Kleiner and Krueger 2013). To update my earlier results to 2008, Figure 1.1 shows the trends in unionization and licensing over time from 1950 to 2008 (Council of State Governments 1952).[3] Licensing data for earlier periods are available only at the state/occupational level; the data gathered through the Gallup and Westat surveys for 2006 and 2008 are denoted with a dashed line in the figure. Despite possible problems in both data series, occupational licensing clearly is rising and unionization is declining. By 2008, approximately 29 percent of workers polled in the Westat survey said they were required to have a government-issued license to do their job, compared with about 12.4 percent who said they were union members in the Current Population Survey (CPS) for the same year. An overview of the data used in this volume is presented in Appendix E.

An interesting anomaly involves the potential substitution between occupational licensing and unionization. For example, in the United Kingdom about 13.5 percent of the workforce must have a license to work, but about 22 percent of the workforce belongs to a union (Humphris, Kleiner, and Koumenta 2011). In contrast, in the United States about 29 percent of the workforce must have a license to work, but only 12.4 percent belongs to a union. In the United States, 41 percent of the workforce either is in a union or is licensed, and in the United Kingdom about 35.5 percent of the workforce is in a union or is licensed. Other nations, such as China, have found the general wage gaps for licensing relative to unregulated workers to be about 13 percent (Chi, Kleiner, and Qian 2013).

For these two countries, the United States and the United Kingdom, there may be substitution of some form of a "web of rules" at the workplace through the institution of either unionization or governmental licensure. However, there may also be complements, since in the United States, as Table 1.1 shows, 45 percent of union members are also licensed, but only about 26 percent of nonunion members are licensed.

Figure 1.1 Percentage of Union and Licensed Workers, 1950–2008, Trends in Two Labor Market Institutions

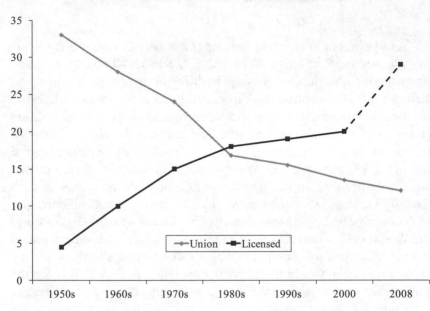

NOTE: Dashed line shows the value of estimates from state-level data of licensing from the Gallup and Westat survey results, including licensing by local, state, or federal governments. More than 800 occupations are licensed on at least one level, according to the Council of State Governments.

SOURCE: Licensing data are estimated from the author's surveys, Department of Labor estimates, a Gallup survey, and a Westat survey; union data are from the Current Population Survey (CPS).

Table 1.1 Percentage of Union and Nonunion Workers Who Are Licensed and Certified

Union status	Licensed		Certified	
	No	Yes	No	Yes
Union	55.4	44.6	95.0	5.0
Nonunion	74.3	25.7	94.0	6.0
Total	71.4	28.6	94.2	5.8

SOURCE: Princeton Data Improvement Initiative (2008).

DEVELOPING STAGES OF OCCUPATIONAL REGULATION

Business enterprises are rarely formed as unionized firms. Similarly, even though occupations develop similar tasks and common procedures for doing a job, they are not begun as licensed occupations. Occupations evolve, organize, and often select licensing as a method to obtain professionalism, quality, and status, as well as to limit the supply of practitioners. They tax their members through dues and engage in political activities that lead to registration, certification, and eventually licensing. The process of regulation across political jurisdictions often takes years or decades to achieve full licensure. Consequently, new occupations are often in varying stages of the regulatory process as they seek to become regulated by units of government. Since regulation mainly influences new entrants, it would take some time before the full effect of licensing would influence either the wages and employment of the individuals in the occupation or the consumers of their services. It usually takes some time for individuals who are grandfathered into the occupation, and have less measured human capital than newly regulated practitioners, to retire or leave the job. Occupations at a more mature stage of regulation would be more likely to have the benefits or advantages of the various stages of licensing than those that have recently sought or obtained regulation at different levels of government.[4]

The occupations that I plan to examine have been selected because they are at varying stages of regulation across states. In addition, they were chosen because they have unique characteristics, such as a potential conflict with another occupation, an example being dentists and hygienists. In other cases, I used an outcome factor, such as health and safety, to evaluate the influence of licensing within the construction industry.

Consequently, the overarching framework used to examine each of the occupations is adapted from the models of economic growth in Walter Rostow's *The Stages of Economic Growth: A Non-Communist Manifesto* (1960). Rostow's model illustrates five stages of growth, from traditional to highly developed, and places nations within these groups. Usually there are events or institutional changes in nations that trigger movement to higher stages of economic growth and development. The stages of occupational regulation are an arbitrary and in many ways a limited way of looking at the sequence of regulation. The stages approach utilizes not merely the uniformities in the sequence of regulation but also—and equally—the uniqueness of each occupation's experience. The trigger to starkly influence the impact of regulation within an occupation is occupational licensing. There is an important time-series element to the stages of occupational regulation. Furthermore, there is the importance of the restrictiveness of entry and the significance of occupation members remaining in good standing, both of which influence the ability of the members of the occupation to influence wages, employment, and other outcomes that are affected by regulation. Occupational licensing, like the economic growth models described by Rostow, does not operate in a linear manner. Rather, time and stages of regulation are key elements in the issues faced by the members of the occupation, consumers, and society.

In this book, I modify the Rostow model to show that the various stages of occupational regulation can be represented by several occupations that are at various levels of regulation by different jurisdictions of government. I also examine the tension that exists between the occupations over the "span of control" of job tasks that are regulated by the state. Each stage of the influence of occupational regulation has its own set of outcome criteria such as wages, housing foreclosures, or health and safety levels. Policies may differ based on the stage of occupational regulation and the tasks that the occupation performs. Furthermore, the length of time an occupation has been licensed matters for labor market outcomes. Generally, the longer an occupation is licensed, the larger the economic gain for being a member of the licensed occupation. I will analyze these occupations to establish whether there is a consistent model of stages of growth or whether there are local occupation-specific conditions for each occupation—in which case the model would not apply to those circumstances or for that time period. The model development, the gathering of new data on regulatory institutions, and the empirical testing all have a common goal: to inform the public and policymakers of the costs and benefits of being at each stage of occupational regulation.

Figure 1.2 shows the seven occupations that I plan to examine in the book, ordered by the number of states requiring practitioners to have a license in 2007. Practitioners of these seven occupations include, on one end of the spectrum, interior designers, who are fully licensed in

Figure 1.2 Number of States Requiring Licensing for Seven Occupations, 2007

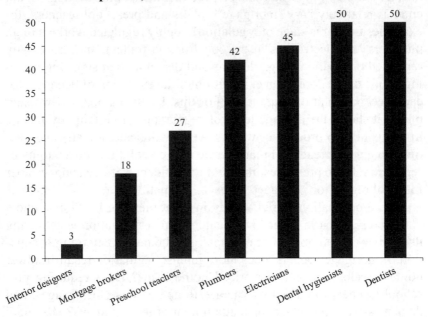

SOURCE: Author's tabulation.

only three states, and, on the other end, dental hygienists and dentists, for whom licensing is mandatory in all states. To the extent that there is much variation in the number of states that require full licensing, the examination of these occupations is likely to show how different stages of regulation may influence workers in these fields and consumers of their services.

FOCUS OF THE BOOK

A goal of this book is to examine a broad variety of occupations that includes blue- and white-collar occupations at different stages of occupational regulation by government. In subsequent chapters, I examine occupations that include ones that are regulated in only a few states (e.g., interior designers), moderately regulated ones where from one-third to one-half of the states license the members of the occupation but entry is relatively easy (mortgage brokers and preschool teachers, for example, are at this stage of regulation), highly regulated workers (e.g., plumbers and electricians in the construction trades), and universally regulated occupations (e.g., dentists and dental hygienists). One unifying theme of the book is an exploration of the evolution of licensing for each occupation at the state level. For this, I utilize a box-and-whisker plot that shows the average level of regulation for certain key factors in the regulatory process, as well as the variation across states and over time, to give the reader a broad picture of the evolution and anatomy of regulation. I also present estimates of the influence of licensing or other forms of regulation on wages for each occupation.

Since occupations differ widely in what they do, I will examine a variety of criteria in order to evaluate whether regulation is achieving its publicly stated goals. For example, for the newly emerging occupation of mortgage brokers, does more intense regulation result in fewer home foreclosures or lower-priced home loans? Does requiring preschool teachers to have a baccalaureate degree raise their wages, and does it assist in the educational attainment of their students? Has more stringent licensing of plumbers and electricians reduced the number of severe injuries and deaths for workers in the construction industry, where such casualties have a higher occurrence than in other industries? When two universally licensed occupations such as dentists and hygienists perform several similar tasks for the patient, how do the regulations determine who gets to do the work, and what are the labor market outcomes for practitioners in both occupations? Should national standards be used in order to reduce any barriers to employment that may be imposed at the local or state level? These are some of the questions the rest of this book addresses. In the final chapter, I summarize the major findings on occupational mobility and examine the role that different stages of occupational regulation over time play in the lives of licensed workers and other constituents. I also examine the implications of occupational regulation for federal, state, and local government in making policies that regulate occupational tasks and entry barriers. Overall, the volume's chapters have commonalities, yet each chapter delves into the unique aspects of a particular occupation and how it is regulated, then looks at the economic consequences.

Notes

1. Unfortunately, no more recent national data are available than the data from 2008, since the federal government does not keep regular data on the number or percentage of workers that are licensed. In contrast, annual data from the Bureau of Labor Statistics tabulate the number and the percentage of union workers and union coverage. Unions form a much smaller percentage of the workforce than licensed occupations (Kleiner 2006).
2. In March 2013, the U.S. Court of Appeals for the Eastern District of Louisiana, in *St. Joseph Abbey et al. v. Paul Wess Castille et al.*, Case No. 11-30756, ruled that the occupational licensing laws issued by the Louisiana Board of Funeral Directors granting funeral homes an exclusive right to sell caskets was unconstitutional because it stifled competition.
3. The method used to calculate the percentage of workers licensed prior to 2006 first involved gathering the listing of licensed occupations in each state by Labor Market Information Units under a grant from the U.S. Department of Labor—see America's Career InfoNet, http://www.acinet.org/acinet/licensedoccupations/lois_occ.aspx?stfips=27&by=occ&keyword=&searchType=&. This was matched with occupations in the 2000 census. If no match was obtained, the occupation was dropped. From the census, the number of people working in the licensed occupation in each state was estimated and used to calculate a weighted average of the percentage of the workforce in the United States that works in a licensed occupation. For 2008 we deleted individuals who were certified from our tally of licensed individuals who were either licensed or certified in our survey conducted by Westat.
4. Modern econometric techniques such as regression discontinuity, field experiments, or difference-in-difference approaches may have difficulty detecting the full influence of licensing on wage determination unless they have long time-series databases.

2
An Initial Stage of Regulation:
Interior Designers

A practice act allows individuals to become licensed with a state board in order to practice a scope of work previously not allowed to non-licensed individuals. These design services vary by state but typically include code affecting work. Most architecture and engineering laws have been written without regard to the capabilities and training of interior designers. This is where legal recognition becomes necessary.

—American Society of Interior Designers (2005)

An overarching goal of many occupations at an initial stage of regulation is to obtain licensing by a governmental entity (Kleiner 2006). The goal of this chapter is to present and evaluate an occupation at an initial stage of regulation. The case study presented in this chapter looks at interior designers, whose profession will serve as a baseline for the other occupations that will be examined and evaluated later in the book.[1]

According to this chapter's epigraph, which comes from the American Society of Interior Designers (ASID), a goal of interior designers is to become regulated by the government. The rationale is that their occupation must become regulated in order to maintain its legitimacy relative to complementary and competitive occupations such as those of engineers and architects. Given the institutional environment of interior designers, where practitioners work with members of other regulated occupations, regulation has become necessary in order to maintain job tasks. The goal of the major association of interior designers is to obtain occupational licensing status across states in order to secure the legitimacy and power to do work under the law—similar to other major occupations that are complementary to interior designers.

Much growth in the regulation of interior designers has taken place during the recent past. In 1993 only 36 percent of interior designers were

15

subject to any type of state regulation, whereas in 2007 over 60 percent of interior designers were subject to occupational regulation.[2] However, interior designers are fully licensed in only three states—Florida, Louisiana, and Nevada—plus the District of Columbia, the fewest number of states for any licensed occupation examined in this book. Alabama was the first state to regulate interior designers, having done so in 1982. The so-called title act gave interior designers the exclusive right to use the term "interior designer" in advertising. Alabama's former practice act resulted in full licensing in 2001, but the act was declared unconstitutional in 2007 by the state supreme court. The court stated that the act "imposes restrictions that are unnecessary and unreasonable upon the pursuit of useful activities" and that those restrictions "do not bear some substantial relation to the public health, safety, or morals, or to the general welfare, the public convenience, or to the general prosperity."[3] By 2009, 22 states and the District of Columbia imposed some level of regulation on interior designers. Two states have registration laws, the most basic type of regulation. States such as Minnesota, however, regulate the use of "certified interior designer" as a title but allow anyone to do interior design work without certification. The District of Columbia and the three states that have full licensing regulations, however, restrict the ability to work in the profession by prohibiting practitioners from doing certain types of interior design work without a license from the government.

This chapter provides an overview of the occupation of interior designers, including regulatory requirements for entry and tasks relative to complementary occupations such as engineers and architects. The analysis then documents the various stages of regulation and shows the growth of the regulation of interior designers over time. Since relatively few states license interior designers, the chapter documents other forms of regulation, such as certification and registration, for workers in the occupation. The chapter also explores the rationale for why the occupation seeks to become fully licensed. Since there is a battle for work tasks in the construction and remodeling industries among civil engineers, architects, and interior designers, not having an equal voice within state licensing boards likely limits the ability of interior designers to legally do certain tasks or take ownership of large projects, which may be the purview only of engineers and architects. Since the construction industry is highly volatile, having experienced large growth in the early 2000s and contraction following 2007, the ability to control supply is important. Furthermore, the ability to regulate specific tasks—either those legally assigned to the occupation or those permissible—is an essential element of the "web of rules" for an occupation's members. The chapter provides a state-specific example of the push to have interior designers fully licensed—in this case, in the state of Minnesota. Finally, it also supplies an empirical analysis of the labor market implications of various forms of regulation on the wage determination of interior designers.

WHY LICENSE INTERIOR DESIGNERS?

The Bureau of Labor Statistics' *Occupational Outlook Handbook* provides a definition of the occupation of interior designers:

> Interior designers draw upon many disciplines to enhance the function, safety, and aesthetics of interior spaces. Their main concerns are with how different colors, textures, furniture, lighting, and space work together to meet the needs of a building's occupants. Designers plan interior spaces of almost every type of building, including offices, airport terminals, theaters, shopping malls, restaurants, hotels, schools, hospitals, and private residences. (BLS 2012d)

In many respects, the work of interior designers overlaps and competes with that of engineers, architects, and other construction workers. The fear that interior designers have of remaining unregulated among these other occupations which are governmentally regulated in all states is captured in the following statement by the ASID: "It is no secret that some other professional groups would like to limit, control, or even eliminate the practice of interior design as a unique profession. It would be naive to believe that they are not making their cases" (ASID 2005). Given that many unregulated occupations, such as perfusionists in health care or the current case of interior designers in construction, view their position as being precarious, the fear that other, similar occupations will achieve through regulatory boards the ability to limit or eliminate their jobs is a driving force behind much of the push toward additional government regulation. The argument has been made that the true measure of a profession lies in the number of educational requirements and sophisticated tasks that determine whether the occupation is licensed (Martin 2008). Thus far, no detailed analytical studies show that licensing significantly reduces dangers to the health and safety of the public as a result of the work of interior designers, which is a major concern of public policymakers. These public health and safety concerns dominate the public debate regarding whether an occupation should be licensed. Recent analysis shows that giving interior designers the ability to provide a "sign and seal" service for drafting documents for final approval of building architecture increases their earnings, and that higher earnings are associated with more individuals entering the occupation. No such labor market effects are observed with regard to the earnings and employment of architects (Kleiner and Vorotnikov 2012).

HISTORICAL EVOLUTION OF THE OCCUPATION OF INTERIOR DESIGN

The occupation of interior design is a relatively recent addition to the purview of governmental oversight. The professional association for the occupation, the American Institute of Interior Designers (AID), was founded in 1931, but it was not until the postwar boom of the 1950s that the organization had grown large enough that it sought to become regulated. In 1968, voluntary certification began through AID, which was designed to pave the way for licensing. The professional organization also began to work with interior design programs to strengthen curriculums and develop continuing education programs for the members of the occupation. In the following decade, AID and another interior design organization merged to form the American Society of Interior Designers (ASID) and were immediately assigned the task of collecting information on state regulations for the profession (ASID 2005). In the 1980s the association began encouraging state-by-state registration regulations, and it signed an accord with the architects' professional association to support only certification and not full licensing, or what became known within the occupation as title acts. The agreement allowed architects to register interior designers in states with these acts and establish joint regulatory boards. Within this context, the agreement gave interior designers with expertise in the field the ability to use this title, and those persons who did not fulfill the qualifications were forbidden from using the term "registered" or "certified interior designer." In 1999, however, the ASID board voted to withdraw from the accord and aggressively pursue full occupational licensing by the states. Such state licenses became known as practice acts.

When government regulation of engineers evolved to include civil, electrical, mechanical, and industrial engineering by the 1960s, the law stated that only engineers can sign off on initial and final construction design and implementation of final construction. As a result, interior designers were relegated to an inferior position within the construction industry. Moreover, architects were held responsible for the development of the initial design of structures, which further diminished the role of interior designers in the eyes of the law. More generally, state and local governments have gradually assumed a more important role in determining how work is to be done in construction. The appropriate types of labor inputs in construction are largely determined through governmental statutes or administrative procedures. Working within the constraints of this institutional environment, interior designers concluded that the only way to obtain access to certain types of work in this growing field was to take steps to become a regulated occupation. With this in mind, they proceeded to push for licensing in a number of states. Here, a case study is instructive. The state of Minnesota is used to illustrate the process of how interior design has evolved over time. This state was chosen because it has regulated the interior design occupation since 1992 and full occupational licensing regulations have been proposed to the legislature in every biennium since 2003.

REGULATION OF INTERIOR DESIGNERS IN MINNESOTA: A CASE STUDY

A law to change interior designers from a certified profession to a licensed one was first introduced in the Minnesota Legislature in 2003. As of 2011, the current law governing interior designers in Minnesota is a titling act that regulates the use of the title "registered interior designer."[4] The stated purpose of this statute is to "safeguard life, health, and property, and to promote the public welfare."[5] Regulations restricting the work to persons meeting certain statutory requirements now affect professions such as architects, engineers, land surveyors, and landscape architects.[6] The statutory amendments proposed in prior sessions of the Minnesota legislature have called for a requirement that interior designers be licensed (Alexander et al. 2009). The current definition of an interior designer under Minnesota law is the following: "One who uses the title, and who designs public interior spaces, including preparation of documents relative to non-load-bearing interior construction, space planning, finish materials, and furnishings."[7] Those without certification cannot use the title in the preparation of plans, specifications, reports, plats, or other interior design projects.[8] They are also precluded from holding themselves up to the public as "certified interior designers."

The proposed law has been introduced in every biennium since 2003. No major changes have been made to the content of the bill since it was originally introduced as a proposed licensing law in 2003. Table 2.1 shows a brief history of the various attempts to obtain full licensing for interior designers in Minnesota.

The key provisions of the proposed legislation would limit the extent of the licensing provisions to larger buildings and construction sites. Specifically, exemptions to the proposed law read as follows:

> Nothing contained in sections . . . shall prevent persons from advertising and performing services such as consultation, investigation, or evaluation in connection with, or from making plans and specifications for, or from supervising, the erection, enlargement, or alteration of any of the following buildings:
>
> (a) dwellings for single families, and outbuildings in connection therewith, such as barns and private garages;
>
> (b) two-family dwellings;
>
> (c) any farm building or accessory thereto; or
>
> (d) temporary buildings or sheds used exclusively for construction purposes, not exceeding two stories in height, and not used for living quarters. (Minn. Stat. § 326.03, subd. 1)

The proposed bill would thus exempt single-family dwellings (which is intended to include homeowners) and farm buildings from being covered by the act, in spite of the general proposition that home-

Table 2.1 Attempts to Pass Licensing Regulations for Interior Designers in Minnesota, 2003–2009

Year	Proposed legislation	Sponsoring legislators	Result
2003	SF 2868 / HF 3066	Sen. Higgins / Rep. Osterman	Never heard
2005	SF 263 / HF 1277	Sen. Higgins / Rep. Thissen	Never heard
2007	SF 788 / HF 991	Sen. Higgins / Rep. Thissen	Never heard
2009	SF 349 / HF 416	Sen. Higgins / Rep. Thissen	Hearing in Senate Committee on Commerce and Consumer Protection, 2/17/09, failed on a voice vote

SOURCE: Alexander et al. (2009).

owners are the least likely to have detailed information about the safety of materials or the proper design of space for best use. A listing of the proposed exemptions to the proposed Minnesota statute is presented in Table 2.2. For example, the flammability of various building materials or the appropriate distances for wheelchair accessibility or handrail height may be unknown to a homeowner. For a large construction company, however, this information would be a routine part of the bidding process. Large private-sector building contractors and governmental builders are more likely to be aware of current building codes and guidelines and be knowledgeable about the qualifications for skilled architects, engineers, and interior designers. Consequently, these occupations would not need the protection of a licensing law. Much of the rhetoric during the discussion of licensing has focused on the comparability of laws covering licensing provisions for other occupations that come under the auspices of the Minnesota Board of Architecture, Engineering, Land Surveying, Landscape Architecture, Geoscience, and Interior Design (AELSLAGID). The argument is that all the other occupations are fully licensed and able to capture work, especially for large buildings. The provisions and administrative procedures established by the AELSLAGID board govern the allocation of work that can legally be done by each of the occupations within its jurisdiction. Therefore, architects, engineers, and land surveyors are able to serve as large-scale project contractors who can legally sign off on the quality of a building, factory, or hospital. In contrast, since interior designers are not licensed, they would not have such authority. This restriction dimin-

Table 2.2 Exemptions to Proposed Minnesota Statute to License Interior Designers

Classifications	Elements that must be met to be exempt
Assembly (as defined by the Minnesota State Building Code [MSBC] under Occupancy Group A2: dining and drinking, fewer than 50 persons)	Not greater than one story with no basement, seating for not more than 20 persons, and not greater than 1,000 gross square footage (GSF)
Business (as defined by the MSBC under Occupancy Group B)	Not greater than two stories with a basement, and not greater than 2,250 GSF
Factory (as defined by the MSBC under Occupancy Group F2)	Not greater than one story with no basement, and not greater than 3,000 GSF
Mercantile (as defined by the MSBC under Occupancy Group M)	Not greater than two stories with a basement, and not greater than 1,500 GSF
Residential (as defined by the MSBC under Occupancy Group R)	Apartment houses/condominiums (three units or less), dwellings, lodging houses, attached single-family dwellings/townhomes, and congregate residences (each accommodating 10 persons or fewer)
Storage (as defined by the MSBC under Occupancy Group S1: aircraft hangars and helistops)	Not greater than one story with no basement, and not greater than 3,000 GSF
Storage (as defined by the MSBC under Occupancy Group S2 except for parking garages, open or enclosed)	Not greater than one story with no basement, and not greater than 5,000 GSF
Utility (as defined by the MSBC under Occupancy Group U except for fences higher than 8 feet, tanks and towers, and retaining walls with over 4 feet of vertical exposed face)	Not greater than one story with no basement, and not greater than 1,000 GSF

SOURCE: Alexander et al. (2009).

ishes their responsibility for risk and perhaps their rate of pay within the construction industry. Therefore, it is in their best interest to tax their members for political contributions and lobby appropriate legislators and the governor for passage of legislation that would enhance their position within occupations that are governed by the board.

Unlike the case with many of the other occupations that are discussed in this book, opposition to the licensing of interior designers is organized. For example, AIA Minnesota, a Society of the American Institute of Architects, and the National Kitchen and Bath Association have both opposed the licensing of interior designers. The arguments put forth state that licensing is not necessary to protect the health, safety, and welfare of the public. Opponents have also argued that licensing is a danger to job growth in Minnesota because it limits the number of interior designers who could practice in the state. Furthermore, the argument goes, licensing would be detrimental to consumers because the limited supply of interior designers would both increase the prices charged for services and limit access to services. And, in testimony provided to the state legislature, witnesses made statements that licensing proponents had not provided any studies to back up their claim that unqualified interior designers are a threat to health and safety. The groups opposing licensing argue that the exemptions in the bill prove that licensing is not about protecting public health and safety, because if unqualified interior designers were a danger to the public in commercial spaces, they would also be a danger in residential spaces, and therefore no exemptions should exist. If any group needs protection from incompetent or unscrupulous vendors, they contend, it is homeowners. They also argue that additional exemptions are allowed for licensed interior designers under the proposed bill that are not allowed for other occupations.

As mentioned earlier, architects also argue that the building code requires that interior designers work under the direction of an architect in most commercial projects. Problems with compliance would arise if some projects were required to be supervised by an architect and others required only a licensed interior designer.[9] Architects have opposed the licensure of interior designers mainly in anticipation of potential battles among the occupations covered by the AELSLAGID for work tasks such as certifying drafts of final drawings in the construction industry (Kleiner and Vorotnikov 2012). This issue is more likely to occur in industries such as architectural, engineering, and related services (NAICS 5413) and specialized design services (NAICS 5414).

ISSUES OF HEALTH AND SAFETY

A central argument for the proposed Minnesota statute has been the importance of licensing for the health and safety of the citizens of the state. The anecdotes that have been presented focus on legal cases involving interior designers, which are detailed in this section. In 1996, a restaurant employee in the title-act state of New York sued an interior designer for injuries related to a fall.[10] The court stated that the interior designer's services were completed prior to the plaintiff's fall, so the court rejected the plaintiff's claim.[11] This determination was based neither on the existence of titling nor on any of the benefits of the act (Alexander et al. 2009).[12] One important aspect of this case is the court's finding that, because the plaintiff was not a party to a contract with the defendant—rather, she was an employee who worked in the facility—the interior designer owed no duty of care to her after the completion of the discrete project for which he had been hired.[13] The court stated that the interior designer was not at fault in the incident.

In another case study involving the state of New York, a building tenant brought an action against an interior designer, among others, for injuries sustained in a fall.[14] The New York State Supreme Court dismissed this action against the interior designer because there was no evidence that the interior designer's specifications were faulty.[15] An additional anecdotal case related to interior design comes from the state of Mississippi, which has no interior design regulation. In Simoneaux v. BSL Inc., a plaintiff slipped and fell while attempting to exit a hotel Jacuzzi tub.[16] The plaintiff in the case sued several parties, including the interior designer.[17] The court in this case ruled that the issue should be decided by a jury and that interior designers were not necessarily responsible for the fall.

This case law suggests that not many legal cases offer clear evidence that the actions of interior designers have caused substantial harm to the public. Even if these cases of injury had been attributed to interior designers, there is no evidence that having licensed interior designers would have avoided the injuries. Moreover, the issues of the role of prices in seeking nonlicensed substitutes, the scrapping of marginal projects because of labor cost concerns, and the reduction in the ability to make private contractual arrangements are costs that should be weighed against the potential benefits of moving interior designers in Minnesota to a more rigorous regime of regulation.

Next I examine whether regulations for interior designers have affected either the wages or employment growth of the occupation.

ANALYZING INTERIOR DESIGNERS

A key element in the examination of interior designers is whether regulations at this stage of licensing have significant labor market effects with respect to the wages or employment growth of the occupation. In order to present evidence on the influence of regulations, I examine the American Community Survey (ACS) from 2007 through 2009. The ACS does not include a specific category for interior designers. However, an earlier analysis of the occupation by Harrington and Treber (2009) developed a template for examining the occupation. They created an interior design classification from occupational and industry codes and used the following occupational codes to identify "designers":

260—Artists and related workers
263—Designers
775—Miscellaneous assemblers and fabricators

I begin with Harrington and Treber's definition and expand it slightly to include individuals with the occupational codes working in architectural services (the industry code for architectural services is NAICS 5413 and for specialized design services is NAICS 5414). In my conversations with both architects and design professionals, I learned that many interior designers work in architecture firms. It is appropriate, then, to assume that individuals coded as "designers" working in the architecture industry are, in fact, interior designers.

DEVELOPING ESTIMATES ON THE INFLUENCE OF THE REGULATION OF INTERIOR DESIGNERS

In order to examine the influence of regulation for interior designers, I initially develop an index of regulation for the occupation. The index includes the following three characteristics of the type of regulation for the occupation: 1) whether the state had any form of regulation; 2) whether it had a full licensing law or a practice act; and 3) whether it had certification of the occupation, known as a title act. Forming the basis of our analysis of the role of regulation in the labor market for interior designers, Table 2.3 shows which states have passed these types of laws, the kind of regulation by state, and the year in which the law was passed.

As the previous comments and examination of the evolution of regulation for this occupation have shown, growth in the regulation of interior designers has evolved over time. Figure 2.1 is a box-and-whisker plot that shows the growth of the mean and variance of the regulation of interior designers for all states from 1990 to 2009. Prior to 1980, no states regulated interior designers, but starting in the early 1990s the number of states regulating interior designers through either a practice act or a title act increased. The figure shows that growth has occurred over time in both the level and the variance of the regulations governing the occupation. Although the figure shows the statutory coverage of the occupation, it does not provide the level of enforcement of the provisions.

Detailed data are available for interior designers from two major data sources: the American Community Survey (ACS) of the U.S. Census Bureau and the Occupational Employment Statistics (OES) survey from the U.S. Bureau of Labor Statistics. The ACS is based on interviews with individuals, whereas the OES is based on a survey of employers. Both databases allow for an examination of wage and employment data by state. A major difference in the ACS is that it allows for many covariates (such as human capital and other types of characteristics of the individual) to be controlled for in estimation procedures. It also has information on income from nonlabor funds, and many of the interior designers were self-employed and reported profits on their enterprises. The OES, however, is a state-based program with few of the covari-

Table 2.3 State Regulations for Interior Designers

State	Type of statute	Year passed
Alabama	Title act	1982
Alaska	None	
Arizona	None	
Arkansas	Title act	1993
California	Title act	1990
Colorado	Permitting statute	2001
Connecticut	Title act	1983
Delaware	None	
District of Columbia	Practice act	1999
Florida	Practice act	1994
Georgia	Title act	1992
Hawaii	None	
Idaho	None	
Illinois	Title act	1990
Indiana	Title act	1990
Iowa	Title act	2005
Kansas	None	
Kentucky	Title act	2002
Louisiana	Practice act	1999
Maine	Title act	1993
Maryland	Title act	1991
Massachusetts	None	
Michigan	None	
Minnesota	Title act	1992
Mississippi	None	
Missouri	Title act	1998
Montana	None	
Nebraska	None	
Nevada	Practice act	1995
New Hampshire	None	
New Jersey	Title act	2002
New Mexico	Title act	1989
New York	Title act	1990
North Carolina	None	
North Dakota	None	
Ohio	None	

(continued)

Table 2.3 (continued)

State	Type of statute	Year passed
Oklahoma	Title act	2006
Oregon	None	
Pennsylvania	None	
Rhode Island	None	
South Carolina	None	
South Dakota	None	
Tennessee	Title act	1991
Texas	Title act	1991
Utah	None	
Vermont	None	
Virginia	Title act	1990
Washington	None	
West Virginia	None	
Wisconsin	Title act	1996
Wyoming	None	

SOURCE: Author's compilation; American Society of Interior Designers (ASID).

ates that are needed to fully examine the occupation, but it does allow the use of state-level covariates. Together, these data sources provide confirmation or evidence of the role of statutory requirements in the regulation of interior designers.

Other Data

In order to take into account other characteristics of the economic environment that may influence the labor market for interior designers, the empirical models control for state per capita income and the growth in state employment. Since other factors may influence the wages and employment growth of interior designers beyond those captured by the statutory factors, additional controls are included for the state and year characteristics of the observations; these additional controls are called state and year fixed effects. This approach provides estimates that are equivalent to difference-in-differences estimators for those states that changed their policies. This technique is useful because it avoids bias due to omitted variables that do not change over time in the use of a panel data set like the ones used in the analysis.

Figure 2.1 Evolution of State Regulations for Interior Designers, 1990–2009

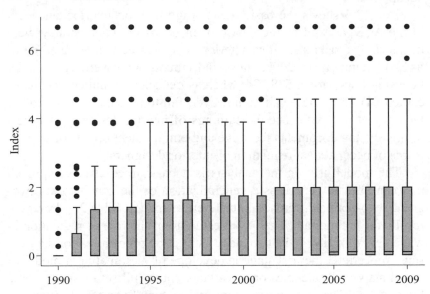

NOTE: This figure shows the growth of the mean and the variance for the regulation requirement index of interior designers from 1990 to 2009. The requirement indexes for each state, which measure the restriction level of regulation, are produced based on a series of requirements to obtain a license or certificate, including minimum education and experience, examination requirement, continuing education requirement, age requirement, and so on.
SOURCE: Author's compilation.

ESTIMATES OF THE INFLUENCE OF REGULATION ON WAGES AND EMPLOYMENT

In order to analyze the influence of state regulation on the labor market of interior designers, the analysis uses the data on the labor market combined with the information on the regulatory regimes of each of the states. The ACS contains detailed economic data for an analysis of the economic characteristics of interior designers. In combination with the trends in the regulation of the occupation over time, the estimates should show to what extent the movement toward more regulation may

30 Kleiner

have influenced the wages and employment of the individuals in the occupation.

Table 2.4 shows the basic mean wage data on interior designers in the ACS, as well as the data broken down by whether they were licensed. The data show that interior designers earned an average of $41,412 annually in 2009; those individuals who were covered by licensing laws earned $38,324, whereas designers in unlicensed states earned $41,750. These values, however, fail to take into account other factors that may influence the earnings of interior designers. The rest of this section documents the wage and employment effects of various forms of occupational regulation of interior designers.

The model used in the analysis is a basic fixed-effects approach that can also be viewed as a generalization of the conventional two-group, two-period difference-in-differences model. Table 2.5 shows the results for both a traditional panel estimate of the role of regulation in wage determination and a two-stage estimation procedure. For the two-stage procedure, the first stage is developed by estimating a model of individual-level outcomes on covariates and a full set of state × time fixed effects. The coefficients on the state × time fixed effects represent state × time mean outcomes that have been "purged" of the variation

Table 2.4 Basic Data on Interior Designers from the American Community Survey (ACS), 2009

	Nonlicensed states		Licensed states		All states	
	mean	sd	mean	sd	mean	sd
Income ($)	41,750	29,890	38,324	26,501	41,412	29,590
Hourly wage ($)	26.26	167.76	22.64	33.49	25.91	159.6
Annual hours	1,872	747	1,912	743	1,876	746
Age	39.54	12.24	41.30	12.47	39.72	12.27
Female	0.54	0.50	0.55	0.50	0.54	0.50
Hispanic	0.08	0.27	0.15	0.36	0.08	0.28
Black	0.04	0.19	0.05	0.22	0.04	0.19
Asian	0.09	0.28	0.03	0.16	0.08	0.27
Bachelor	0.50	0.50	0.44	0.50	0.49	0.50
Master	0.09	0.28	0.08	0.27	0.09	0.28
No. of observations	10,889		1,287		12,176	

NOTE: sd = standard deviation.
SOURCE: ACS.

associated with the within-cell variation in the covariates. In the second stage, these "adjusted cell-level means" are estimates on the policy variables and fixed effects. The two-step approach is a way of performing aggregation while still allowing for adjustment of individual-level covariates, which is a limitation of pure aggregation. The basic panel estimates, which are also shown in the table, include individual covariates as well as state and year fixed effects.[18]

Using data from the ACS, Table 2.5 shows the influence of economic variables on the logarithm of hourly earnings. The key variables from the ACS are as hypothesized, with key human capital factors such as education and age having a major influence on wage determination. In order to show the influence of regulation on wage determination, the model includes measures of regulation in the estimation equations. The basic economic variables such as age and gender show consistent results, and there seems to be little influence of the individual regulation variables on measures of hourly wage determination. However, using an F-test of the joint significance of the variables on wage determination finds that they are positive and significant using either the one- or the two-stage specification of the earnings model. Perhaps at very low levels of state regulation, which is the case for the occupation, the influence of regulation on earnings appears to have a small magnitude.

Licensing may behave in a manner similar to unionization, where initially the influence of regulation on wages may be small, but the influence is likely to grow over time (Freeman and Kleiner 1990). Analysis for interior designers and architects shows that this is the case for provisions such as sign-and-seal for these occupations as well (Kleiner and Vorotnikov 2012). Furthermore, since only three states and the District of Columbia have a practice act, which is the most restrictive form of occupational regulation and the type of regulation that is most likely to limit competition, the result may be that neighboring or nearby states are able to provide these services. As with any form of regulation, a key issue is enforcement, and in building, remodeling, and construction, where architects, engineers, and interior designers work closely together, the issue of licensing may have a smaller role and less enforcement than in occupations where the work tends to stand alone, as in the case of dentistry, detailed in a later chapter.

Although these estimates on wage determination provide some evidence of the overall effects of regulation on wage determination, a case

Table 2.5 An Analysis of the Role of Occupational Regulation on the Labor Market Outcomes of Interior Designers Using the ACS, 2001–2009

Interior designer–logged hourly wages

Variables	One-stage model B	SE	t	Two-stage model B	SE	t	One-stage model B	SE	t	Two-stage model B	SE	t	One-stage model B	SE	t	Two-stage model B	SE	t
Regulation	0.100	0.081	1.24	−0.189	0.203	−0.93												
Practice act							0.311	0.083	3.74	0.176	0.210	0.84	0.212	0.017	12.57	0.359	0.121	2.97
Title act							0.100	0.081	1.24	−0.192	0.204	−0.95						
State fixed effects	Y			Y			Y			Y			Y			Y		
Year fixed effects	Y			Y			Y			Y			Y			Y		
Covariates	Y			Y			Y			Y			Y			Y		
F statistic for joint significance							78.91***			4.53**								
First stage N	12,176			12,176			12,176			12,176			12,176			12,176		
Second stage N	n/a			454			n/a			454			n/a			454		

NOTE: The covariates included in all models are indicators for gender, race, education, and a quadratic function in age. The one-stage models are estimated using ordinary least squares (OLS) with state and year fixed effects. The two-stage models adjust for covariates in a first-stage regression of individual logged wages on covariates and a full set of state × year fixed effects. In the second stage, the state × year fixed effects (covariate-adjusted mean wages) are regressed on the regulation variables and state and year fixed effects. The second-stage regressions are weighted by the inverse of the state × year cell sample sizes. In all models, the standard errors are robust and allow for clustering at the state level. *significant at the 0.10 level; **significant at the 0.05 level; ***significant at the 0.01 level. Y = yes; blank = not applicable; SE = standard error; t = t-score; B = coefficient.

SOURCE: ACS.

study is particularly instructive, and the state of Alabama provides an interesting one. The state implemented a practice act in 2001, which was then ruled unconstitutional in 2007 by the state supreme court. If a practice act had increased wages for interior designers, we would then have expected to see a substantial increase in wages between 2002 and 2007 in Alabama. For example, interior designers in Alabama saw a wage increase of 46 percent under a practice act (see Figure 2.2), along with wage changes in the occupation nationally. By comparison, the national mean wage increased by 17 percent over the same period of time (Alexander et al. 2009). This case study demonstrates the influence of licensing on wage determination for the occupation in Alabama in comparison with other states.

The BLS data provide the impetus for further analysis of wages in the interior design industry. Although these differences in means certainly provide substantial evidence in support of the hypothesis, they are not conclusive. Many possible explanations can account for wage

Figure 2.2 Annual Interior Designer Wages, Alabama vs. National Average, 1999–2009

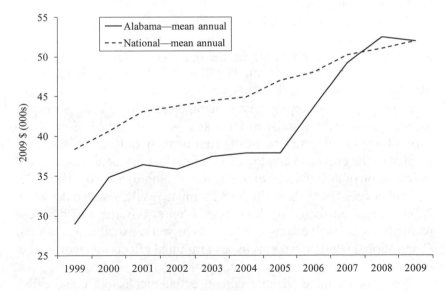

SOURCE: Occupational employment and wage estimates for various years, www.bls .gov/oes/oes_data.htm, from the U.S. Bureau of Labor Statistics (BLS).

differences between designers in one state and another. For example, a reasonable assumption is that interior designers in regulated states have attained a higher level of education, on average, than those in unregulated states because of the presence of educational requirements for licensure. In the subsequent section, statistical analysis is used with the data from the ACS in an attempt to isolate the effects of regulation on wages and explain the gap in earnings between regulated and unregulated designers.

One additional factor is the influence of regulation on the employment of interior designers. In order to determine this, the analysis provides two different data sets. In Table 2.6, the model is estimated using the ACS for the influence of regulation on annual hours of labor supplied. The estimates in Table 2.6 show that having a practice act reduces annual hours worked by approximately 16 percent based on the significant estimates in column three of the table. (This is the -330.3 coefficient value divided by the standard number of hours worked of 2,080 per year.) More rigorous regulation may drive up earnings enough for practitioners to take some of those earnings in the form of leisure. Moreover, occupational regulation may restrict the supply of labor available within the occupation.

In order to provide additional sensitivity estimates for the analysis, the OES is used because it provides more detailed and potentially reliable employment data by state for the occupation. The estimates from the statistical model are presented in Table 2.7. The basic model examines the influence of the three types of regulation of interior designers on employment and employment growth, controlling for the per capita income in the state. Similar to the wage estimates, none of the measures of regulation were statistically significant in influencing either the level of or the growth in employment of interior designers. Independent examination of the influence of regulation on employment by Alexander and colleagues using the ACS found similar results (Alexander et al. 2009). Based on these estimates, regulation at this stage of development produces small employment effects as well as small wage effects. Occupational regulation seems to have minimal effects on labor market outcomes at the earliest stages of regulation.

Next we examine whether certain economic factors could affect whether regulations for interior designers are enacted into law.

Table 2.6 Effects of Interior Designer Regulation on Annual Hours of Labor Supplied by Interior Designers Using ACS, 2001–2009

| | Interior designer annual hours of labor supply | | | | | | | | | | | | | | | | | |
| | One-stage model | | | Two-stage model | | | One-stage model | | | Two-stage model | | | One-stage model | | | Two-stage model | | |
Variables	B	SE	t	B	SE	t	B	SE	t	B	SE	t	B	SE	t	B	SE	t
Regulation	−138.3	227.5	−0.61	190.3	156.3	1.22												
Practice act							−330.3	231.1	−1.43	−228.3	174.2	−1.31	−193.2	20.63	−9.36	−413.9	146.9	−2.82
Title act							−138.1	227.6	−0.61	194.5	157.1	1.24						
State fixed effects	Y			Y			Y			Y			Y			Y		
Year fixed effects	Y			Y			Y			Y			Y			Y		
Covariates	Y			Y			Y			Y			Y			Y		
F statistic for joint significance							44.61***			4.08**								
First stage N	12,176			12,176			12,176			12,176			12,176			12,176		
Second stage N	n/a			454			n/a			454			n/a			454		

NOTE: The covariates included in all models are indicators for gender, race, education, and a quadratic function in age. The one-stage models are estimated using OLS with state and year fixed effects. The two-stage models adjust for covariates in a first-stage regression of labor supply on covariates and a full set of state × year fixed effects. In the second stage, the state × year fixed effects (covariate-adjusted mean hours of labor supply) are regressed on the regulation variables and state and year fixed effects. The second-stage regressions are weighted by the inverse of the state × year cell sample sizes. In all models, the standard errors are robust and allow for clustering at the state level. * significant at the 0.10 level; ** significant at the 0.05 level; *** significant at the 0.01 level. Y = yes; blank = not applicable; SE = standard error; t = t-score; B = coefficient.

SOURCE: ACS.

Table 2.7 Role of Occupational Regulation on Employment Levels and Growth of Interior Designers, 2001–2009

Variables	(1) lnemp	(2) lnemp	(3) lnemp	(4) empgr	(5) empgr	(6) empgr
regulation	0.163			−0.0003		
	0.128			0.273		
practice		0.427	0.274		0.352	0.357
		0.278	0.250		0.505	0.430
title		0.160			−0.005	
		0.128			0.273	
lnpcinc	−2.769***	−2.738***	−2.648***	1.291	1.323	1.320
	0.768	0.768	0.766	1.450	1.452	1.437
State fixed effects	Y	Y	Y	Y	Y	Y
Year fixed effects	Y	Y	Y	Y	Y	Y
Observations	369	369	369	328	328	328
R-squared	0.747	0.748	0.747	0.440	0.441	0.441

NOTE: * significant at the 0.10 level; ** significant at the 0.05 level; *** significant at the 0.01 level. Y = yes.
SOURCE: Occupational Employment Statistics (OES) survey, from the U.S. Bureau of Labor Statistics (BLS).

DETERMINANTS OF THE PASSAGE OF LAWS REGULATING INTERIOR DESIGNERS

Could some economic factors affect whether regulations for interior designers are enacted into law? In order to determine whether the economic climate in a state matters, in Table 2.8 a hazard model is estimated for the period 2001 through 2009 to examine whether a titling law was enacted during this period. This approach examines the time to the passage of a titling law based on the characteristics of the state. The results show that none of the three factors—1) the annual wage, 2) the state per capita income, and 3) the employment growth rate—was statistically significant in determining the passage of a titling law. In a similar manner, Panel A of the table provides estimates of a hazard model for the period 2001 through 2009 for the passage of a titling act, and Panel B shows the passage of a practice act, or a full licensing of interior designers. No additional licensing laws granting full licensing to the occupation have been passed since 2000. Again, the economic factors in the state are not related to the eventual passage of a licensing law. Perhaps political issues or a major event in a state may have led to the passage of a law either giving interior designers the right to exclusive title and use of the term "interior designer" within the law or granting them the right to perform certain tasks. The results of the analysis in this area, however, were inconclusive.

Next I examine whether unlicensed interior designers pose any serious risks to public health and safety.

PRELIMINARY EVIDENCE ON THE HEALTH AND SAFETY OF CONSUMERS

If the licensing of interior designers does indeed protect public safety, then licensing would reduce the probability of negative outcomes for consumers. In the case of interior designers, such negative outcomes could include whether a building collapses, the impact of injuries caused by slippage on improperly coated floors, and the destruction of buildings by fire. Alexander et al. (2009) examine results from insur-

Table 2.8 Possible Economic Factors Leading to Passage of Legislation Regulating Interior Designers

Panel A: Hazard model estimates of time to adoption of titling law
for interior designers' regulation, 2001–2009

Variable	Hazard ratio	Coefficient
Average annual wage, 1999–2001	2.400	0.876
	(9.786)	(4.077)
Average state per capita income, 1999–2001	16.780	2.820
	(89.803)	(5.352)
Average state employment growth rate,	0.356	−1.032
1999–2001	(0.410)	(1.152)
Observations	28	

NOTE: Standard errors are in parentheses.

Panel B: Hazard model estimates of time to pass practice act
for interior designers, 1990–2000

Variable	Hazard ratio	Coefficient
Average annual wage, 1990	42264.3	10.652
	(291206.5)	(6.890)
Average state per capita income, 1989–1992	4.867	1.583
	(22.395)	(4.601)
Average state employment growth rate,	3.124**	1.139**
1989–1992	(1.828)	(0.585)
Observations	45	

NOTE: Standard errors are in parentheses. The wage is calculated from the 1990 census Public Use Microdata Sample (PUMS). The five states (Alaska, Montana, North Dakota, South Dakota, and Wyoming) with the fewest interior designers in the micro-sample are excluded from the estimation. * significant at the 0.10 level; ** significant at the 0.05 level; *** significant at the 0.01 level.
SOURCE: Author's calculations using PUMS.

ance brokers who cover interior designers and the structures they normally work on. In addition, they performed an empirical analysis across states where firings might have been the result of shoddy work. Their analysis, in which they considered together insurance premiums and fire death rates, indicated no clear effect of the quality of interior design licensing. They did not find conclusive evidence to support the claim that interior design licensing will provide greater protection of public health and safety. Furthermore, Richard Carpenter of the Institute for Justice, using data on complaints to the Better Business Bureau in his research, found no difference in the number of consumer complaints filed against interior designers in states that had just certification (title acts) and those that had full licensing (Carpenter 2008). Carpenter cites testimony in Wisconsin that showed that officials in that state could not find health and safety reasons for regulating interior designers (Callender 1995).

Thus far, the ASID has not demonstrated that unlicensed interior designers have generated significant harm or loss to society relative to those that are regulated (Harrington and Treber 2009). Proponents of interior design licensing have asserted that the interior finish and content of building materials are contributing factors to fires and thus responsible for deaths, injuries, and costly property damage (Martin 2008). But building occupants themselves may have been responsible for creating interior environments more conducive to the ignition and lethality of fires. Thus far, no rigorous empirical evidence supports the assertion that failure to regulate interior designers would result in more fires, deaths, or injuries to the consumers of interior design services. Overall, the preliminary empirical evidence contained in the current research does not support the public safety rationale for the licensing of interior designers (Harrington and Treber 2009).

CONCLUSIONS

One could summarize the role that licensing plays in regulating interior designers in this statement by Glenn Wilson, former commissioner of the Minnesota Department of Commerce, regarding occupational licensing within his department: "What you think we do, we don't do."

Wilson explains that the ability to monitor or enforce regulatory provisions on individuals who are licensed by his department is minimal. Consequently, he says, the general enforcement ability of government on licensing regulations is minimal.[19]

For occupations at this initial stage of regulation, where certification rather than licensing dominates, evidence that regulation raises wages or does much to improve quality is conflicting. The estimates by Harrington and Treber (2009) show some influence of regulation on wage determination. Similarly, Alabama interior designers' wages grew much faster than the national growth rate after implementation of full-scale licensing in the state. More recent national data from the ACS analysis through 2009, however, show that the regulation and licensing of interior designers has a small and insignificant influence on wage determination.

An examination of the employment growth of interior designers during the period 2000–2009 shows that regulation has a small influence on employment growth once state economic characteristics are taken into account. Furthermore, the economic factors available for the analysis were not important in determining whether a law was passed. Perhaps the organizational or political skills of the leaders of the profession were the more important factors in determining whether interior designers were licensed. Another event in the state, such as a building collapse or other catastrophic event, may have galvanized support for the regulation of the occupation. However, in my research I was unable to find such events that might have triggered the eventual licensing of interior designers.

An examination of the evidence shows that interior designers are seeking regulation in order to maintain the status of the organization in comparison to both engineers and architects. From their perspective, this goal is reasonable because these other licensed occupations have the ability to legislate work for their members, which comes at the expense of interior designers—especially when construction jobs decline, as they did from 2007 through 2010. Although this goal is an important one for the more than 72,000 interior designers in the United States and their families, it may not warrant additional regulation based on the criteria of health and safety that are established in most states (BLS 2011). Moreover, the dominant criterion for regulation in state government is the quality of the practitioner; it does not take into account that limiting members of the occupation might affect consumers. Consequently, what may be good for the members of the interior design occupation relative to other competing occupations may drive up prices without any clear evidence of higher-quality buildings or improved consumer health and safety.

An examination of the regulation of interior designers serves as a foundation from which to compare more intensely regulated occupations. The next several chapters examine occupations with longer and more intense experiences with licensing. These chapters evaluate the performance of the members as well as the influence of these regulations on consumers.

Notes

1. I would like to thank Jing Cai for her extraordinary assistance with the chapter.
2. See Harrington and Treber (2009) for a detailed listing of the issues involved with this increase.
3. Alabama v. Lupo, 984 So. 2d 395 (Ala. Sup. 2007).
4. Minn. Stat. § 326.02. ("No person may use the title certified interior designer unless that person has been certified as an interior designer or has been exempted by the board.") Registered architects can seek certification as interior designers without meeting any additional requirements, and the act does not preclude an individual from saying he or she can do interior design work.
5. Minn. Stat. § 326.02, subd. 1.
6. Minn. Stat. § 326.02, subd. 2.
7. Minn. Stat. § 326.02, subd. 4b.
8. Minn. Stat. § 326.03, subd. 1.
9. Minnesota Senate, Hearing on S.F. 349 before the Senate Committee on Commerce and Consumer Protection, 86th Minn. Leg., Reg. Sess. (Feb. 17, 2009), available at http://www.senate.leg.state.mn.us/media/media_list.php?ls=86&archive_year=2009&archive_month=02&category=committee&type=audio#monthnav (audio).
10. Neil v. City of New York, 642 N.Y.S. 2d 661 (1996).
11. Ibid, 662.
12. Ibid.
13. Ibid.
14. Rubin v. First Avenue Owners Inc., 618 N.Y.S. 2d 793 (1994).
15. Ibid.
16. Simoneaux v. BSL Inc. WL 2165208 S.D. Miss. (2008).
17. Ibid.
18. The approach taken in Tables 2.5 and 2.6 produces results that are consistent with the more commonly used panel estimation approach. Given the type of data gath-

ered in the book on the influence of regulation on the labor market, we present the
panel estimation approach for the other occupations that are analyzed in detail.
19. Glenn Wilson, personal communication with the author, December 22, 2010.

3
The Rise, Fall, and
Regulation of Mortgage Brokers

People think they can make a quick buck, but they're not in it for the long haul. We'll see every shoe salesman and photocopier salesman will all of a sudden be a mortgage broker, but come next year they'll all be gone.

—Mary McGarity (2001, p. 41)

Mortgage brokers are intermediaries who both match potential mortgage borrowers with lenders and assist them in completing the loan origination process for the purpose of purchasing property.[1] Brokers have typically operated as independent service providers, not as agents or employees of either borrowers or lenders, and they are compensated by fees paid by the borrower and sometimes the lender as well.[2] They are generally small businesses. Approximately 83 percent of companies are licensed in only one state and employ from one to five mortgage loan originators. Additionally, 87 percent of these companies have only a single location. Data for individual mortgage loan originators reflect similar trends (Nationwide Mortgage Licensing System and Registry 2012). Their role in the U.S. mortgage market skyrocketed from an insignificant few in 1980 to a predominant position in the home purchasing market in 2007, just before the collapse of the housing market in the United States. In 2004, about 53,000 mortgage brokerage firms were operating in the United States and were directly or indirectly involved in the origination of as many as 68 percent of all mortgages that year (Wholesale Access 2005).[3] As the mortgage broker business grew, so did questions about the industry's role and its effects on consumer welfare. However, with the financial crisis of 2008 and the decline in the housing market, mortgage brokers declined dramatically, so that by 2009 there had been a 72 percent decline in the number of mortgage brokerage firms from its peak (Olson 2007). By 2010, there were only half as many mortgage brokers, about 246,000, as had been working in the occupation in 2006. In addition, by 2010 all states required state licensure of loan officers, except for those who had the title of independent brokers (Berry 2010). This decline and move to more regulations reflects the opening quotation of this chapter. The goal of the chapter is to examine the role of the governmental regulation of mortgage brokers on wage determination and on outcomes for consumers for this highly volatile occupation. Within this context, this occupation is one that has moderate levels of occupational regulation, judged by the fact that it takes relatively little specific education and few other job-specific requirements to become licensed. Nevertheless, the governmental requirements that practitioners must meet in order to do the work have been increasing over time, with clear implications for the members of the occupation and the consumers of their services. Workers in financial services are much more regulated than interior designers, the focus of the previous chapter, but they still represent an occupation at an initial stage of occupational regulation in comparison with those that will be examined later in this volume.

This chapter examines the relationships between mortgage broker licensing and labor market and consumer outcomes, focusing on the period of growth of the services provided and the occupation. The chapter gives some background on the occupation and reviews the rationale for how licensing can affect outcomes in both the labor market for mortgage brokers and the consumer product market for mortgages. The examination of the occupation then introduces and summarizes a compilation of mortgage broker licensing requirements from the 50 states and the District of Columbia for the period 1996–2006, initially developed by Pahl (2007). The data are used to analyze whether mortgage broker licensing or any of its components have significant relationships with labor or service market outcomes. Estimates are presented from an index of regulation that attempts to construct overall indices of the difficulty of mortgage broker regulation, but the analysis finds that they are not significantly related to labor market or consumer market outcomes. The index examines many of the separate components of state mortgage broker regulation and finds that one component—the requirement in many states that mortgage brokers maintain a surety bond or maintain a minimum net worth—has a significant and fairly consistent statistical association with fewer brokers, fewer subprime mortgages, higher foreclosure rates on subprime mortgages, and a higher percentage of mortgages carrying high interest rates.[4] These results are often viewed as a counterintuitive finding by those who suggest that occupational regulation either does not matter or can have positive influences on labor markets and consumer financial well-being. The results developed in this chapter provide more evidence of the influence of regulation on the quality and prices of the services in this financial sector (Ambrose and Conklin 2012; Shi 2012).

UNDERSTANDING THE INDUSTRY AND OCCUPATION

The number of mortgage broker firms nationwide is expected to fall a staggering 72 percent from its peak back in 2005, according to Wholesale Access chief David Olson, who spoke with National Mortgage News. —Colin Robertson (2009)

From one perspective, the rise of mortgage brokering was just one part of a broader vertical disintegration of the lending business which is thought to have made mortgage credit more widely and cheaply available to many households following the savings and loan crisis of the 1980s. Mortgage brokers have played a role in the evolution of the highly specialized and efficient mortgage market. In particular, brokers can make the complicated task of shopping and applying for the increasingly wide array of mortgage products more manageable and efficient for borrowers and lenders alike. Millions of households, including many affluent and sophisticated consumers, have frequently arranged mortgages through brokers. The brokers' services seem to be operating in reasonably competitive markets, as evidenced by the repeat business and the recommendations of their services to others.

Critics of the members of the occupation have argued that too many mortgage brokers are not honest or, more broadly, that market failures prevent competition from effectively disciplining brokers' profits and quality of service. These market failures, mainly through information asymmetries, allow mortgage brokers to profit at the expense of mortgage borrowers as well as lenders. These issues are said to be especially problematic in the subprime mortgage market, where mortgage brokers dominated originations from the late 1990s through the middle of the next decade (Schloemer et al. 2006). For example, data from New

Century Financial Corporation show that brokers earned an average of $5,300 per funded loan for all loans in New Century's sample of the loans made through mortgage brokers (Berndt, Hollifield, and Sandås 2010).

In response to these concerns, a variety of policy measures have been discussed. One of the most common responses of policymakers has been to increase the regulatory practices to include occupational licensing standards for mortgage brokers. In a study for the Federal Reserve Bank of Minneapolis, Pahl (2007) documents how state licensing of mortgage brokers increased both in the number of states and the intensity of the statutes, as measured by more restrictions per state between 1996 and 2006. Since then, a surge in mortgage foreclosures has provided even greater political momentum for the enactment of further regulation. Policymakers seem to have concluded that a lack of market discipline and regulatory oversight allowed many mortgage brokers to originate expensive and risky mortgages. They tend to view a more comprehensive system of mortgage broker licensing as part of the solution in order to reduce consumer problems in these financial markets. Yet little is known about how or even whether licensing influences the labor market for brokers or their customers.

The evolution of mortgage brokering in the United States and the policy issues that arose with it have been well described in other sources; this chapter summarizes them to motivate and provide background for the analysis of mortgage broker occupational licensing.[5] In particular, mortgage brokering has become an economically significant industry surrounded by controversy about the extent of benefits it provides to consumers and lenders. This section describes some of the key pricing and quality issues that policymakers try to address with licensing programs.

The National Association of Mortgage Brokers (NAMB) delineates the roles of the mortgage lender and the mortgage broker as follows:[6]

> The wholesale lender underwrites and funds the home loan, may service the loan payments, and ensures the loan's compliance with underwriting guidelines. The broker, on the other hand, originates the loan. A detailed application process, financial and credit worthiness investigation, and extensive disclosure requirements must be completed in order for a wholesale lender to evaluate a consumer's home loan request. The broker simplifies this process for the

borrower and the wholesale lender, by conducting this research, counseling consumers on their loan package choices, and enabling them to select the right loan for their home buying needs.

The mortgage loan process can be arduous, costly, and seemingly impossible to the consumer. The broker works as the liaison between the borrower and the lender to create a cost effective and efficient loan process.

As an independent contractor, the broker allows wholesaler lenders to cut origination costs by providing such services as preparing the borrower's loan package, loan application, funding process, and counseling the borrower. (NAMB 2013)

The services of mortgage brokers were virtually nonexistent 30 years ago. At that time, the mortgage industry was made up almost entirely of banks and savings and loans that managed the entire process of bringing borrowers and investors together. They located depositors and borrowers and recommended from a small subset the appropriate type of mortgage, analyzed borrowers' creditworthiness and the value of their collateral, closed the loans, serviced the loans, and made payments to the investors. The banks used simple criteria of 20 percent down payment—or higher fees for those with lower down payments—and a fixed-rate mortgage over the life of the mortgage.

By 2000, the mortgage market had changed radically (U.S. Department of Housing and Urban Development [HUD] 2002; Jacobides 2005). Technological change (fax machines, the Internet, and other technologies), financial innovation (credit scoring, automated underwriting, securitization of mortgages, and so forth), and deregulation (e.g., repeal of state usury limits) abetted extensive specialization and vertical disintegration in the industry, so that separate firms could focus on particular steps in the process, such as loan marketing and closing, underwriting, initial funding, servicing, pooling, and long-term funding. At the same time, the range of potential participants within each such niche broadened; for example, nondepository mortgage banks competed with depository institutions to originate and sometimes service, pool, or fund mortgages. In addition, new types of mortgages (e.g., adjustable rate mortgages [ARMs]) and differentiated products aimed at a wider array of consumers, and these new products captured significant shares of the market.

These developments both affected and were affected by the rapid growth of mortgage brokering. As the decision to grant credit became less based on subjective assessments of the loan applicant and more based on credit scores and other objective underwriting standards, underwriting moved to the back office, and loan officers employed by depository institutions focused increasingly on sales and loan closing services. Improved communications technology—fax machines and later the Internet and PDF documents—fostered the physical separation of the sales function from the underwriting function, and this in turn made it possible to outsource either or both.

Mortgage brokers take outsourcing one step further, in that they work for themselves, as independent contractors dealing with multiple lenders. As such, brokers allowed both established mortgage lenders (the depository institutions) and new competitors (nondepository mortgage banks) to specialize and to rapidly scale up or down their sales efforts and loan origination volumes in response to market cycles and competitive opportunities (HUD 2002; Apgar, Bendimerad, and Essene 2007).

Low overheads and the resulting ability to efficiently market themselves within residential neighborhoods helped brokers in the early 2000s penetrate the emerging subprime market, which included many households that were somewhat unfamiliar with traditional mortgage lending institutions. Much of the growth of the mortgage broker industry took place through the addition of new firms, as the average size of firms remained small, about 10 individuals, during most of the period of the analysis (Sichelman 2003).

Mortgage brokers, by consolidating information on multiple products from multiple lenders, offered consumers a convenient way to examine a variety of home loans for which they were financially qualified. The result was the creation of a viable intermediary role and rapid growth in the mortgage broker industry from the late 1990s to 2008.

The transformation of the U.S. mortgage market after 1980 created significant benefits for U.S. consumers by increasing home ownership and improving the efficiency of mortgage processing, and mortgage brokers claimed a share of the credit. Brokers served millions of customers from all parts of society; their repeat business and the multiyear growth in their market share until the financial crisis in 2008 suggest that many of their customers had been pleased with their services. Brokers helped to shorten the loan closing process and made it cheaper, and they enabled the mortgage industry to meet enormous variations in demand. However, the transformation of the mortgage industry created new problems, and mortgage brokers were blamed for many of these.

Critics of mortgage brokers generally focus on incentive problems stemming from the fact that the broker is an intermediary whose pay depends directly on the size and number of loans he or she originates and only indirectly on whether the borrower received appropriate representation on the deal and whether the borrower makes payments as expected (Schloemer et al. 2006). The incentive issues arise because of informational asymmetries among the borrower, lender, and broker. It has been well documented that borrowers are confused by the language and terms of mortgage contracts and related documentation (Guttentag 2000; Woodward 2003; Pappalardo and Lacko 2007). Borrowers frequently fail to understand basic facts about the mortgages they signed and are even more confused about the other mortgage options available to them. Many have argued that the complexity created by having so many legal documents to sign in a short period of time makes the financial part of home purchases nearly impossible to understand. Many borrowers are willing to follow the advice of a professional, such as a mortgage broker, even though they may be unable to verify the quality of the advice even after the fact. This creates an opportunity for professionals, including mortgage brokers, to abuse that trust by, for example, recommending a mortgage that has a higher interest rate than the customer qualifies for, in order to obtain a higher fee.[7] The following three points, taken from Guttentag, are among the most frequently cited consumer issues regarding mortgage brokers and other financial intermediaries with similar incentives:

1) Brokers steer borrowers "to mortgages that provide higher compensation to the broker but are not necessarily the lowest cost or most advantageous to the consumer," and they do so deliberately and disproportionately with subprime, minority, elderly, or poorly informed customers.

2) They market aggressively to maximize origination fees, in particular by persuading borrowers to take out loans they cannot afford or to refinance too frequently based on their income and financial status.

3) They receive fees from borrowers and lenders that are more than commensurate with services rendered, especially from minority or unsophisticated borrowers.

Asymmetrical information, or information that one side possesses but the other does not, also makes lenders concerned about the quality of mortgage brokers' services. Brokers' fees typically are paid only when loans are closed. Consequently, brokers' immediate incentive is to earn their fees by getting lenders to approve and close loans, and they do not have a direct stake in subsequent loan performance. This incentive has been seen as raising the following major issues for lenders regarding brokers:

1) Brokers may corrupt the information about the borrower that is submitted for underwriting in order to increase the chances that the lender will approve the loan, with the result that loans handled by brokers are more likely to default than loans processed by the lender's own loan officers (Alexander et al. 2002). The incomplete or inaccurate information can arise from either carelessness or deliberate misrepresentation or fraud (Schloemer et al. 2006). For mortgage brokers there are, potentially, clear elements of either incompetence or unscrupulous behavior.

2) Contrary to contractual agreements with their lender clients, brokers encourage the clients' existing borrowers to refinance, so that prepayment rates on the lenders' broker-originated mortgages are higher than on mortgages originated by the lenders' own loan officers (LaCour-Little and Chun 1999).

One view is that the marketplace can mitigate these consumer and lender information and incentive problems and correct or alleviate the market failures that have been alleged in housing finance. For example, over time lenders can monitor the quality of the loans submitted by a given broker and either stop dealing with or pay lower fees to inferior brokers. Although some lenders began monitoring in this way, industry experts assert that, at least until recently, these efforts have not been sufficiently strict or widespread to significantly change aggregate outcomes (Alexander et al. 2002; Apgar, Bendimerad, and Essene 2007). Some lenders mitigated losses by pricing broker-originated loans differently, using higher interest rates on these loans to offset default risk or imposing prepayment penalties to offset higher prepayment risk. On the consumer side, confusion about mortgages contributed to enhanced efforts at home buyer financial education, but with only limited results. Guttentag (2000) suggests a new contractual arrangement, the Upfront Mortgage Broker certification, under which mortgage brokers would serve as the borrower's agent in return for fixed, fully disclosed fees. However, only a small fraction of brokers work under this arrangement. As of 2007 the market responses have not eliminated concerns about bad outcomes caused by asymmetric information and incentive conflicts in the mortgage broker market. Partly as a result, many mortgage lenders have cut back on or ceased accepting broker-originated loans, exacerbating the steep decline in mortgage brokering since 2006. More importantly, the recession that was triggered by the financial collapse in 2008 saw financial institutions dramatically reduce their reliance on brokers because of the drop in demand for housing and because of the actual and potential abuses that were associated with brokers.

RATIONALE FOR THE REGULATION OF MORTGAGE BROKERS

With mainly market-based responses to financial crises not eliminating concerns about mortgage broker incentives and actions, public policymakers have entered the fray. The federal financial regulatory agencies have promulgated new guidelines and requirements regarding mortgage information disclosures and subprime loan underwriting and pricing. Many states and local governments have enacted antipredatory lending laws that restrict mortgage interest rates, fees, and contract terms. In addition, state legislators and regulators, often with the support and help of mortgage broker trade associations, have broadened and tightened the requirements for mortgage broker firms and individual loan officers to obtain the licenses that they need to operate legally. In the Housing and Economic Recovery Act of 2008, Congress established new minimum requirements for state mortgage broker registration and regulation. This section reviews the rationale for and previous empirical studies of occupational licensing. The following sections summarize the specifics of mortgage broker licensing in the United States and assess how state differences in mortgage broker licensing are associated with outcomes in the labor and mortgage markets.

Licensing requirements generally take the form of unspecified fixed costs controlled by the licensing authority, broadly similar to typical licensing requirements such as payment of an annual licensing fee or maintenance of a surety bond, which would be the case for mortgage brokers. Utilizing a commonly used perspective on the rationale for governmental regulation, skill affects the relative cost of producing high-quality services, and licensing takes the more specific form of a minimal human capital requirement, similar to actual requirements that entrants and sometimes incumbents take certain training programs or pass an exam (Shapiro 1986). Apart from these special fixed costs, entry into and exit out of the occupation are unrestricted, which ensures that providers earn zero economic profits in equilibrium—or, in other words, no excess profits.

In applying any of this rationale to mortgage broker licensing, a worthwhile consideration is what would be observed in the credit market if mortgage brokers provided higher-quality services. The nature of the service is to match a borrower and lender efficiently, so that loans are made with a favorable combination of lower search-plus-processing costs than if a broker had not been involved. However, because credit markets are also subject to information asymmetries, the credit market results of high-quality brokering are potentially counterintuitive. For example, higher quality might include the consideration that the broker provides the lender with more complete and accurate information about the borrower, so that loans are underwritten and priced more accurately. If so, it is conceivable that better brokers could be associated with a greater proportion of high-priced loans in the credit market, because lenders would be more willing to price risk rather than ration credit if they had more trust in the information brokers were submitting. In other words, the quality of mortgage brokering can affect the breadth of the credit market and thus the range of creditworthiness among loan applicants and recipients, and this can complicate the impact of higher-quality brokering on some credit market outcomes.

However, if we control for the creditworthiness of loan applicants, better brokering services would be associated with lower search- and processing-related costs, such as a lower percentage of loan applications being denied, a lower rate of bad matches that lead to delinquency or foreclosure, and a shorter time between loan application and loan closing or denial. The effects of better services provided by the occupation on interest rates, controlling for creditworthiness, are less clear. Borrowers might be willing to accept higher interest rates in a brokered transaction, compared with a nonbrokered transaction, if there were more-than-offsetting reductions in search costs, just as lenders might be willing to accept lower interest rates if there were more-than-offsetting reductions in marketing and processing costs. The role for public policy presumably is to ensure that borrowers obtain a higher-quality service by the members of the profession, and that outcomes such as foreclosures are diminished by having brokers oversee the process.

Table 3.1 shows the extent to which the individuals surveyed who were interested in these financial services checked with the government to see if the person who was providing the service was licensed. The results from the survey show that only 14 percent checked to learn whether the individual was licensed; 84 percent did not check on the licensing status of the individual, and 2 percent didn't know whether they had checked. One conclusion from the survey is that licensing is not a major factor in the perceived quality of the service. On the other hand, the survey results could show that consumers assume that these services are already of high quality or that regulation is not essential for the service provider.

Table 3.1 Financial Consumer Monitoring of Licensing

Survey question	Eligible respondents	Answers	Percentage
Have you ever checked with a state or federal regulator regarding the background, registration, or license of a financial professional?	Respondents who have used a financial professional ("Yes" to any of k_1 to k_5)	Yes	14
		No	84
		Don't know	2
		Prefer not to say	0
	N		14,918

SOURCE: FINRA Investor Education Foundation (2013).

MEASURING THE INFLUENCE OF OCCUPATIONAL REGULATION ON MORTGAGE BROKERS

In order to examine and analyze the role of the regulation of mortgage brokers both for the members of the occupation and for consumers of their services, a method needs to be devised to determine the level of regulation over time for each state. To associate mortgage broker licensing with market outcomes, a method was developed for the measurement of the extent of mortgage broker licensing. Cindy Pahl, as part of her work at the Federal Reserve Bank of Minneapolis, implemented a compilation of these regulations in the 50 states and the District of Columbia for the period 1996–2006, just prior to the dramatic decline in housing prices and the recession (Pahl 2007). Pahl shows that a wide variety of licensing provisions may apply specifically to mortgage brokerage firms. The following are examples of such provisions:

- The entity's *controlling individual(s)* may be required to be of minimum age; maintain in-state residency; meet minimums for professional prelicensing education, experience, or examination results; provide evidence of ethical fitness and absence of criminal background; and complete required continuing education.

- The entity may be required to name an individual as *managing principal*, and the managing principal may be subject to requirements similar to those for controlling individuals as well as requirements to maintain a minimum net worth or surety bond or to obtain a license as an individual mortgage broker or loan officer.

- The entity itself may be required to maintain a minimum net worth or a surety bond. Entities, sole proprietors, controlling individuals, and managing principals may be required to pay fees for licensing, application processing, application investigation, or license renewal.

- Entities and sole proprietors may be required to meet minimum physical office requirements, such as maintaining a physical office in states where they operate. To open a branch office, entities and sole proprietors may be required to provide notification, obtain a license or certificate, pay various fees, maintain branch-specific amounts of net worth or surety bonds, or name a branch manager who may be required to meet provisions similar to those listed above for managing principals. In some states, the loan officers who work for mortgage brokerage firms may also be required to meet standards of the same type as those listed above for managing principals, but often at a lower level. Additional provisions may specify that a loan officer can work for only one firm at a time. However, some states allow certain other professionals, such as real estate agents or attorneys, to engage in some aspects of mortgage brokering without obtaining a specific mortgage broker license; these exemptions may be subject to limits on the maximum number or volume of loans brokered.

For each state and the District of Columbia for each year from 1996 through 2006, the index assigns an integer value for the intensity of each of 24 regulatory components. Most of the components deal with the regulation of human capital requirements. For example, regarding the controlling of individuals in mortgage brokerage firms, the codes separate intensities for prelicensing education, prelicensing experience, prelicensing examinations, and continuing education requirements. Pahl codes the same four variables for managing principals, branch managers, and the firms' employees, for a total of 16 human capital components. Three components reflect, respectively, the degree of individual licensing required of managing principals, branch managers, and employees. At the firm level, the index is coded by intensity; in other words, entry requirements are more difficult for both net worth and surety bonding requirements, so the intensity of surety bonding required for branches is separately coded. Finally, the codes show whether an in-state office is required and the extent of exemptions that allow other professions to engage in mortgage brokering activities.

The analysis uses two overall indices of the intensity of mortgage broker regulation in a state: a simple sum of all 24 of Pahl's individual intensity values (*the summated rating scale*) and a statistically weighted nonlinear index (*the Rasch index*).[8] This combined index can capture the major regulatory provisions affecting the occupation using both linear (summated rating scale) and nonlinear (Rasch index) measures of the level of regulation.

In addition to these composite indices, the analysis also examines subsets of the 24 regulatory components that were collected.[9] Much of the analysis includes a dollar-valued measure of the bonding and net worth regulations, which were created by examining the details of each state's requirements and selecting what was judged to be the smallest dollar option by which new entrants could meet either the bonding or the net worth requirement. These values were also examined by subtracting the bonding and net worth indices from the composite indices. There was an examination of other subindices and individual components, such as those for the provisions regarding training and examinations, provisions that apply only to the management of brokerage firms, provisions that limit brokerage firm branches, and provisions that apply only to employees of brokerage firms. Some of these regulatory variables were significant in regressions with one or more of our labor and mortgage market–dependent variables, and in a few cases their presence materially weakened the significance of the bonding and net worth variable. The major focus was on the bonding and net worth provisions in order to show the broadest and most consistent pattern of significant relationships with market outcomes.

Using the measures of regulatory restrictiveness, Table 3.2 shows the top seven and bottom five states ranked by the restrictiveness of their summated scale of mortgage broker licensing. Florida has the most statutory provisions regulating mortgage brokers. The five states with the least restrictive statutes in 2004, such as Alaska and Wyoming, are less populous. Montana and Texas had the greatest increase in the regulation of mortgage brokers during the period 1999–2004. In general, larger industrial and urbanized states were more likely to impose broader and deeper regulatory provisions on mortgage brokers, Montana being an exception.

Figure 3.1 shows the more general growth and variation of regulation over time from 1996 to 2006, using a box-and-whisker plot. The mean value of the summated rating scale for all states was 3.2 in 1996 and increased to almost 8.0 by 2005, using the index developed by Pahl (2007). The variations in state practices also rose. As the membership in the occupation expanded in response to growth in the demand for broker services, more states began regulating the members of the occupation. This may have occurred because members in the occupation

Table 3.2 Regulation in the Most, Least, and Greatest Changer States

Rankings	Regulation value
Top seven regulated states, 2004	
Florida	16
Montana	14
New Jersey	13
Ohio	12
Texas	12
North Carolina	12
Nevada	12
Bottom five regulated states, 2004	
Colorado	0
Wyoming	0
Alaska	0
South Dakota	1
Maine	2
Top seven states by change in regulation, 1999–2004	
Montana	14
Texas	12
North Carolina	11
Oklahoma	8
Connecticut	7
Nevada	7
Utah	7

SOURCE: Developed from Pahl (2007).

sought regulation or because of public concern about brokers allegedly charging excessive fees or leading customers into overly risky loans.

Because of their significance for the subsequent analysis, it is important to understand the nature of bonding requirements.[10] When brokers are required to have a bond of $50,000, for example, this typically means that they pay an annual premium, ranging from several hundred to a few thousand dollars, to a surety bond company. It does not mean that the broker must own and place in trust a fixed-income security with a market value of $50,000. Under specified conditions of broker nonperformance of duties spelled out in the governing laws and regulations, third parties, such as the broker's customers, may collect up to the amount of the bond from the surety company. The role of the

Figure 3.1 Growth and Variation of Occupational Regulation over Time

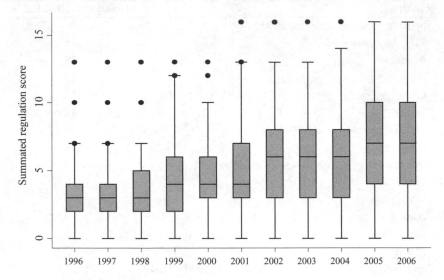

NOTE: This box-and-whisker plot shows annual values of the median, interquartile range, and outliers of the summated rating scale derived from the catalogue of state (and District of Columbia) mortgage broker regulations. The line in the middle of the box represents the median. The bottom and top edges of the box are the first and third quartiles, respectively. The whiskers extending from the box represent the most extreme point within the range of one and a half times the interquartile range (the difference between the third and first quartiles). The remaining points represent outliers that do not fall within the range of the whiskers.
SOURCE: Pahl (2007).

surety company is to ensure that a valid claim will be promptly paid.[11] If this occurs, the surety company will seek full compensation from the broker for the amount it paid out to the third party, plus expenses. The broker's annual premium or the basis of his or her salary is thus a fee paid to guarantee a line of contingent credit up to a legally required amount. In setting the annual premium it charges a broker, a surety company considers both the expected value of claims against the broker and the probability of collecting from the broker for any amounts paid out. Consequently, the bond company may conduct detailed screening of applicants, similar to credit underwriting, before issuing the bond.

The basic hypothesis is that this type of screening could make bonding one of the most significant barriers to entry in states requiring bonds of $50,000 or more, especially given that the educational requirements for mortgage brokers do not usually require more than one year of classes or other tasks. Some support for this view comes from Barker's (2008) finding that state bonding requirements mattered in a related occupation—real estate brokerage—where they were associated with higher-quality service, as measured by a lower rate of consumer complaints. An industry expert, David Olson (2007), provides additional support. He notes that one factor that kept mortgage brokers from originating many Federal Housing Administration (FHA) mortgages was the FHA's requirement that originators provide a formal audit, costing about $5,000 each year. He suggests that more mortgage brokers would originate FHA loans if this audit requirement were dropped in favor of having brokers maintain a $75,000 surety bond. For established mortgage brokers with good credit, the cost of this bond would be about $750, but Olson notes that "brokers with low net worth and fewer years in the business will have a more difficult time getting a bond at all." In such cases, the broker could seek a more costly bond from a surety company that specializes in serving higher-risk clients, but premiums from this type of company often reach 10 to 15 percent of the amount of the bond, compared with 1 to 2 percent for low-risk mortgage brokers. Thus, on just a $50,000 bond, a high-risk premium could match or exceed the $5,000 audit cost that Olson judged to be prohibitive for most brokers. This requirement may serve to increase the quality of brokers but reduce their quantity. For some who need the services of a broker for negotiating price, picking an appropriately structured mortgage, or maintaining payments on an existing mortgage, having the financial advice of a competent and honest broker may enhance their economic welfare.

ESTIMATING RELATIONSHIPS

In order to calculate the influence of regulation of mortgage brokers and their labor market and consumer market outcomes, multivariate statistical models were developed of these relationships. These two types of relationships—1) labor markets and 2) consumer markets—are the key ones for evaluating the social costs and benefits of the institution of licensing for this occupation. The model controls for other factors affecting these markets. The analysis takes two main forms: 1) panel data analyses using repeated annual cross sections of labor and mortgage market data, and 2) cross-sectional analyses of hundreds to thousands of individual mortgages issued in 2005. Most of the panel data regressions utilize state-level average data, but for mortgage broker earnings the observations are combined on individual mortgage professionals with state-averaged data. The panel data regressions allow for fixed effects in each state as well as time trends. As a check on the results, a re-estimation was developed of the cross-sectional regressions on a sample restricted to mortgages just in metropolitan statistical areas (MSAs) that cross state boundaries, so that MSA fixed effects for the prices of mortgages could be included.

ESTIMATES FOR LABOR MARKET VARIABLES

Table 3.3 provides descriptive statistics for key labor market variables as well as other mortgage market and regulatory variables used in the analysis. The table shows the growth in occupational regulation and a measure of hourly wages and earnings from the annual American Community Survey (ACS) of mortgage brokers and related lending professionals.[12] The ACS is conducted annually by the Census Bureau and replicates the formerly used long form on the decennial census. It provides large samples of individuals even for relatively detailed occupational classifications such as loan officers and brokers.

To take advantage of the variation across both space and time to analyze relationships between the intensity of licensing and key labor market variables such as mortgage brokers' employment (relative to that of the population) and earnings, a panel data set is created. These relationships could be either positive or negative, based on the hypotheses discussed above. An additional complication, not reflected in the theoretical models, is that brokers may accelerate entry into the occupation before the standards become fully effective, leading to a spurious positive relationship between subsequent regulation and the number of practitioners in the short run. This was the case in accounting, where anticipated new regulations resulted in a surge of applications just

Table 3.3 Summary Statistics for the Labor Market, Service Market, and Legal and Bonding Provisions

State-level and individual variables	2000 mean (sd)	2005 mean (sd)
Broker/loan officer hourly wage ($)	20.12	25.15
	(12.74)	(16.87)
Annual broker/loan officer earnings ($)	40,973.43	52,748.68
	(26,177.80)	(41,526.24)
Employment (loan officers and brokers/population, %)	0.15	0.17
	(0.06)	(0.17)
Years of experience	18.49	19.51
	(10.54)	(11.51)
Years of schooling	14.54	14.69
	(1.79)	(1.80)
Mean number of loans	537,109.57	736,032.00
	(679,999.52)	(880,192.82)
Mean number of subprime loans	13,995.13	95,726.69
	(15,213.93)	(129,101.6)
Mean number of loans in foreclosure	6,214.27	8,580.52
	(8,883.82)	(9,444.91)
Mean state population	5,471,375.84	5,757,977.29
	(6,101,905.36)	(6,498,035.30)
Median household income ($)	58,574.57	63,504.76
	(7,641.51)	(10,326.91)
Licensing index (1996)	2.33	
	(1.96)	
Licensing index (2005)	6.84	
	(3.68)	
Bonding/net worth index (2000)	1.7	
	(1.37)	
Bonding/net worth index (2005)	1.88	
	(1.35)	
Real bonding/net worth requirement ($) 1996[a]	15,825.12	
	(18,963.83)	
Real bonding/net worth requirement ($) 2005[a]	27,479.08	
	(25,928.68)	

NOTE: Standard deviations in parentheses.
[a] Base year 2000.
SOURCE: American Community Survey (ACS) of the U.S. Census Bureau; Occupational Employment Statistics wage survey.

before more stringent educational requirements took effect (Cumming and Rankin 1999).

The analysis begins by relating regulation to the employment of brokers and associated lending professionals. Initially, the results find that neither the linear-summated rating scale nor the Rasch index is significantly related to mortgage broker employment at the state level. The basic findings hold, whether the specification and estimation are done with the more rigorous fixed effects or with random effects. The estimation strategy chosen uses the fixed effects approach since it helps avoid omitted variable bias due to unobserved heterogeneity.

Table 3.4 shows the relationship between bonding and net worth requirements and state-level employment relative to population from 2000 to 2005. The measure of employment is based on the ACS data and represents the number of mortgage brokers and related lending professionals per capita by state. The use of the ACS is in many ways preferable to the OES because the OES does not cover self-employed individuals, and, as was noted earlier, up to 80 percent of licensed mortgage brokers are either self-employed or work in small group practices that may not be covered in the OES (BLS 2013b). The model uses pooled time series and cross-section data that allow an estimate with year fixed-effects models and a set of human capital, labor market, and service market state controls. The results show that the bonding and net worth requirement is significant and negatively associated with employment. Using the values at the mean of the distribution, the estimates show that doubling the bonding requirement is associated with an approximately 8 to 10 percent decrease in the number of brokers and related lending professionals in the state relative to the population. The bonding requirement may have a stronger relationship to employment than the other licensing components for several reasons: it may be both relatively onerous and easily enforced up front and thus may reduce entry into the occupation. One would expect that states with older mortgage brokers and related lending professionals were the ones with lower per capita levels of employment within the occupation. This may simply reflect the fact that most new entrants are younger, so that impeding entry tends to both age the profession and reduce employment. It could also be that, as the occupation matures and public policies on regulation evolve, the political clout of mortgage brokers will grow, possibly leading to adoption of more rigorous educational and experience requirements that will complement those on bonding.

Table 3.4 Fixed-Effects Models of Loan Officer Employment/Population by State

	(1)	(2)
Summated regulation index, lagged once (no net worth/bonding)/100	0.068	0.058
	(0.206)	(0.173)
Real net worth/bonding requirement, lagged once /1,000,000	−0.545	−0.795
	(0.431)	(0.350)**
Summated regulation index, lagged twice (no net worth/bonding)/100	−0.026	
	(0.235)	
Real net worth/bonding requirement, lagged twice /1,000,000	−0.418	
	(0.403)	
Mean experience by state	−0.004	−0.004
	(0.003)	(0.003)
Mean experience by state squared/10,000	0.993	0.994
	(0.659)	(0.658)
Mean years of school by state	−0.001	−0.001
	(0.005)	(0.005)
Lag median state household income/100,000	0.218	0.211
	(0.162)	(0.161)
Lag state unemployment rate	0.010	0.010
	(0.006)*	(0.006)*
Lag state home ownership percentage	−0.001	−0.002
	(0.002)	(0.002)
Constant	0.172	0.187
	(0.176)	(0.175)
Year dummy controls (2001–2005), base 2000	Y	Y
Observations	300	300
Number of states	50	50
R-squared	0.12	0.11
F-test for one- and two-period lags of summated index	0.06	—
F-test for one- and two-period lags of bonding/net worth	3.16**	—

NOTE: The two columns contain two different estimates for the influence of those factors on employment of loan officer population to employment. The second column shows a sensitivity analysis of using a different statistical specification. Robust standard errors in parentheses. * significant at the 0.10 level; ** significant at the 0.05 level; *** significant at the 0.01 level. Y = yes. — means no estimates were developed for these cells. Blank means the variable was not used in the second specification.
SOURCE: ACS data.

Restricting entry could have a direct effect on earnings. To examine this relationship, a model is estimated showing the association between the bonding requirements and annual earnings, using individual-level data in the ACS. Table 3.5 presents estimates of the relationship between regulation and annual earnings from 2000 to 2005 using the individual practitioner data for each year. The basic earnings equation can be stated as follows:

$$(3.1) \quad \ln(Earnings_{it}) = a + b_1 R_{it} + b_2 X_{it} + u_{it},$$

where $Earnings_{it}$ stands for the annual earnings of person i in time period t; R_{it} is the tightness of mortgage broker licensing through bonding and net worth requirements in person i's state in time period t; the vector X_{it} includes covariates measuring characteristics of each person and state, along with year time trends; u_{it} is the error term; and a, b_1, and b_2 are the coefficients we estimate. Since regulation generally influences only new entrants, it would take some time before the full effect of regulation would influence wages and employment of the individuals in the occupation. We find a positive relationship between mortgage broker licensing and mortgage broker earnings, ranging from an imprecisely estimated 7 percent to a marginally significant 6 percent.[13,14] As shown in Table 3.5, the coefficients on the nonregulatory explanatory variables were consistent with the labor economics and human capital literature. Using an F-test in column 1, the joint regulation variables are statistically significant.

The findings show that tighter requirements for bonding and for net worth are also associated with lower volumes of loans processed and a higher percentage of high-priced loans originated. One interpretation of this set of results is that the demand for mortgage broker services is approximately of unit elasticity, so that as the numbers of brokers and loans processed contract, brokers' fees per loan processed rise by enough to just offset the lower loan volume and higher operating costs that result from tighter licensing, leaving the average broker's net earnings only slightly higher.

Table 3.5 Pooled Ordinary Least Squares (OLS) Models of Log Annual Earnings, 2000–2005

	(1)	(2)
Summated regulation index, lagged once (no net worth/bonding)/100	0.290	−0.485
	(0.520)	(0.204)**
Real bonding/net worth requirement, lagged once/100,000	0.076	0.060
	(0.099)	(0.033)*
Summated regulation index, lagged twice (no net worth/bonding)	−0.009	
	(0.006)	
Real bonding/net worth requirement, lagged twice/100,000	0.148	
	(0.113)	
Experience	0.057	0.057
	(0.004)***	(0.004)***
Experience squared/1,000	−1.018	−1.020
	(0.089)***	(0.090)***
Log years of school	1.262	1.263
	(0.059)***	(0.059)***
Lag median household income/1,000,000	10.823	10.786
	(1.677)***	(1.668)***
Lag state population/1,000,000	4.950	4.653
	(1.721)***	(1.702)***
Lag state unemployment rate/100	−0.231	−0.046
	(1.465)	(1.453)
State homeownership percentage/100	−0.088	−0.070
	(0.226)	(0.222)
Constant	6.430	6.407
	(0.262)***	(0.262)***
Year dummy controls (2001–2004), base 2000	Y	Y
Observations	6,699	6,699
R-squared	0.13	0.13
F-test for one- and two-period lags of summated index	3.54**	—
F-test for one- and two-period lags of bonding/ net worth	1.97	—

NOTE: Columns (1) and (2) show sensitivity analyses using different statistical specifications to see if the results are stable. Robust standard errors in parentheses. * significant at the 0.10 level; ** significant at the 0.05 level; *** significant at the 0.01 level. Y = yes. — means no estimates were developed for these cells.
SOURCE: ACS data.

DOES BROKER REGULATION INFLUENCE FINANCIAL OUTCOMES FOR CONSUMERS?

A key part of the investigation shows the relationship between mortgage broker licensing, the volume of subprime lending, and the rate of mortgage foreclosures. As discussed above, stricter licensing could reduce the number of subprime loans, for example, by restricting the number or work effort of mortgage brokers. Alternatively, stricter licensing could boost effective loan demand by enhancing the quality of broker services, thereby increasing the willingness both of marginal borrowers to step forward to use their services and of lenders to also see these services as being of high quality. To probe these potential outcomes, the following model is estimated:

$$(3.2) \quad \ln(sp - loans\ originated_{it}) = \alpha + \beta_1 R_{it} + \beta_2 X_{it} + \mu_{it},$$

where $sp - loans\ originated_{it}$ is the number of new subprime mortgages in state i over period t; R_{it} represents the state-level mortgage broker licensing indices in time period t; the vector X_{it} includes covariates measuring the characteristics of each state, along with year time trends; μ_{it} is the error term; and α, β_1, and β_2 are the coefficients we estimate. Subprime loans originated were measured as the number of all originations in a state for a given year that were made by lenders on the U.S. Department of Housing and Urban Development's list for that year (or for the most recent year available) of institutions whose mortgage activity is primarily in the subprime market.

The state fixed-effects results estimated over 2001–2005 with the bonding/net worth requirements are presented in Table 3.6. The results show that the two-lag specification of bonding requirements is associated with fewer loans originated. These estimates are consistent with those on employment. The results show that imposing bonding requirements correlates with fewer brokers and fewer subprime loans originated in the state. Quantitatively, the coefficients imply that a doubling of the mean bonding requirement to approximately $54,000 would be associated with a cut in the number of subprime loans originated by about 220,000 per year in 2004, or approximately 9 percent.

**Table 3.6 Fixed-Effects Estimates of the Log of State Subprime Loan
Originations**

Constant	(1)	(2)
Summated regulatory index, lagged once (no net worth/bonding)	−0.023 (0.011)**	−0.020 (0.010)*
Real net worth/bonding requirement, lagged once/100,000	0.104 (0.253)	−0.321 (0.223)
Summated regulatory index, lagged twice (no net worth/bonding)	−0.002 (0.012)	
Real net worth/bonding requirement, lagged twice/100,000	−0.741 (0.219)***	
Lag state unemployment rate	−0.017 (0.034)	−0.014 (0.035)
Lag state population/100,000	0.024 (0.010)**	0.022 (0.010)**
Lag median state household income/100,000	0.622 (0.938)	0.511 (0.965)
State homeownership percentage	0.050 (0.012)***	0.049 (0.012)***
Constant	4.661 (1.048)***	4.823 (1.076)***
Year dummy controls (2002–2005), base 2001	Y	Y
Observations	254	254
Number of states (including DC)	51	51
R-squared	0.76	0.74
F-test for one- and two-period lags of summated index	2.78*	—
F-test for one- and two-period lags of bonding/ net worth	6.91***	—

NOTE: Columns (1) and (2) show sensitivity analyses using different statistical specifications to see if the results are stable. Standard errors in parentheses. * significant
at the 0.10 level; ** significant at the 0.05 level; *** significant at the 0.01 level. Y =
yes. — means no estimates were developed for these cells.
SOURCE: ACS data.

If there are fewer loans with stricter licensing, does the quality of those loans, as measured by fewer negative outcomes such as foreclosures, also vary with licensing requirements? If state licensing improves the quality of broker services, the effects might include more appropriate loan selection and more accurate loan underwriting, resulting in fewer foreclosures. Alternatively, foreclosures could be positively correlated with tighter licensing, perhaps because a reduced availability of brokers leads to less accurate underwriting or because states that have higher foreclosure rates for other reasons (e.g., low or volatile incomes) are more likely to enact tighter restrictions. To assess these possibilities, we estimate two versions of the following model with regard to owner-occupied properties, one for only subprime mortgages and one for all mortgages:

$$(3.3) \quad Home\ Foreclosures_{it} = \alpha + \beta_1 R_{it} + \beta_2 X_{it} + \mu_{it},$$

where *Home Foreclosures$_{it}$* is the percentage of mortgages (on owner-occupied properties) in foreclosure for state i over period t (as measured in the National Delinquency Survey of the Mortgage Bankers Association, 1979–2005); R_{it} represents the state-level measures of mortgage broker bonding/net worth requirements in time period t; the vector X_{it} includes covariates measuring characteristics of each state, along with year time trends; μ_{it} is the error term; and α, β_1, and β_2 are the coefficients we estimate.

As shown in Table 3.7 for the estimation period 1999 through 2004, there is a significant positive relationship between bonding/net worth requirements and foreclosure rates for both subprime and all mortgages when state-level labor market and service market factors are also controlled for. The estimates are consistent with the view, discussed above, that occupational regulation reduces the quality of an occupation's output. However, the results do not clarify the mechanism by which mortgage broker bonding would lead to higher foreclosures. One could speculate that fewer brokers, which is the outcome of tougher regulation, may reduce the "nudging" to maintain the serviceability of loans that brokers may have consummated (Thaler and Sunstein 2008).

Given the positive relationship between bonding and foreclosures that could arise because states enact bonding or net worth requirements in response to previous periods of high foreclosure, additional quality safeguards are provided. As a check on this possibility, an estimated subsequent passage of a bonding or net worth requirement is developed. Table 3.8, which uses a Weibull hazard model with covariates similar to those in Tables 3.6 and 3.7, shows that the relationship is not statistically significant, indicating an absence of this form of simultaneity bias. This statistical approach is used to measure the time to the adoption of the licensing bill based on the major socioeconomic characteristics in the state.

One final issue we address in this section is presented in Table 3.9, which shows the relationship of bonding/net worth requirements to homeownership. Using the same type of model as Table 3.7, we show estimates of the relationship of mortgage broker bonding/net worth requirements and homeownership. The findings show that income is positively related to homeownership, but there is no statistically significant relationship between the measures of regulation and homeownership. Although bonding may matter for the quantity and quality of subprime mortgages, it does not seem to vary with the overall rate of state homeownership. It might reflect the fact that mortgage originations are flow variables and hence can change more from year to year than a stock variable like homeownership.

FURTHER PROBING OF REGULATION AND FINANCIAL OUTCOMES FOR CONSUMERS

Brokers have short-term incentives to sell high-priced loans to consumers. The federal banking regulators track high-priced loans through the Home Mortgage Disclosure Act (HMDA) data collection, which records most home mortgage applications and originations in the United States. The focus is on first-lien mortgages in our analysis. A high-priced first-lien mortgage is defined as one whose annual percentage rate (APR) is 3 or more percentage points above the contemporaneous 30-year Treasury bond yield. APR is defined essentially as an internal rate of return, taking into account initial fees and introductory rates and setting any index variables in the contract at current market values, assuming they remain constant for the scheduled maturity of the loan.

70

Table 3.7 Fixed-Effects Models of the Percentage of Loans (subprime and all loans) in Foreclosure

	(1) subinfclose	(2) subinfclose	(3) allinfclose	(4) allinfclose
Summated reg. index, lagged once (no net worth/bonding)	0.022	0.004	0.016	0.021
	(0.093)	(0.078)	(0.016)	(0.014)
Real net worth/bonding requirement, lagged once/100,000	1.357	3.186	0.217	0.540
	(1.585)	(1.245)**	(0.280)	(0.226)**
Summated reg. index, lagged twice (no net worth/bonding)	−0.100		0.013	
	(0.104)		(0.018)	
Real net worth/bonding requirement, lagged twice/100,000	3.659		0.476	
	(1.598)**		(0.283)*	
Lag state unemployment rate	0.873	0.970	0.222	0.251
	(0.224)***	(0.196)***	(0.040)***	(0.036)***
Lag state population/100,000	−0.005	−0.059	−0.032	−0.033
	(0.069)	(0.055)	(0.012)***	(0.010)***
Lag median state household income/100,000	−5.080	−7.396	−1.560	−3.003
	(6.709)	(6.059)	(1.187)	(1.100)***
State homeownership percentage	−0.292	−0.319	−0.057	−0.057
	(0.087)***	(0.080)***	(0.015)***	(0.014)***
Constant	27.444	28.629	6.617	6.673
	(7.197)***	(6.168)***	(1.273)***	(1.120)***
Year dummy controls (2000–2004), base 1999	Y	Y	Y	Y
Observations	255	306	255	306
Number of states (including DC)	51	51	51	51

R-squared	0.66	0.63	0.42	0.43
F-test for one- and two-period lags of summated index	0.50	–	1.46	–
F-test for one- and two-period lags of bonding/net worth	5.51***	–	3.29**	–

NOTE: Columns (1) and (2) and columns (3) and (4) show sensitivity analyses using different statistical specifications to see if the results are stable. Standard errors in parentheses. * significant at the 0.10 level; ** significant at the 0.05 level; *** significant at the 0.01 level. Y = yes. — means no estimates were developed for these cells.

SOURCE: Home Mortgage Disclosure Act (HMDA) data from FFIEC (2007); U.S. Census Bureau, Census of Population and Housing, various years.

Table 3.8 Hazard Model Estimates of Time to Adoption of a Net Worth or Bonding Bill, 1998–2005 (using a Weibull distribution of duration)

	(1)	(2)	(3)	(4)
Avg. percentage of subprime loans in foreclosure, '98–'00	0.17	0.15		
	(0.19)	(0.26)		
Avg. percentage of all loans in foreclosure, '98–'00			0.53	0.98
			(0.75)	(1.25)
Avg. state unemployment rate, '98–'00		0.186		0.185
		(0.386)		(0.390)
Avg. state population, '98–'00/1,000,000		−0.030		−0.050
		(0.062)		(0.072)
Avg. state median household income, '98–'00/1,000		−0.047		−0.042
		(0.062)		(0.064)
Avg. state homeownership percentage, '98–'00		−0.005		0.003
		(0.085)		(0.089)
Constant	−3.742	−2.029	−3.422	−2.858
	(1.274)***	(7.921)	(1.113)***	(8.308)
Observations	17	17	17	17

NOTE: Columns (1) and (2) and columns (3) and (4) show sensitivity analyses using different statistical specifications to see if the results are stable. Standard errors in parentheses. * significant at the 0.10 level; ** significant at the 0.05 level; *** significant at the 0.01 level.
SOURCE: HMDA data from FFIEC (2007); U.S. Census Bureau, Census of Population and Housing, various years.

If mortgage broker licensing succeeds in protecting consumers, high-priced loans may be reduced.[15] There is a further assessment of the empirical relationship between mortgage broker regulation and the probability that a mortgage will be high-priced. For broker-originated loans the model assesses how broker regulation affects the chance that any mortgage, brokered or not, is high-priced. This also would be plausible, since mortgage brokers compete strongly with other mortgage origination providers. However, looking at the entire mortgage market could weaken the model's ability to detect the direct effects of mortgage broker regulation, so there is a preference to focus as closely as possible on broker-originated mortgages.

Focusing on brokered mortgages, however, presents a problem because the HMDA data do not indicate whether a mortgage was brokered. A couple of strategies can deal with the issue of this missing information. For federally regulated banks and thrifts, there is the potential to use the borrowers' location (available at the census tract level from the HMDA data) to condition on whether the loan was made outside the lender's Community Reinvestment Act (CRA) assessment area. Under the CRA, federally regulated banks and thrifts must declare an assessment area where the degree of services they provide will be evaluated for compliance with the CRA. Typically these areas include the lender's principal retail offices, and lenders generally have fewer offices outside their assessment area. Federally regulated lenders are presumed to rely on their retail offices to originate the majority of their mortgages within their assessment areas but are presumed to rely much more on brokers to reach mortgage customers outside their assessment areas. Accordingly, for federally regulated banks and thrifts, the focus is on mortgages originated outside each reporting lender's CRA assessment area.[16]

For mortgage banks not subject to the CRA, there is a reliance on reports from industry publications and industry experts to identify a set of lenders known to rely almost exclusively on mortgage brokers for loan applications. For one lending company, Option One, in 2005, the year examined in this study, the firm obtained almost all of its mortgage applications through brokers. Thomas LaMalfa, formerly managing director of Wholesale Access (2005), helped identify nine other "broker-dependent" mortgage originators in 2005: 1) Taylor, Bean, and Whitaker Mortgage Company; 2) First Magnus Financial Corporation;

Table 3.9 Fixed-Effects Models of State Homeownership Percentage

	(1)	(2)
Real bonding/net worth requirement, lagged once/100,000	0.881 (1.154)	1.206 (0.943)
Real bonding/net worth requirement, lagged twice/100,000	0.582 (1.188)	
Lag state unemployment rate	−0.194 (0.155)	−0.191 (0.155)
Lag state population/100,000	0.066 (0.043)	0.066 (0.043)
Lag median state household income/100,000	10.896 (4.778)**	11.029 (4.763)**
Constant	61.428 (3.004)***	61.415 (2.999)***
Year dummy controls (2000–2004), base 1999	Y	Y
Observations	306	306
Number of states (including DC)	51	51
R^2	0.26	0.26
F-test for one- and two-period lags of net worth/bonding requirements	0.94	—

NOTE: Columns (1) and (2) show sensitivity analyses using different statistical specifications to see if the results are stable. Standard errors in parentheses. * significant at the 0.10 level; ** significant at the 0.05 level; *** significant at the 0.01 level. Y = yes. — means no estimates were developed for this cell.
SOURCE: HMDA data from FFIEC (2007); Census of Population, various years.

3) American Mortgage Network; 4) Loan City; 5) Green Point Mortgage Funding; 6) Argent Mortgage Company; 7) New Century Mortgage Corporation; 8) Nova Star Home Mortgage; and 9) Résumé.[17]

In Table 3.10, an estimated linear probability model for whether a loan is high-priced, using four different data sets, is developed.[18] Observations are clustered by state to compute robust standard errors that allow for less than full independence among the observations in each state. This controls for the state regulatory environment, the borrower's income and racial/ethnic identity, the loan amount, and several economic and demographic properties of the census tract where the property is located (the distribution of credit scores, unemployment rate, median age of applicants, median age of housing stock, percentage of minority population, median income, and the percentage of owner-occupied and vacant housing units).

For mortgage refinancing, the results are fairly consistent. There is a clear difference in the size of the constant term, which is low for the CRA lenders outside their assessment areas (0.10) and higher for the 10 broker-dependent lenders (0.38). The 2005 national average was 0.26 for first-lien refinance mortgages. Although this gives a very different starting point to the two refinancing regressions, the marginal effects of many of the explanatory variables are similar. The coefficients on the mortgage broker regulatory variables for 2004, which was the only year there were data for, are of primary interest here. In Table 3.10 the coefficient on the bonding/net worth requirement is positive and significant, indicating that a $100,000 increase in this requirement is associated with, respectively, a 5.4 or a 3.5 percentage-point increase in the probability that a refinancing is high-priced in these two columns. The coefficient on the index of other mortgage broker regulations is not significant in Table 3.10.

The results for two other regulatory variables—an index of state antipredatory-lending laws and an indicator of states that prohibit deficiency judgments—are also consistent across the refinancing regressions in Table 3.10. The coefficient on the index of antipredatory-lending laws is negative but not significant at the 0.10 percent level. The coefficient on the indicator of no deficiency judgments is significant but with an unexpected negative sign, suggesting that high-priced loans are less likely in states that do not allow creditors to pursue deficiency judgments. A possible explanation is that lenders ration credit more strictly in states that rule out deficiency judgments but use risk-based pricing to lend to a wider selection of applicants where they have the right to pursue a deficiency judgment.[19]

The coefficient on the percentage of adults in the census tract of the mortgaged property who have very low credit scores is consistently positive and significant in Table 3.10. A 10-percentage-point increase in the percentage of adults in the tract with a very low score is associated with about a 5- to 6-percentage-point increase in the probability that a mortgage refinance loan in that tract will be high-priced.[20]

African American, Hispanic, and female borrowers are significantly more likely to get a high-priced mortgage refinancing than are non-

**Table 3.10 Logarithmic Probability of a High-Priced Loan in a Cross
Section of 10 Broker-Dependent Lenders' Mortgages**

	Mortgage refinance	Home-purchase mortgage
State broker bonding/net worth requirement ($100,000)	0.054 (0.021)**	0.050 (0.028)*
Index of other state broker licensing requirements	0.002 (0.003)	0.002 (0.003)
Index of state antipredatory-lending laws	−0.012 (0.008)	0.004 (0.009)
State prohibition of deficiency judgments (dummy variable)	−0.130 (0.029)***	−0.098 (0.027)***
Borrower's income ($1,000)	−0.505 (0.077)***	−0.280 (0.068)***
Borrower's income squared ($1,000,000)	0.093 (0.020)***	0.035 (0.011)***
Adults in census tract with very low credit score (%)	0.005 (0.001)***	0.006 (0.001)***
African American borrower (dummy variable)	0.146 (0.018)***	0.173 (0.011)***
Asian American borrower (dummy variable)	−0.060 (0.019)***	−0.032 (0.023)
Hispanic borrower (dummy variable)	0.074 (0.013)***	0.119 (0.019) ***
Female borrower (dummy variable)	0.039 (0.006)***	0.163 (0.006)***
Constant	0.382 (0.073)***	0.537 (0.069)***
Number of state clusters for standard errors (DC included)	51	51
R^2	0.095	0.107
N	273,365	185,773

NOTE: * significant at the 0.10 level; ** significant at the 0.05 level; *** significant at the 0.01 level.
SOURCE: HMDA data from FFIEC (2007); U.S. Census Bureau, Census of Population and Housing, various years.

Hispanic white male borrowers. The largest effect is for African American borrowers. For example, for mortgage refinance loans by federally regulated banks and thrifts lending outside their CRA assessment areas, the probability of getting a high-priced loan increases by 21 percentage points for an African American borrower, compared with increases of 9 percentage points for Hispanics and 4 percentage points for women. For other racial groups, we find no significant effects, except that Asian Americans refinancing with the 10 broker-dependent lenders are about 6 percentage points less likely to get a high-priced loan.

The results for the regulatory variables are not as strong or as consistent with home-purchase mortgages as with mortgage refinance loans. The bonding/net worth variable is positive and significant at a 0.10 level for the 10 broker-dependent lenders but has an insignificant and small negative coefficient for the CRA-regulated lenders on loans outside their assessment areas. The index of the remaining mortgage broker regulations is insignificant in the home-purchase regressions, as is the index of antipredatory-lending laws. The indicator of no-deficiency judgments is again negative and significant for the broker-dependent lenders, but it is now insignificant for the CRA-regulated lenders' loans outside their assessment areas. Apparently, the process for making home-purchase loans differs in important ways from the process for making mortgage refinance loans, at least at the CRA-regulated institutions.[21]

As Avery, Brevoort, and Canner (2006) note, CRA-regulated lenders' mortgage underwriting appears to be quite different inside, compared with outside, their assessment areas. The authors speculate that one explanation may be the use of differing marketing channels, including greater use of brokers outside assessment areas.

To limit the potential influence of unmeasured location-specific effects, a reestimation is developed with a sample restricted to only observations in MSAs that straddle state borders, similar to the methods in Holmes (1998) and Bostic et al. (2007). The data used were on 51 MSAs that cross state boundaries, touching parts of 39 states.[22] They estimate the same equations in Table 3.10 but with fixed effects for each MSA, which has the advantage of controlling for location-specific factors not measured by the other variables, such as the percentage of loans with adjustable rates or the level or rate of change in housing prices (LaCour-Little 2007c). This is useful, in that the nature of interest-rate data (a single cross section) precludes controlling for these factors by means of state fixed effects, because they would be collinear with the state-level policy variables.

For the data from the broker-dependent lenders, the results on the sample from multistate MSAs for the bonding variable (and most of the other variables) are similar to those in Table 3.10.[23] In particular, for mortgage refinancing loans by the broker-dependent lenders, the coefficient on the state broker bonding variable has a t-statistic of 2.05 and a coefficient of 0.048, compared with 0.054 in Table 3.10. For home-purchase mortgages from the same lenders, the coefficient on the bonding variable has a 1.96 t-statistic and a coefficient of 0.041, compared with 0.050 in Table 3.10. For home-purchase loans by CRA lenders outside their assessment areas, the coefficient on the bonding variable is −0.004 and insignificant for the multistate MSA sample with fixed effects, very similar to the results in Table 3.10.

Thus the results for Table 3.10, which uses data almost exclusively on broker-originated loans, are reasonably robust to location-specific effects not explicitly controlled for in the model. These results are also robust to the omission of data from the 12 states without multistate MSAs, including California. However, the same is not true of the results for mortgage refinance loans by CRA lenders outside their assessment areas, which probably consist of a mixture of broker-originated and other loans. The coefficient on the bonding variable for those loans becomes marginally insignificant when observations from the 12 states without border-crossing MSAs are dropped from the full sample or when they are estimated on the multistate MSA sample without fixed effects. With fixed effects on the multistate MSA sample, the coefficient becomes clearly insignificant.

ILLUSTRATIONS OF THE POLITICS OF ENHANCING HIGHER BONDING REQUIREMENTS

To examine the potential endogeneity or lack of a causal relationship of mortgage broker regulations, information was gathered on the legislative history information from industry sources and regulators in eight states that have raised their bonding requirements at least once. Overall, these conversations suggest a somewhat long and complicated chain of legislative causality. Successful efforts to raise bonding requirements tend to originate from the mortgage broker industry or from state regulators, rather than directly from consumer groups. However, consumer advocacy and issues still can motivate the industry or give rise to regulatory proposals, and there are also some signs of grassroots industry opposition to proposals made by state mortgage broker associations. In addition, the gestation time between an initial legislative proposal and final passage and implementation may go several years, so any market outcomes that initiated the legislative process may have changed by the time of implementation. Consumer issues seem to serve as the background from which industry and regulatory agency–initiated bonding requirements emerge, often during a multiyear process.

Of the nine increases we discussed, five were described as first proposed or drafted by the state's mortgage broker association (Ohio 1999, Texas 1999, North Carolina 2002, Idaho 2004, and Montana 2004), and four were described as initiated by the state regulatory authority (New Jersey 2001, Tennessee 2001, Ohio 2002, and Minnesota 2007). The distinction is somewhat blurred by the industry's frequent practice of vetting its proposals with state regulators, which often yields at least technical drafting suggestions but sometimes yields more affirmative legislative support from the regulator. No successful bonding proposal was said to have been opposed by state regulators. Sometimes earlier proposals that had not been vetted with the regulator had failed. As a result, regulators have been involved, actively or passively, in most of the successful bonding bills we examined.

The stated motivations of the industry and the regulators differed. Industry proposals were described as attempts to make the occupation more professional and to provide a degree of consumer protection by inhibiting some forms of fraud, thereby enhancing the occupation's reputation. However, industry-supported increases to bonding requirements were sometimes motivated on narrow grounds (e.g., North Carolina 2002), such as to ensure that consumers could be compensated if a broker absconded with the relatively small amount of cash the customer had entrusted to the broker, but not to help the consumer collect on larger judgments for less narrow forms of fraud or negligence. By contrast, proposals initiated by the regulatory authorities tended to have bonding requirements that were higher and broader in scope, with the apparent intention of providing both more resources to compensate consumers and more incentives for appropriate broker behavior.

None of the sources (which did not include consumer groups) suggested that the bonding requirement that passed had been either first proposed or subsequently opposed by consumer advocates. However, the industry's proposal in Texas was in part a response to a much higher bonding proposal previously introduced by a legislator on the grounds of consumer protection, and in at least two other cases (Ohio 1999, North Carolina 2002) the industry's proposal was said to be motivated in part by competing regulatory proposals (not including bonding) from consumer groups. Opposition to the bonding bills that passed was said to be limited and mainly from legislators who were concerned that it might be onerous enough to hurt their constituents who were in the business. In some cases, this was thought to reflect, in part, grassroots lobbying by mortgage brokers at odds with their own industry association's position.

CONCLUSIONS

Mortgage brokers make up a relatively new occupation that has recently been regulated in the United States. About 40 years ago, there were almost no mortgage brokers, because individuals who wanted a loan to buy or refinance a house went to a bank or savings and loan. With deregulation of financial services and technology improvements that allow easy development and dissemination of credit scores, this picture began to change, and in 2004 as much as two-thirds of all housing finance was initiated through a mortgage broker. However, by 2009 there had been a dramatic drop in the number of brokerage companies and brokers.

This chapter examines the relationships between state regulation of mortgage brokers, outcomes in the labor market, and outcomes for consumers of these services during the period of growth. The occupation, although at an early stage of regulation, is much more regulated than that of interior designers, the focus of Chapter 2. The findings show that the relationship between mortgage broker licensing and market outcomes differs among the types of licensing requirements; in particular, financial bonding or net worth requirements are associated with somewhat higher earnings, with modest reductions in the number of mortgage brokers and the number of subprime loans originated, and with somewhat higher foreclosure rates and higher interest rates on brokered loans.

Much of the empirical analysis for this chapter ends in 2006, just as U.S. foreclosure rates on nonprime adjustable-rate mortgages began to surge. Financial markets reacted to the raft of foreclosures by raising the cost and cutting the availability of funding for both subprime and mortgage-broker-originated mortgages. State regulators have tightened regulations on mortgage contracts, mortgage origination, and mortgage broker licensing as well, and the Housing and Economic Recovery Act of 2008 brings federal oversight to mortgage broker licensing. Such a result would be consistent with the findings of Law and Kim (2005), which show that during the early periods of occupational regulation in the United States, the monopoly impacts were modest. As in other occupations that have evolved with near-universal licensing in the states, mortgage brokers, having survived the Great Recession and the bust of the housing market, could also eventually benefit through higher earnings and the ability to control both entry and quality. At this early stage of regulation, it is not surprising to find only modest effects. This is perhaps similar to the case of unions, which have only modest effects on wages when they first organize a firm, but in subsequent stages of negotiations may have larger effects on wage determination (Freeman and Kleiner 1990). In the case of occupational regulation, the initial stages of regulation may have modest effects, but over time may reach long-run estimates of about 15 percent (Kleiner and Krueger 2010). The next chapter examines the regulation of an occupation that is in the takeoff stage of regulation—the low-paying occupation and industry of early childhood education.

Notes

1. I thank Richard Todd, vice president of the Federal Reserve Bank of Minneapolis, for his work on and assistance with this chapter. This chapter is based on and uses material from Kleiner and Todd (2007).
2. Some states have recently moved to enact or more strictly enforce laws that make the broker an agent of the borrower, but this was not a factor during much of the period of the empirical part of the study.
3. By 2006, the number of firms had changed little, but their share of originations was estimated to have declined to about 58 percent (Wholesale Access 2007). With the volume of subprime lending apparently having fallen significantly in 2007, mortgage broker numbers may decline further, as brokers had originated the majority of subprime mortgages and these types of loans have all but disappeared in the post-2008 crash period (Olson 2007).
4. Some of the other components of mortgage broker regulation also are significant in some of the specifications and may deserve further research, but here the focus is on the bonding and net worth requirements because they were more broadly and consistently significant.
5. For example, see Guttentag (2000); Engel and McCoy (2002); U.S. Department of Housing and Urban Development (HUD) (2002); Woodward (2003); El Anshasy, Elliehausen, and Shimazaki (2005); Apgar, Bendimerad, and Essene (2007); Essene and Apgar (2007); Jackson and Burlingame (2007); and LaCour-Little (2007b).
6. The term "broker" is generally used to refer to a firm offering mortgage brokerage services, whereas the term "loan officer" is commonly used to refer to an employee of a mortgage broker who actually performs these services. We adopt this common usage, with certain exceptions, as for instance in note 7, where "broker" means the individual. Indeed, terminology in the industry is not uniform (HUD 2002) and can be confusing, not least because the actual roles of brokers, loan officers, lenders, and others are not rigidly bounded and distinctions often blur. For a wry but useful summary of the overlapping roles and confusing jargon in the mortgage origination business, see Tanta (2007).
7. This potential is not limited to mortgage brokers, however. It extends to loan officers at mortgage lending banks when they are paid incentives based on the size and interest rate of the loans they originate.
8. This index is from a Rasch-type model (Andrich 1988) that places each of the variables within a logical structure based on frequency of outcome and an integer scale. The empirical measure of the Rasch model we use is known as a partial credit model—a nonlinear model that assigns weights that are consistent with an implicit structure to the regulatory system. This approach assumes that the distance between parameters is equal and that the categories are equal integers. The development of the Rasch scale uses maximum likelihood estimation to calculate a unique index for each state. The estimates derived from using the Rasch index did not differ qualitatively from those of the nonlinear approach.

9. The anatomy of the regulatory system for brokers by state is generally consistent. Simple correlations among the individual items in our index were mostly positive, and a large number were statistically significant. None of the negative correlations among the components of the index were statistically significant.
10. For background on the market for surety bonds in general and mortgage broker surety bonds in particular, see www.jwsuretybonds.com.
11. Surety companies investigate the validity of claims before paying out. We are referring here to claims they consider valid.
12. As a check on the results using the ACS, I also use the Occupational Employment Statistics (OES) wage survey, which has produced employment and wage estimates for over 800 occupations by state on a biennial basis from 1999 on. The OES also includes a category for loan officers and brokers. In both the ACS and OES, the data we use include mortgage loan officers and agents, collection analysts, loan servicing officers, and loan underwriters. These state OES figures are highly correlated ($r = 0.81$) with the National Mortgage Broker Association's count of membership by state. Similar high correlations were found between National Mortgage Broker Association memberships and the ACS figures. The ACS figures are presented because of their ability to show additional individual- and state-level covariates to reduce omitted variable bias in the estimates.
13. Estimates for hourly earnings showed generally similar results. We use total earnings in our estimates because of the variable nature of compensation for brokers that are commission-based. In addition, since many brokers are in small offices where profits are shared, the earnings variable will capture this form of compensation.
14. Estimates for changes in licensing and changes in wages also showed no statistically significant impact. In none of the earnings or wage estimates were the licensing index variables significant when we used state-level controls. We also estimated nonlinear models of the licensing variables, and they were also not significant. Furthermore, tests using the OES found significance for the licensing variables only when the X_{it} controls were omitted. The estimates are also available from the authors.
15. Two separate studies, based on proprietary data from selected major lenders' mortgages that originated in 2002, suggest that, on average, consumers using brokers did get lower-priced loans than other borrowers, when other factors were controlled for. See El Anshasy, Elliehausen, and Shimazaki (2005) and LaCour-Little (2007a). Results to the contrary were found by LaCour-Little (2007b).
16. HMDA data from CRA-regulated mortgage originators was used.
17. Their respective HMDA respondent ID numbers are 7499100008, 7979400002, 1788100000, 7428900001, 13-3210378, 1917700009, 7900200006, both 1512400000 and 1707500002 for Nova Star, and 1991500005. To make the data more manageable, an estimated 50 percent random sample was developed.
18. An estimated probit model for each of these regressions obtained very similar results.
19. Karen Pence, assistant director of the Board of Governors of the Federal Reserve System in Washington, D.C., raised this issue.

20. In the full regression results underlying Tables 3.9 and 3.10, the coefficient on another credit score variable—the percentage of adults with a credit file who lack a credit score—is significantly positive but smaller for the CRA-regulated lenders but not significant for the 10 broker-dependent lenders.

21. For the home-purchase mortgages examined in Table 3.10, the coefficients on the credit score and racial/ethnic variables have a pattern of statistical significance not too different from that of the mortgage refinance loans in Table 3.9, although the size of the coefficients often differs substantially. In results not shown but available from the author, we repeated the estimates in Table 3.10 for mortgages made within the CRA assessment areas of CRA-regulated lenders. None of the regulatory variables were statistically significant except the coefficient on the indicator of no-deficiency judgments, which was significant and positive for home-purchase mortgages. The insignificance of the mortgage broker regulation variables in these regressions is consistent with our presumption that loans within a CRA assessment area are much less likely to involve a mortgage broker. We have no clear explanation yet for why the results for the indicator of no-deficiency judgments change.

22. These states are Alabama, Arkansas, Delaware, the District of Columbia, Georgia, Idaho, Iowa, Illinois, Indiana, Kansas, Kentucky, Louisiana, Maryland, Massachusetts, Michigan, Minnesota, Mississippi, Missouri, Nebraska, New Hampshire, New Jersey, New York, North Carolina, North Dakota, Ohio, Oklahoma, Oregon, Pennsylvania, Rhode Island, South Carolina, South Dakota, Tennessee, Utah, Vermont, Virginia, Washington, West Virginia, Wisconsin, and Wyoming.

23. The parallels are even closer if we estimate on just the split MSAs without fixed effects.

4
Occupational Regulation
of Child Care Services

with Matthew Hendricks
University of Tulsa

Empirical research cannot tell us for sure how zealously the government should promote quality in child care or Head Start or pre-K programs, but it can draw our attention to quality variables that really matter. Strong empirical research, combined with clear values, can promote a more enlightened public debate on early child care and education. Already, it has helped us to distinguish between good and bad arguments and good and bad policies.

—William Gormley (2007)

INTRODUCTION

The regulation of child care services presents a unique opportunity to examine occupational regulation for a service that is provided in both the public and private sectors.[1] Given the growing policy issue of the funding and effects of early childhood education on economic development, an empirical examination of the issue of government and regulation, as Gormley suggests in the chapter's opening quotation, is an important way to enhance the ability of policymakers to judge the efficacy of various policies (Grunewald and Rolnick 2006; Bartik 2011). Furthermore, the way that child care centers have evolved in the United States has resulted in their serving both as small schools and as babysitting services for young children. The chapter presents an analysis of occupational regulation in a unique and growing sector of the U.S. economy, where licensing is fairly new and generally lax (Hotz and Xiao 2011). As with the other occupations that are examined in this book, day care teachers, assistants, and administrators have seen an increase in state regulation over time. Given this institutional setting, the regulation of day care labor is at an early stage of regulatory evolution relative to most of the other occupations discussed in the book.

As the rate of mothers' labor market participation has increased over time, so has the number of children in regular nonparental care (Smolensky and Gootman 2003). Estimates from surveys conducted in the early 2000s suggest that 43 percent of children under age five and 53 percent of children between the ages of three and four are in some type of nonparental child care, the majority of which is provided by professional child-care providers (U.S. Census Bureau 2008). Increasingly, nonparental child care is also recognized as an important context for children's development, particularly for promoting school readiness. Although nonparental care has become more popular, the variability in the quality of early education and care has become a concern to parents and policymakers. Prior analysis of the issue suggests that the quality of nonparental care is highly variable and that a substantial portion of children's experiences is of questionable value to the child's educational attainment (Helburn 1995; Kontos et al. 1995; Helburn and Howes 1996).

In contrast, several analytical research studies have shown that the skills, habits, and attitudes developed in early childhood can have important effects as children grow into adults. Parental care giving, including investments of time and money, has long been recognized as an important influence on children's early human capital development (Becker 1991; Shonkoff and Phillips 2000). The impetus to regulate child care initially grew out of safety concerns for children and the view that many children receive poor quality of care, as measured by safety or the quality of learning (Phillips and Zigler 1987). Proponents argued that government licensure assures parents of a basic level of quality in the provision of child care. Moreover, it ensures greater monitoring and transparency in the provision of care and the quality of services provided. In addition, through both standards and enforcement actions, governmental regulation provides a system to enforce penalties in the event of poor quality care.

For child care providers and other regulated industries and occupations, occupational licensing can reduce competition and thereby increase revenues for existing providers of the service or product. Quality and access to high educational outcomes are of major importance to policymakers and legislators, as states consider several alternative initiatives to improve early education outcomes and child care quality of service. For example, Hotz and Xiao (2011) show that regulatory provisions for child care and early education facilities by states grew by more than 39 percent from 1983 to 1997, and the estimates derived for this chapter show the overall growth of regulation from 1983 to 2007 to be more than 40 percent. Although the breadth of coverage has grown, the intensity of coverage is still modest.

Despite this increase in regulation, analysis of relevant data on how regulation affects children and their families is limited. In order to examine these issues in more detail, this chapter addresses three important issues on child care regulation. First, a theory on the evolution of the role of government regulation will show the potential for an increase in the educational outcomes of the regulated, but the potential also to possibly increase child care prices, thus pricing some families out of the formal center-based child care market. That result causes them to substitute informal care or to reduce maternal labor supply to the labor market. Second, if regulation reduces the number of individuals who can become workers in early childhood facilities, then wages will go up. Prior studies have found that stricter regulations both decrease the availability of center-based care and increase the price of such care. Third, the analysis in the chapter examines whether state child care regulations affect children's school readiness as measured by preacademic score outcomes. Although prior research has investigated how child care regulations are related to health outcomes (Currie and Hotz 2004), the effects of regulation on children's cognitive and early academic measures have not been analyzed in such detail.

In order to address the issues specified above, the chapter is organized as follows. Initially, background information is provided on the regulatory environment for the preschool industry in the United States. Next, there is an explanation of the theoretical background and prior literature on the effect that government regulation has on both the quality of child care and the potential consequences for supply and demand. The section after that gives the empirical models used in the analysis. Next, an overview of the data and descriptive statistics is provided. The empirical analysis shows the effects of regulation on the wages of child care workers, child access to regulated forms of care, and finally the influence of these regulations on childrens' early academic achievement. The summary and conclusions section develops a discussion of the policy implications of the findings.

GOVERNMENT REGULATION AND THE CHILD CARE INDUSTRY

As has been discussed earlier in this book, over the past 60 years, the United States has witnessed a major growth in the number of individuals who require occupational licensing from the government (Kleiner 2006). By 2008, about 29 percent of the members of the U.S. workforce indicated that they worked in an occupation licensed by either local, state, or federal governments (Kleiner and Krueger 2013). The three types of occupational regulation used by various levels of government are licensure, certification, or registration. Licensing is the most restrictive form of occupational regulation and the most frequently used. State-appointed boards generally have oversight on the licensing process, including setting entry and continuing practice standards to include education requirements and testing for entry, creating codes to govern behavior, and creating penalties for violations of the rules. Procedurally, licensing an occupation means an individual must pass the board's requirements before practicing in the profession. Individuals who fail to meet the licensure requirements face financial or criminal penalties if they try to practice the profession for pay. More specifically, entry requirements vary across occupations; common licensure requirements include formal education, experience, an entry test, good character, and a period of residency.

In general, the jurisdiction that regulates occupations is at the state level, which is also the case in the child care industry (Mocan 2001; Kleiner 2006). Every state regulates the child care industry to some degree, since child care establishments must obtain licensure to enter the market (Hotz and Xiao 2005). In 2005, nationwide, there were approximately 335,520 licensed child care providers. Of these, one-third were center-based and two-thirds were family-based providers (National Association for Regulatory Administration [NARA] and National Child Care Information and Technical Assistance Center [NCCIC] 2006).

State rules regarding the licensing of both center-based child care and family-based child care fall into two main categories: structural and safety. Structural regulations are those that mandate maximum child-to-staff ratios, minimum experience/education requirements, ongoing education requirements, and maximum classroom size. The child ratios and classroom sizes vary, depending on the age of the children in the program. Safety regulations include stipulations regarding staff training in CPR/first aid, immunizations, criminal background checks, and compliance with the provision of nutritional meals. In addition, some states have licensing rules and policies about the use of developmentally appropriate activities. States also establish guidelines for monitoring programs to ensure that they are complying with child care licensing requirements.

A common and important distinction among child care providers is whether the program is center-based or family-based. Center-based programs are more academically oriented and generally refer to programs offered in a dedicated facility or nonhome environment (church, synagogue, community center, and so on). "Family-based" refers to programs offered in a caregiver's private residence for children related and unrelated to the caregiver (family-based care does not include informal care provided by a family's relative). States regulate each of these types of child care differently. In addition, regulations may differ by the age of the children. For example, states often set lower child-to-caregiver ratios for infants than for toddlers or for children age three to kindergarten.

OVERVIEW OF THE HISTORY OF DAY CARE AND REGULATIONS IN THE UNITED STATES

The origins of day care are often traced to the welfare and reform movements of the nineteenth century. "Day care grew out of a welfare movement to care for immigrant and working class children while their . . . mothers worked," write Scarr and Weinberg (1986, p. 1140). The early nurseries cared for children of working wives and of widows of merchant seamen. Settlement houses were especially active in promoting day care for immigrant children. Jane Addams, the highly regarded

Chicago social worker and activist, developed nurseries for poor children who needed supervision and care, note Scarr and Weinberg. During World War II, the federal government sponsored day care for more than 400,000 preschool children. The focus was the effort to increase female labor-force participation during the war. Following the war, the federal government stopped subsidizing preschool child-care facilities and got out of both the regulation and the funding of preschools (Boschee and Jacobs 1997).

When the federal government reduced its heavy involvement in day care, a number of firms established their own centers, which created a substantial benefit for women with children. Firms such as Kaiser, Stride Rite, and Marriott established day care centers either on their property or with a subcontractor. In recent years, organizations such as the National Association of Child Care Resource and Referral Agencies and the National Association for Regulatory Administration have argued for more and tougher licensing requirements both for the facilities and for workers such as teachers and assistants, stating that licensing is the path toward higher-quality outcomes for children and toward quality assurance for their parents. The first study that gathered data on licensing of facilities and their workers was developed by Kay Hollestelle, former executive director of the Children's Foundation, in the early 1980s. The report documented the types of regulations that each of the states adopted and their coverage (NARA and NCCIC 2010). Many states require child care centers, including those in private homes, to be licensed if they care for more than a few children (the number varies by state). In order to obtain their licenses, child care centers may require child care workers to pass a background check, get immunizations, and meet a minimum training requirement.

CHILD CARE REGULATION AND CHILD CARE EDUCATION QUALITY

The stated goal of the regulators is that licensing of the child care market is an attempt by the state to ensure that the provision of child care guarantees the safety of children and meets a minimum quality standard. Analysts of child care outcomes distinguish between two types of quality indicators: 1) process measures and 2) structural measures (Blau and Currie 2006). Process quality refers to children's experiences in child care settings, including children's interactions with caregivers and peers, developmentally appropriate activities, and health and safety measures. Structural characteristics include the child-to-adult ratio, the size of each group of children, and the level of caregiver education and training (Vandell and Wolfe 2002). Structural characteristics, which are most often the target of regulations, are thought to affect children's development, primarily by shaping the quality of providers' caregiving (National Institute of Child Health and Human Development [NICHD] 2002). Developmental analysts found some evidence of linkages between child outcomes and the quality of care—both process and structural—that children experience. Beginning in the 1960s, higher quality caregiving is associated with improved school readiness and better early academic skills (Shonkoff and Phillips 2000; Vandell and Wolfe 2002; Smolensky and Gootman 2003).

The effect of state-level regulations on the level of quality in the regulated child care market remains uncertain, primarily because the few studies that have addressed this question face methodological challenges. Nevertheless, previous theory and evidence suggest that higher levels of state regulation are linked with higher process measures of quality care in regulated types of care, including family- and center-based care (see Chipty 1995; Hofferth and Chaplin 1998; Blau 2003; Heeb and Kilburn 2004; Raikes, Raikes, and Wilcox 2005; Rigby, Ryan, and Brooks-Gunn 2007). In particular, the work by Hotz and Xiao (2011) has found that stringent child-staff ratios have the effect of increasing the probability that providers who stay in the market will seek to obtain accreditation from the National Association for the Education of Young Children (NAEYC), since this is one of the requirements of that organization. This suggests that the given amount of regulation may indirectly cause child care centers to pursue accreditation, which may be one way in which regulation improves quality and signals to the market that it provides high-quality child care services.

Although all of these factors may influence the effects of stricter regulation on child care quality, there remain two potential reasons why stricter regulation may not lead to improvements in structural or process quality. First, the link between the health and safety quality of care, children's experiences, and measures of academic indicators of quality (regulated or otherwise) may be modest. There is some evidence that provider education and training is associated with child care outcomes (Burchinal, Howes, and Kontos 2002; Clarke-Stewart et al. 2002; NICHD 2002). However, the magnitudes of estimated associations between structural and process measures of quality are small.

Second, child care regulations may not be adequately implemented or enforced, which implies that the effects of regulation would be weaker than intended. For example, centers rarely lose their accreditation or are fined, and teachers also infrequently lose their licenses. This suggests that in order to estimate the effects of stricter regulations, it is also necessary to examine the enforcement mechanism across states, which include financial penalties and the number of monitors per state. Unfortunately, these data are not readily available, either nationally or on a state-by-state basis.

THE POTENTIAL INFLUENCE OF CHILD CARE REGULATION ON PRICE, SUPPLY, AND DEMAND

This section develops the rationale for the role of regulation on the key economic factors in child care. The long-term trend of increasing participation by women in the labor force has been a key factor in the increasing number of children who are in nonparental child care or early education centers. A basic rationale for child care provisions suggests that three factors work in concert to affect parents' labor market and child care decisions: 1) availability, 2) price, and 3) quality (as perceived by parents). If regulation is intended, in part, to produce a higher quality of child care for those who attend, then there is good reason to suspect that it will also affect the economics of child care, such as price, supply, and demand for those services. Moreover, within a family production function, if the inheritance and passing along of skills and education to a new generation is viewed as positive, then early childhood education and skill development would be perceived as a normal good that would increase as the income of the household grew.

Stricter regulations might increase the perceived quality of regulated care because the downside risks of care are reduced, and with this risk reduction, the demand for nonparental care is increased. For example, some advocates of regulation suggest that the establishment of minimum quality standard regulations sends a signal to parents that providers are guaranteed to meet basic requirements (Akerloff 1970). This quality signal can, in turn, stimulate demand because it reduces parents' uncertainty or unease about their children's experiences in non-parental child care.

Similarly, increased regulation may reduce the supply of formal care arrangements. For example, by increasing the minimum education required for a care provider and decreasing the child-to-staff ratio in care facilities, the government could decrease the number of eligible care providers willing to work for a given wage. Hotz and Xiao (2011), for example, find that regulation of center-based child care reduces the supply of child care centers, by increasing the costs of providing care and thereby outweighing the demand effects. Their analysis makes a distinction between regulations related to child-to-staff ratios and minimum education requirements. The child-to-staff ratio requirements deterred provider entry and reduced supply. Minimum education requirement regulations did not deter entry, but they did reduce profits and ultimately the supply of child care providers. Though important, these economic effects did not address wage effects, access, or the influence of regulation on child educational outcomes.

In each case, increased demand or decreased supply would suggest that the price of formal care arrangements will increase. As a result, not all consumers benefit from any quality-enhancing effects of regulation. Some consumers will, in the absence of a subsidy, be priced out of the market for child care and be forced to substitute another arrangement, often choosing either parental care, unregulated informal care, or family-based monitoring of children. This potential price increase is likely to have the greatest impact on some of the most at-risk children, since children from low-income families are most likely to be priced out of regulated child care markets. This may result in children from lower-income categories starting school behind other children. In child care, as in most forms of licensing, there is usually a trade-off between access and quality.

The empirical analysis of regulation has consistently found a significant relationship between regulations, price, and demand for day care (Lowenberg and Tinnin 1992; Hotz and Kilburn 1994; Hofferth and Chaplin 1998; Heeb and Kilburn 2004). These findings show that regulation of an input, especially a costly one such as labor in producing child care, will restrict the supply of these services. Combining this supply restriction with potentially increased demand for regulated care is associated with an increase in the price of a good or service. The analysis of the topic suggests that lower-income individuals lose in quantity but that higher-income consumers gain both in the number of providers of the service and in the quality of the service (Shapiro 1986; Hotz and Xiao 2011).

The choice of the type of day care facility that parents select has been influenced by government regulation. Several studies have focused on a family's choice of the mode of child care (Hotz and Kilburn 1994; Hofferth and Chaplin 1998; Currie and Hotz 2004; Heeb and Kilburn 2004). In particular, Currie and Hotz examine the effect of regulation on the probability that a child will be enrolled in regulated modes of child care (center- or family-based care). They find that families are less likely to enroll their children in center-based care as regulations and prices rise. Their results suggest that, as regulations increase, families substitute away from formal care arrangements (family- and center-based) into informal child care arrangements (parental care or relative monitoring of children). The empirical models of enrollment effects closely follow those of Currie and Hotz. However, these analysts employ a relatively small sample in their estimation, which prevents the inclusion of techniques such as state fixed effects in their specifications. Several of the approaches presented in this chapter improve on the Currie and Hotz specifications by including state and year fixed effects in a larger sample. The models also include a rich set of individual-level controls offered by the Early Childhood Longitudinal Study (ECLS) and the National Longitudinal Survey of Youth (NLSY) surveys.

Prior research on state regulations and the child care and early education markets has established that stringent child care regulations affecting labor costs have the effect of restricting the supply of child care in the regulated sector. In addition, the reduction of supply can lead to a higher price for child care and early education in the regulated sector as parents and guardians bid for fewer child care slots. This development would disproportionally disadvantage children from lower-income households that cannot obtain need-based subsidies.

EMPIRICAL ANALYSIS OF EARLY
CHILDHOOD REGULATION

Analytical studies have been slow to consider the associations between state or local regulation of early child care and education and children's early academic skills. If, as suggested by prior research, stricter regulation improves child care quality, then we would expect that such regulation will also improve children's early academic skills, at least in the short run (Anderson 2008). In particular, intuition suggests that stricter structural quality–related regulations such as those related to staff training, adult-to-child ratios, and class size would have a positive influence on academic achievement. Yet there is a possibility that regulation will increase child care prices, thereby reducing access to formal care arrangements, particularly for lower-income families who do not have subsidies for child care such as offered through Head Start or other government programs. This could potentially lead parents to choose unregulated child care arrangements (or none at all), which suggests that any possible benefits accruing to those enrolled in more highly regulated care may be offset by these unintended negative consequences of regulation. The analysis that follows will measure these potential effects of regulation for early childhood services. Specifically, the intent of the remainder of the chapter is to examine the following set of issues: First, can occupational licensing and other regulations raise the wages of child care workers? Second, to what extent do regulations influence the likelihood of children enrolling in a center-based day care facility? Third, to what extent does more regulation cause an increase in early child academic achievement for those children attending a formal day care facility?

Several data sources are used to estimate the influence of regulation on wages, enrollment, and educational attainment. These data sources include the Early Childhood Longitudinal Study's kindergarten and birth cohorts (ECLS-K and ECLS-B), the National Longitudinal Survey of Youth (NLSY), the American Community Survey (ACS), and a detailed database of child care regulations for all 50 states from 1983 to 2007. The following section provides a description of the relevant variables in each of these data sets.

CHILD CARE REGULATIONS

The child care regulation database was originally compiled by Hotz and Kilburn (1994) for the years 1983–2000. The regulation database provides key information on the nature of the state regulatory environment under which family-based and center-based child care facilities operated over the period. The database was updated from 2000 to 2007. It provides a wide variety of information regarding state requirements for child care facilities. For example, it indicates which states require child development programs, the training and minimum education level necessary for directors of child care facilities as well as for instructors and their assistants, the required child-to-teacher ratio, and the physical requirements of the facilities (e.g., building size and playground requirements).

The regulation data include state-level child care regulation indices to quantify the degree and intensity of regulation by state for center-based and family-based child care. Eight summated indices were created that summarize the strength of a state's requirements in separate categories. They include an overall index, as well as indices for development of children, staff requirements, education within the center, the environment of the facility, the ratio of children to staff, health issues, and oversight and monitoring of the facility. The components of each of these indices are listed in Appendix Tables A.1 and A.2. The overall summated index captures the overall intensity of state regulations by adding up all of the regulations that apply to child care providers. The other indices covering various categories include these seven:

1) The development index sums those regulations that are intended to encourage child development. These variables include measures of experience and training of the staff, the ratio of children to staff members in the facility, and whether the state requires a child development program.

2) The staff index sums any regulations that stipulate requirements of the staff at child care providers. These regulations include education, experience, age, and training requirements, as well as criminal background checks and first aid certification.

3) The education index measures the strength of a state's regulations related to the minimum education requirements for the staff, including their assistants.

4) The environment index attempts to capture the strength of a state's regulations regarding the physical environment of the care facility. These regulations include the amount of indoor and outdoor space required.

5) The ratio index captures the strength of a state's regulations related to child-to-staff ratios for a provider.

6) The health and safety index measures the strength of a state's regulations related to the health and safety of children. The components of this index include requirements for immunization, health evaluations, policies regarding sick children, first aid training requirements for the staff, and criminal background checks.

7) Finally, the oversight index measures a state's ability to provide oversight or enforce its regulatory provisions. Included in the index are variables such as whether the state can impose fines, whether parents have free access to the facility, and whether the state has the ability to revoke a license. Unfortunately, enforcement data were not available in the data sets that were used for the analysis.

Measured by the overall summated index, the strength of state regulation of child care facilities has steadily increased over the period 1983–2007. Figure 4.1 displays a box-and-whisker plot for each year of the summated index for center-based (Panel A) and family-based (Panel B) care. The figure is a visualization of the mean (over states) and standard deviation of the summated ratings over time. The figure shows an increase in the mean number of state regulations facing child care providers over the years 1983–2007. The declining range of the whiskers in the plot also indicates that the variance among states in the strength of regulation has steadily decreased over time. Figure 4.1 also suggests that state regulation of child care has become stronger on average and is becoming less variable across states.

Although there is considerable variation in the level of regulation across time, as shown in Figure 4.1, there is also variation across states.

**Figure 4.1 Box-and-Whisker Graph Showing the Growth and Variation
of Child Care Regulations by State over Time**

Panel A: Center-based summated regulation scores, 1983–2007

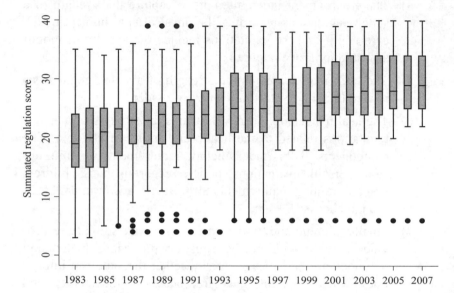

Panel B: Family-based summated regulation scores, 1983–2007

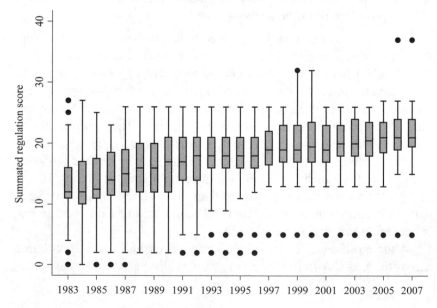

SOURCE: Hotz and Xiao (2011); authors' compilation of data from 2000 to 2007.

Table 4.1 shows variation in the overall summated child care regulation index across all states in 2007. For example, in 2007 the most highly regulated state for center-based care (Rhode Island) had a score of 40 in the overall summated rating index, whereas the least regulated state (Idaho) had a score of only 6. Table 4.1 also depicts considerable variation of state regulations within a particular state over time. For instance, from 1983 to 2007, Mississippi increased its overall regulation score for center-based care by 24 points and for family-based care by 14 points; these values were among the largest increases in these scores. The empirical analysis that follows exploits this variation in regulation, in general and along specific dimensions, within states over time and across states to estimate the influence of regulation on wage determination, access, and child care outcomes.

LABOR MARKET DATA

This section provides an explanation of the data used to examine the labor market effects of regulation of child care workers. The American Community Survey (ACS) provides annual information on wage, education level, race, age, geography, and work experience for a nationally representative sample of child care workers and preschool teachers from the "child day care services" industry classification for the years 2000–2007. The data are used to estimate the influence of regulation on the hourly wages of child care workers, while holding constant other individual characteristics that are related to wages. The ACS provides a large sample of preschool teachers and day care workers with which to analyze the wage effects of state child care regulations. In each year, the ACS has more than 2,000 observations, and in the later years of the survey there are a minimum of 16,000 observations. The ACS provides the standard control variables found in analyzing census data that can be used in estimating wage equations such as race, education level, and years of experience. Table 4.2 shows the summary statistics in the ACS sample covariates used in the estimation of the models that are presented later in the chapter. The table provides information for all preschool workers, child care workers, and preschool teachers.

**Table 4.1 State Levels and Changes in Child Care Regulations,
1983–2007**

State	Overall center-based		Overall family-based	
	1983	2007	1983	2007
Alabama	25			22
Alaska	10	23	11	24
Arizona	7			
Arkansas	16	25	14	23
California				21
Colorado	24	31		25
Connecticut			9	21
Delaware		25		19
District of Columbia		39		27
Florida	9		17	
Georgia	15	22	12	16
Hawaii		22		21
Idaho	3	6	4	5
Illinois	28	35	17	
Indiana	25	33	4	18
Iowa		23		15
Kansas		24		
Kentucky	9	27	11	20
Louisiana				
Maine		35		
Maryland		34		
Massachusetts		39		24
Michigan	16		14	
Minnesota	32	36	27	
Mississippi	5	29	10	24
Missouri	21	25	14	18
Montana		26		25
Nebraska	25	27	12	20
Nevada	15		14	21
New Hampshire	25	26	19	24
New Jersey	20		0	
New Mexico	16		13	
New York	28	36	16	37
North Carolina		32	11	25

Table 4.1 (continued)

	Overall center-based		Overall family-based	
State	1983	2007	1983	2007
North Dakota	10	32	8	19
Ohio	13	27	25	24
Oklahoma	18	26	23	
Oregon	21	30		22
Pennsylvania	24	34	12	20
Rhode Island		40		
South Carolina	6		2	
South Dakota				
Tennessee	17	29	12	
Texas		24	10	
Utah	22	32		24
Vermont	19		10	23
Virginia	16		9	18
Washington	21		14	
West Virginia	20			20
Wisconsin	35		17	
Wyoming				21

NOTE: Blank = data not available.
SOURCE: Hotz and Xiao (2011); authors' compilation.

Measures of Child Care Outcomes

The ECLS-K provides information on child outcomes and child care arrangements and consists of a cross-sectional data set of over 20,000 children and their parents in all 50 states from the kindergarten class of 1998–1999. This chapter uses the restricted confidential version of the ECLS-K, which provides information on child care arrangements and the state in which the children live, as well as individual academic skill assessments (reading and math skills). It also provides extensive background information on the children's parents, including education level, employment status, income level, marital status, race, and further details of the socioeconomic characteristics of the children and their families. Although the data are rich in covariates, they have few observations for many of the smaller states, making the analysis generally applicable only to larger states.

Information on child academic achievement is particularly important as an outcome variable of the influence of occupational regulation. The ECLS-K provides general knowledge, math, and reading skill
assessment scores for all children. These scores were collected in the fall
of the children's kindergarten year and should reflect their experiences
prior to school entry. In mathematics, children are tested on their ability
to identify one-digit numbers, recognize geometric shapes, count, read
two-digit numerals, recognize sequences, solve simple addition and
subtraction problems, and additional questions on cognitive ability. The
reading test consists of measuring the child's ability to identify upper-
and lowercase letters, associate letters with sounds, recognize common
words, and read words in context. In each case, the child's overall skill
in each test is given as an item response theory (IRT) skill score, which
measures their overall aptitude in reading and math skills. These IRT
scores are then standardized across children and are the key dependent
variables in our empirical models measuring the effect of regulation on
academic achievement.

In the analysis, a match was made with children's type of child care
along with the appropriate level of state regulation. The goal was to
classify children by the type of care they received in the year prior to
entering kindergarten. Information was used from the parent survey to
categorize the type of care a child received in the year prior to kindergarten as follows: center-based care (including preschool, day care,
and prekindergarten, but excluding Head Start), family-based care
(nonrelative care provided outside the child's home), nonrelative care
(nonrelative care in the child's home), and relative care. Because information was also collected on how many hours of each type of care
children typically received, the analysis is able to construct variables
that capture whether children receive any of each type of care as well
as designate one type of care as the primary care arrangement (i.e., the
care category in which children spend the largest number of hours). In
order to match our state regulation data with the children included in
the ECLS-K, we match those children that attended center-based care
with the center-based state regulation variables in 1997 (the year before
the children entered kindergarten). Similarly, a match was obtained for
those children that attended family-based care (nonrelative care outside
of the home) with state-level family-based regulation variables in 1997.

Table 4.2 Summary Statistics: American Community Survey (ACS) for All Preschool Workers, Child Care Workers, and Teachers

All				
Variable	Mean	sd	Min.	Max.
years of education	13.05	2.30	0	20
potential experience (age – educ – 6)	19.60	14.44	0	78
potential experience squared	592.78	711.11	0	6,084
female	0.97	0.18	0	1
married	0.57	0.49	0	1
race—white	0.77	0.42	0	1
race—black	0.14	0.35	0	1
N = 64,914				

Child care workers				
Variable	Mean	sd	Min.	Max.
years of education	12.57	2.29	0	20
potential experience (age – educ – 6)	20.07	15.15	0	78
potential experience squared	632.43	760.46	0	6,084
female	0.96	0.19	0	1
married	0.55	0.50	0	1
race—white	0.76	0.43	0	1
race—black	0.14	0.35	0	1
N = 45,054				

Preschool teachers				
Variable	Mean	sd	Min.	Max.
years of education	14.14	1.93	0	20
potential experience (age – educ – 6)	18.52	12.64	0	74
potential experience squared	502.81	573.83	0	5,476
female	0.98	0.14	0	1
married	0.63	0.48	0	1
race—white	0.79	0.41	0	1
race—black	0.14	0.34	0	1
N = 19,860				

NOTE: Models include full set of year and state dummies. The value for *potential experience* is derived from the person's age minus that person's years of education minus six (the age of first enrollment in school).
SOURCE: American Community Survey (ACS).

An additional source of data for the study is the ECLS-B, a nationally representative birth cohort of 14,000 children born in 2001. This longitudinal study follows children from birth until kindergarten and includes both parent interviews and direct child assessments. For the ECLS-B, information was collected when the children were approximately nine months old (2001–2002), two years old (2003), four years old (2005–2006), and at kindergarten age (2006–2007 and 2007–2008).

The kindergarten 2006–2007 round of the ECLS-B provides child achievement assessments that are compatible with the ECLS-K kindergarten test scores. The preschool round of the ECLS-B contains reading and math test scores for children that are nearly the same age as those in the ECLS-K. The reading and math assessments are similar in each data source.

The ECLS-B data also provide detailed information about child care experiences, information on the child's state of residence, primary child care arrangement throughout the child's first five years, including in the year before kindergarten, and family background. The observations in the data include information (up to four years of age) regarding children's primary child care arrangements in a way similar to the ECLS-K, distinguishing between center-based care, family-based care, Head Start, and relative care. Also, similar to the ECLS-K, the ECLS-B has a large amount of information that measures or proxies for influential family processes such as income, mother's education level, poverty status, the number of children in the household, and the family structure.

The empirical analysis combines the ECLS-K and ECLS-B data so that there is a repeated cross section across states. This allows an estimate of the empirical models using various sensitivity approaches. The ECLS-K provides a sample of children across all 50 states who attended child care in the year 1997, and the ECLS-B provides a sample of children attending child care in 2005. Each provides information on the child's primary child care arrangement in the year before kindergarten, the child's reading and math aptitude measured in kindergarten, and the child's individual and family characteristics.

Table 4.3 shows summary statistics of key variables for the analysis by survey type: the ECLS-K or the ECLS-B. The table suggests that the individuals, including the children, in the ECLS-K have comparable average characteristics with the children in the ECLS-B sample. However, a slightly higher proportion of children in the ECLS-B belong to

Table 4.3 Summary Statistics from the ECLS-K and ECLS-B Surveys

Variable	ECLS-K		ECLS-B	
	Mean	sd	Mean	sd
standardized reading score fall of kindergarten	0.04	1.01	0.03	1.00
standardized math score fall of kindergarten	0.09	1.00	0.03	1.00
childcare = center care	0.48	0.50	0.50	0.50
childcare = family-based care	0.10	0.30	0.05	0.23
childcare = head start	0.10	0.30	0.13	0.34
childcare = nonrelative care	0.01	0.09	0.02	0.13
childcare = relative care	0.14	0.35	0.12	0.33
childcare = parental care	0.17	0.38	0.17	0.38
child age KF (months old)[a]	68.49	4.29	65.13	3.75
reside in city	0.41	0.49	0.30	0.46
reside in suburb	0.37	0.48	0.42	0.49
reside in town	0.11	0.32	0.12	0.33
boy	0.51	0.50	0.50	0.50
race is white	0.61	0.49	0.41	0.49
race is black	0.16	0.36	0.15	0.36
race is Hispanic	0.14	0.34	0.21	0.40
race is Asian	0.05	0.21	0.13	0.33
mother works part-time	0.22	0.42	0.19	0.39
mother works full-time	0.47	0.50	0.42	0.49
number of children in household	2.44	1.11	2.52	1.17
family structure: step	0.08	0.28	0.05	0.22
family structure: single parent	0.21	0.40	0.19	0.39
family structure: adoptive or other	0.03	0.17	0.02	0.13
household below poverty threshold	0.16	0.36	0.23	0.42
speak English at home	0.92	0.27	0.78	0.42
mother's education: high school diploma	0.30	0.46	0.25	0.43
mother's education: voc. degree or some college	0.34	0.47	0.30	0.46
mother's education: bachelor's degree	0.19	0.39	0.20	0.40
mother's education: advanced degree	0.07	0.25	0.12	0.32
very low birth weight (less than 3.125 lb.)	0.01	0.10	0.09	0.28

(continued)

Table 4.3 (continued)

Variable	ECLS-K		ECLS-B	
	Mean	sd	Mean	sd
low birth weight (between 3.125 lb. and 5.5 lb.)	0.06	0.25	0.15	0.36
hhincome = $5,001 to $10,000	0.05	0.22	0.04	0.20
hhincome = $10,001 to $15,000	0.06	0.24	0.06	0.23
hhincome = $15,001 to $20,000	0.06	0.24	0.06	0.24
hhincome = $20,001 to $25,000	0.07	0.25	0.08	0.27
hhincome = $25,001 to $30,000	0.07	0.26	0.06	0.25
hhincome = $30,001 to $35,000	0.06	0.23	0.05	0.23
hhincome = $35,001 to $40,000	0.07	0.26	0.05	0.23
hhincome = $40,001 to $50,000	0.11	0.32	0.09	0.28
hhincome = $50,001 to $75,000	0.20	0.40	0.16	0.37
hhincome = $75,001 to $100,000	0.13	0.33	0.13	0.34
hhincome = $100,001 to $200,000	0.07	0.26	0.14	0.34
hhincome = $200,001 or more	0.02	0.13	0.04	0.19

NOTE: Sample sizes limited to complete observations: ECLS-K survey, $N = 13,679$; ECLS-B survey, $N = 5,534$.
[a] *child age KF (months old)* means the child's age in months at the start of the fall semester of kindergarten.
SOURCE: Early Childhood Longitudinal Study, Kindergarten Cohort (ECLS-K); Early Childhood Longitudinal Study, Birth Cohort (ECLS-B).

a racial minority, and children in the ECLS-B are more likely to have a low birth weight. The age of children (listed as 68.5 in the ECLS-K and 65.1 in the ECLS-B) is in months. Given the youth of the children in the samples these differences may matter more than would be caught with just a listing by their age in round years. Beside those differences, the children in the ECLS-K and ECLS-B come from families with similar structure and socioeconomic status, are about the same age at the time of math and reading testing, and have similar levels of child care arrangements.

A Further Measure of Child Outcomes: National Longitudinal Survey of Youth (NLSY)

The NLSY 1979 Maternal and Child Supplement is a panel of children born to mothers who were between the ages of 14 and 21 in 1979.

Starting in 1986 and continuing on a biennial basis, direct child assessments were conducted for all children born to women in the original NLSY sample. Children born early in the study had comparatively young and disadvantaged mothers. However, by the 1990s, the data were far more representative. Although not nationally representative, the data are national in scope and remain one of few such data sets that have repeated panel data with school readiness assessments for young children. For this part of our analysis, a selection was made of all cohorts of children who were between ages three and four between 1986 and 2004. This is important because it eliminates children born to the youngest mothers from the analysis (these children were older than four when first observed in 1986). Moreover, because the mother's age at birth is known, this variable can be controlled for in the analysis. To further test the sensitivity of the results, given the large sample size, one can also remove young mothers or earlier cohorts of children from the analysis.

The analysis indicates the NLSY provides about 5,300 complete-record observations of children at ages three through six. In this data set, and with the others that focus on educational outcomes, the data that are available suggest that there are sufficient observations for large states, but little can be said about educational attainment in smaller states. Permission was obtained from the Bureau of Labor Statistics to work with the restricted-use geocode version of these data. The restricted-use NLSY provides much of the same information as the ECLS-K: state residence, information on child-care arrangements, child cognitive and academic skill assessments (standardized assessment of receptive vocabulary and academic skills), and parental and household characteristics. Information on care arrangements is available for all children for the first three years of life (collected prospectively and retrospectively, depending on the specific year of the survey). Mothers were asked about up to three arrangements for each child, and the data have been coded so that one can distinguish between center-based care, family-based care (nonrelative care in others' homes), and other nonrelative or relative care. As with the ECLS-K, the data allow a determination of whether children regularly experienced any of these types of care, as well as the type of care that was considered the primary care arrangement at age three.

For children's achievement, the NLSY provides measures of the Peabody Picture Vocabulary Test (PPVT), measured at age three or four, which assesses children's receptive vocabulary, and the Peabody Individual Achievement Test (PIAT), a widely used reading recognition and math assessment, measured at age five or six. Although these are different measures of achievement from the ECLS-K or the ECLS-B, they provide another outcome variable in order to test the role that state regulation has in children's academic achievement. Similar to the ECLS data, the NLSY has a wide variety of child and family information that can be employed as covariates. In particular, it has extensive demographic information as well as measures of the child's temperament, the mother's health behaviors, the quality of the home environment, and behavioral attitudes.

INFLUENCE OF REGULATION ON WAGE DETERMINATION

As noted earlier, government regulation of child care may influence the price of child care both by increasing the demand for the regulated service and by reducing supply. On the demand side, theory suggests that certain regulations, given that they increase the quality of care provided, could increase demand for formal care because its quality has risen. On the supply side, increased regulation may have a direct impact on the provider's costs.

Two examples of how regulation can influence provider costs are by 1) requiring providers to hire more highly educated workers or by 2) requiring providers to maintain a higher staff-to-child ratio. Either of these regulations may increase the wages of child care workers in a state. For example, if a state requires providers to hire workers with a college education, wages will tend to increase if the provider would have otherwise hired workers with less education. Similarly, if the state ratio requirement forces providers to hire more staff than they would have otherwise, assuming workers have limited mobility, the ratio requirement will tend to raise the wages of child care workers in the state.

In this section of the chapter, an empirical specification is developed to test for a relationship between state regulation and the wages of child care providers. If state regulation tends to increase wages, regulation may have a direct influence on the supply of regulated child care. If regulation increases wages, then the quantity of child care supplied to the market will be lower for a given price per child. Consequently, raising wages and prices reduces the number of children in day care, all else being equal. Without subsidies to low-income families, their children will be shifted to either parental or other family care.

Analyzing these relationships suggests that we estimate the following log-wage model, which provides an estimate of the determinants of wages for individual child care workers:

$$(4.1) \quad \ln(wage_{ist}) = \delta z_{st} + x_{it}\beta + w_s + v_t + \varepsilon_{ist}.$$

In Equation (4.1), $wage_{ist}$ is the wage of child care worker i in state s at time t, x_{it} is a vector containing observable individual-level variables that influence wages, w_s and v_t are state and time fixed effects, respectively, and ε_{ist} represents individual-level unobservables that influence the wages of workers. Finally, the key explanatory variable in this model is z_{st}, which represents the strength of regulation of care in state s during year t. In the models, z_{st} is restricted to regulations (either indexed or measured individually) that are related to staff-to-child ratios and education requirements. In this model, δ represents an estimate of the causal effect of stricter education and ratio requirements on the wages of child care workers.

The next section examines whether these regulations would provide benefits to children through enhanced academic performance.

REGULATION AND ENROLLMENT IN PRESCHOOL PROGRAMS

As noted earlier, more stringent state regulation of formal child care arrangements may increase the price of care. Moreover, stricter regulation may increase demand for formal care because the perceived and actual quality may increase, and stricter regulation may decrease supply because the increased standards would reduce the number of openings and workers in the industry. More specifically, stricter regulation may reduce the number of children attending formal care arrangements and increase its price if regulation increases provider costs without fueling greater demand.

In contrast, if greater regulation increases the demand for center-based care by increasing the quality of preschools, while having a relatively small influence on the cost of providing formal care, then regulation could have a net effect of increasing child enrollment in formal care arrangements. Regulations that are binding and affect the provider's costs of operation are expected to have an influence on enrollment in formal care arrangements. The expectation is that stricter government limitations on child-to-staff ratios, higher minimum education requirements, limitations on the size of the establishment, and other government regulations will reduce the supply of formal care. This would be similar to the results suggested by Blau and Currie (2006) and by Hotz and Xiao (2011). In turn, assuming that the demand effects of regulation are negligible, the expectation is that states that have stricter regulations with respect to formal care will also have lower child enrollment in formal care providers.

The estimation of the effect of state regulation on the type of child care chosen by parents employs a multinomial logit model of the individual choice of the type of care a child receives (center-based care, family-based care, Head Start, or other, informal care arrangements), conditional on state regulation indices and state fixed effects, year fixed effects, and family and individual controls. In this framework, the estimations are able to assess the influence of state child care regulations on the probability that a child will enroll in formal care arrangements conditional on individual- and state-level characteristics.

ACADEMIC PERFORMANCE OUTCOMES

A basic relationship of the effect of government regulation on academic skills can be modeled using the following specification. The model of childhood achievement assumes that academic skills are determined by the following variables, which differ for individuals in center care ($j = c$) and family care providers ($j = f$):

(4.2) $y_{ist}^j = \delta^j z_{st}^j + x_{it}\,\beta^j + w_s^j + v_t^j + \varepsilon_{ist}^j$, where $j = c, f$.

The variable y_{ist}^{j} is the achievement measure (reading or math test score measure) for which the data are available for child i at time t in state s in care type j, x_{it} is a row vector of individual characteristics affecting a child's outcome, w_s^j is a state fixed effect for care type j, z_{st}^{j} is the state child care regulation index for care type j in state s at time t, where an increase in z_{st}^{j} represents stricter state regulation of care type j, v_t^j is a time fixed effect for care type j, and ε_{ist}^{j} is an error term containing unobserved variables that affect a child's achievement measure. The vector β^j and scalar δ^j are other covariates that will be used to control other factors that may determine test scores. The values for δ^j give the partial effect of government regulation of child care type j on a child's achievement measure.

ESTIMATES OF THE INFLUENCE OF REGULATION

The next section of the chapter is divided into three parts. The initial section presents estimates of the influence of regulation on wage determination of child care workers in the ACS. Next, estimates of child care enrollment are presented. Finally, results of the effect of regulation on children's early academic achievement are shown. At this early stage of regulation and with the mobile labor market of young, generally less-educated workers that work in the industry, there is likely little influence of regulation on the labor market, enrollment in types of programs, or educational outcomes. The remainder of the chapter documents how the estimates were derived and their implications for child care services and for the succeeding chapters, which cover more heavily regulated occupations at more advanced stages of regulation.

The Influence of State Regulation on Wages of Child Care Providers

Initially, estimates are provided of the potential labor costs of regulation. Since labor costs are the largest single cost item for day care centers, they would likely contribute a great deal to the overall price of the service. Given the loose regulatory framework covering preschool teachers and their aides, it would be surprising to find a strong influence of regulation on wage determination. Table 4.4 shows the influence of regulation on wage determination of preschool teachers with (column 2) and without (column 1) state fixed effects. The key variables are education requirements, experience, and teacher-to-child ratios. In a similar manner, using a model consistent with Table 4.4, Table 4.5 gives estimates of the influence of regulation of other kinds of child care workers who are not teachers, with and without state fixed effects. In addition, given the low levels of skill requirements and the ability to replace child care workers, the influence of regulation is expected to be low. The model uses one-period lags, although estimates using two- and three-period lag variables showed similar results. The estimates in these two tables demonstrate that the role of education requirements, experience, and teacher-to-child ratios are small and generally not statistically significant in either Table 4.4 or Table 4.5. On the whole, the explanatory power of the model is fairly low. Furthermore, since the estimates on many of the variables have opposing signs, the use of an F-test for the joint significance of the variables would not provide additional information about the direction of the regulation effects. In the case of preschool education, where workers are easy to replace and where requirements are both new and relaxed, there does not appear to be much of an influence of regulation on wage determination. Similar to the findings by Hotz and Xiao (2011), the estimates vary and show small effects of regulation on wage determination.[2] When government regulation requirements are in an occupation where it is easy to replace these workers, and where regulations are not onerous, then the economic effects appear to be minimal.

The Influence of State Regulation on Enrollment in Formal Day Care Facilities

The previous section of the chapter noted the lack of a consistent result for regulation on wage determination. However, there may be other regulatory factors beyond wage determination that influence whether children are enrolled in formal or center-based preschool programs or in family-focused ones. For example, there may be quality effects of regulation that enhance the enrollment in center-based care, or the staff-student ratio requirements may drive up the prices of these services and send children to family-based care. This section empiri-

Table 4.4 Estimates of the Influence of State Regulation on the Wages of Preschool Teachers in the Day Care Industry, 2000–2008

Variables	(1) lnwage	(2) lnwage
education required in years, aide, day care center	0.00	−0.01**
	(0.00)	(0.00)
education required in years, director, day care center	−0.01	−0.04*
	(0.01)	(0.02)
education required in years, teacher, day care center	0.01***	−0.01
	(0.00)	(0.01)
education required in years, family home provider	−0.00	−0.00
	(0.00)	(0.00)
experience required in years, aide in center	−0.02	0.34***
	(0.02)	(0.07)
experience required, director of center	−0.00	0.03***
	(0.01)	(0.01)
experience required, teacher in center	0.06**	0.08
	(0.03)	(0.06)
experience required, family provider	0.02	0.03
	(0.01)	(0.07)
max. child-to-caregiver ratio for age 48–59 months, center	−0.02***	−0.01***
	(0.00)	(0.00)
max. child-to-caregiver ratio for age 48–59 months, family-based	−0.00	0.00***
	(0.00)	(0.00)
State fixed effects	No	Yes
Observations	16,667	16,667
R-squared	0.089	0.115
N	13,380	13,380

NOTE: Dependent variable is log of wage. Sample restricted to preschool teachers in the child day-care services industry. All models include full set of year dummies. All covariates are lagged one year. Standard errors, in parentheses, are robust to clustering by state. * significant at the 0.10 level; ** significant at the 0.05 level; *** significant at the 0.01 level. Column 1 shows the influence of regulation on wage determination of preschool teachers without state fixed effects; column 2 shows it with state fixed effects.

SOURCE: ACS.

Table 4.5 Estimates of the Influence of State Regulation on the Wages of Child Care Workers in the Day Care Industry, 2000–2008

Variables	(1) lnwage	(2) lnwage
education required in years, aide, day care center	0.00	−0.01
	(0.00)	(0.01)
education required in years, director, day care center	−0.00	−0.05
	(0.01)	(0.04)
education required in years, teacher, day care center	0.01***	−0.00
	(0.00)	(0.00)
education required in years, family home provider	−0.00*	−0.00
	(0.00)	(0.00)
experience required in years, aide in center	0.00	0.06
	(0.02)	(0.09)
experience required, director of center	−0.01	−0.00
	(0.01)	(0.01)
experience required, teacher in center	0.03*	0.02
	(0.02)	(0.02)
experience required, family provider	0.04**	0.03
	(0.02)	(0.03)
max. child-to-caregiver ratio for age 48–59 months, center	−0.00	0.00
	(0.00)	(0.00)
max. child-to-caregiver ratio for age 48–59 months, family-based	−0.00**	0.00***
	(0.00)	(0.00)
State fixed effects	No	Yes
Observations	39,339	39,339
R-squared	0.082	0.094

NOTE: Dependent variable is log of wage. Sample restricted to child-care workers in the child day-care services industry. All models include full set of year dummies. All covariates are lagged one year. Standard errors, in parentheses, are robust to clustering by state. Robust standard errors in parentheses. * significant at the 0.10 level; ** significant at the 0.05 level; *** significant at the 0.01 level. Column 1 is without state fixed effects; column 2 is with state fixed effects.
SOURCE: ACS.

cally examines whether these factors matter in determining the type of care preschool children are enrolled in. A relationship between regulation and enrollment could indicate that state regulations are influencing the price or the availability of certain types of care. Unfortunately, reliable price data do not exist in the data that are examined. The process could be that as regulation raises the price of care and reduces its availability, one would expect to find fewer children attending regulated center care in states where regulation is stronger. However, if regulation increases the quality of care, then demand for formal care arrangements may increase. Specifically, this section of the chapter examines whether increased state regulation of center-based and family-based care increases or reduces a child's probability of enrollment in each care type.

Estimating this relationship involves the use of child care enrollment data from the ECLS-K, the ECLS-B, and the NLSY. Table 4.6 displays a tabulation for the various types of child care enrollment for children in the NLSY and the ECLS-K and ECLS-B in 2007. The tabulations from the three data sets show somewhat different measures of enrollment. In the ECLS-K and ECLS-B, overall enrollment of preschool children is provided in the year before kindergarten, when the children are either age four or five. In the NLSY database, the children are age three. As shown in Table 4.6, the most popular care arrangement in the ECLS-K and ECLS-B data set is center-based care, with 46 percent of children attending some form of center care. The next most popular forms of day care are parental care (19 percent), relative care (15 percent), family-based care (10 percent), Head Start (10 percent), and nonrelative care (1 percent). These values are different from those in the NLSY because the proportion attending center-based care in the NLSY is much lower and the proportion attending parental care is much higher. In the NLSY, only 17 percent of children attend center-based care, and 55 percent receive parental care. This disparity is due in part to the sampling differences used in each of the databases.

Table 4.7 goes beyond the descriptive statistics in Table 4.6 and shows the influence of regulation on preschool children's attendance. The table shows the influence of regulation when other characteristics are accounted for in the empirical analysis. More specifically, the estimates in the table attempt to show whether government regulation, controlling for individual characteristics, influences child care enroll-

Table 4.6 Proportion of Enrollment in Various Types of Child Care, Using ECLS-K and ECLS-B Data, NLSY Data, 2007

Panel A: Primary child care arrangement in the year before kindergarten, ECLS-K and ECLS-B

	n	%
Center care	6,268	45.7
Parental care	2,541	18.5
Relative care	2,049	15.0
Family-based care	1,420	10.4
Head Start	1,315	9.6
Nonrelative care	109	0.8
Total	13,702	100.0

Panel B: Primary child care arrangement at age 3, NLSY

	n	%
Center care	1,581	17.3
Parental care	5,037	55.1
Relative care	1,396	15.3
Family-based care	931	10.2
Nonrelative care	197	2.2
Total	9,142	100.1

NOTE: Total in Panel B does not sum to 100.0 because of rounding.
SOURCE: ECLS-K, ECLS-B, National Longitudinal Survey of Youth (NLSY).

ment. The results show the influence of regulation for center-based and family-based day care, using both the ECLS-K and ECLS-B in Panel A and the NLSY in Panel B. The estimates are a series of marginal effects from a multinomial logit model of the type of care for child enrollment that relates to state regulation and individual characteristics. Overall, the results show no consistent or conclusive results. Nevertheless, for the ECLS data used in the table, the results in Panel A show that greater state regulation is negatively associated with enrollment in center-based preschool programs (given in column one)—programs are calculated to be about 7 percent less at the mean value of the distribution used in Table 4.7. Since different age groups are in the two data sets, the estimates on enrollment are consistent with the anticipated results. None of the other major categories of preschool enrollment show significant

Table 4.7 Effect of Regulation on Preschool Attendance for Center-Based and Family-Based Day Care, Using ECLS-K and ECLS-B Data and NLSY Data

	Panel A: ECLS-K and ECLS-B—2005			
Variables	Center	Family	Head Start	Other
overall center	−0.03***	0.0068	−0.0005	0.0235**
	(0.01)	(0.0058)	(0.0040)	(0.0106)
overall family	0.0053	−0.0046	−0.0051	0.0044
	(0.0126)	(0.0056)	(0.0041)	(0.0117)
Observations	16,363	16,363	16,363	16,363

	Panel B: NLSY Overall Regulation Enrollment Effects		
Variables	Center	Family	Other
overall center	−0.0032	0.0024	0.0009
	(0.0033)	(0.0027)	(0.0041)
overall family	−0.0051**	−0.0001	0.0052
	(0.0026)	(0.0020)	(0.0032)
Observations	3,481	3,481	3,481

NOTE: Standard errors in parentheses. Model includes a full set of year and state dummies and includes a full set of individual and family controls. Estimates are marginal effects at the mean (MEM) from the multinomial logit model. Overall regulation indices are lagged one year in Panels A and B (1996 or 2004). * significant at the 0.10 level; ** significant at the 0.05 level; *** significant at the 0.01 level.
SOURCE: ECLS-K, ECLS-B, NLSY.

results for the role of regulation. Furthermore, the estimates using data from the NLSY in Panel B also show no influence of regulation on preschool enrollment for center-based care, but these results are for only three-year-olds. The estimates in Panel B show only a modest negative influence for family-based care. Looking at both national data sources, it is difficult to find a clear pattern for the role of regulation in affecting enrollment in preschool programs over the period for the data analysis shown in Table 4.7, but to the extent the estimates are informative they suggest a negative influence of regulation on center-based enrollment.

Finally, the rest of the chapter focuses on the potential effect of regulation in influencing test scores as a proxy for academic achievement.

The Influence of Regulation on Preschool Children's Academic Skills

If regulation accomplishes its goals of improving quality, a measure of that goal would be an enhancement of test scores for children in regulated preschool environments. The outcomes would occur because regulation would produce more highly qualified teachers and staff or because the regulations would result in more attention being devoted to students through lower staff-to-student ratios (Kleiner 2011). Based on the results examined earlier in the chapter, it appears that occupational regulation does not influence either wage determination or the selection of the type of day care facility. However, other regulatory provisions may affect the quality of student achievement, which then shows up in enhanced student performance. This section of the chapter focuses on this issue.

Estimates of student achievement from the ECLS-K

Table 4.8 shows the effect of each summated regulation index on math and reading scores for children sampled in either the ECLS-K or the ECLS-B data. The dependent variable is the child's item response theory math or reading score in the fall of his or her kindergarten year (measured in 1998), which provides a measure of academic aptitude prior to kindergarten. The samples used for the estimates include children whose primary care arrangement was center-based (including preschool, day care, and prekindergarten, but excluding Head Start) or family-based care (nonrelative care provided outside the child's home) in the year prior to kindergarten (1997–1998).

The table matches each child in the ECLS-K and ECLS-B samples with the appropriate state regulation indices (family-based or center-based, depending on which type of care the child received) for the year 1997–1998. The match occurs for each child, with the regulation index using information from the child's home state in the year 1997. The sample sizes vary based on the regulation data that was available for each state. They match with the state regulation indices for that individual, which measure an overall value along with ones for development, health, staff, environment, ratio, oversight, and education. The coefficients on these variables measure the relationship between a child's test score and the strength of state regulation in each area, given that the child was exposed to the measured regulation. The estimates are an approximation of the effect of the strength of government regulation on early childhood academic achievement. This interpretation, however, depends heavily on controlling for factors that influence average test scores within a state, and the factors are correlated with the number of regulations within the state. To reduce the risk of potential bias, the estimates include several covariates in these models, which control for individual-, family-, and state-level characteristics that may be related to test scores. The individual-level variables include race, gender, and birth weight. In addition, family-level covariates include family income, father's and mother's education and employment status, family type, and residence type. Finally, these estimates include state controls, such as state per capita income and spending on welfare, and regional dummy variables to control for a wide range of differentials in children's test scores by state and region of the country.[3]

The results show that state regulation of center-based providers in terms of environmental and educational requirements is positively related to math and reading scores among children who attended center-based care. The coefficients suggest that additional state regulation in either of these areas is associated with an increase in math and reading scores by roughly a tenth of a standard deviation. To put this in perspective, a tenth of a standard deviation increase in test scores is roughly equivalent to the black-versus-white test score gap (0.13 of a standard deviation) and is more than three times larger than the gender gap (0.03 of a standard deviation), which is estimated as part of the same model that is shown in Table 4.8. While the results suggest that educational and environmental requirements carry an important impact, there is no evidence in the ECLS that stronger regulation of other aspects of the provider's operation has an effect on child test scores.

Estimates of student achievement from the NLSY

To test for robustness and consistency of the estimates in the ECLS-K and ECLS-B samples, the NLSY is examined. This is another database that contains information on preschool academic achievement. Using data on student achievement, Table 4.9 shows results of the estimates of the influence of regulation. Again, the sample sizes vary based on the regulation data that was available for each state. The NLSY estimates find a similar result for the role of educational requirements on

Table 4.8 Regulation's Influence on Student Academic Outcomes, Using the Combined ECLS-K and ECLS-B Data

Panel A: Influence of center-based regulations on math scores

Variables	(1) Math	(2) Math	(3) Math	(4) Math	(5) Math	(6) Math	(7) Math
overall center	−0.02 (0.02)						
development center		−0.02 (0.02)					
health center			0.02 (0.05)				
staff center				0.00 (0.02)			
environment center					0.10*** (0.01)		
ratio center						−0.02 (0.05)	
education center							0.11*** (0.03)
Observations	4,810	5,806	8,918	5,852	8,802	9,537	8,712
R^2	0.265	0.266	0.281	0.269	0.283	0.282	0.283

NOTE: Columns show the influence of regulation on math scores, according to the type of preschool program the child attended. The ECLS-K and ECLS-B provide detailed information by type of preschool program. Robust standard errors in parentheses. Estimates include set of year and state dummies and individual and family controls. Sample includes only children attending center care in the year prior to kindergarten. Standard errors are robust to clustering at the state level. * significant at the 0.01 level; ** significant at the 0.05 level; *** significant at the 0.01 level.
SOURCE: ECLS-K, ECLS-B.

reading scores. However, the result for math scores is insignificant. The NLSY estimates also fail to reveal an effect of regulations related to the environment, as was found in the ECLS. The NLSY results reveal a positive relationship between health- or safety-related regulations and test scores. The estimates in Table 4.9 show the effect of each summated regulation index on math and reading scores for children sampled in the NLSY. The method of presentation in Table 4.9 is similar to that for the combined ECLS estimates. The dependent variables in Panel A are the PIAT (Peabody Individual Achievement Test) math scores measured at age six, on average. The dependent variables in Panel B are the PIAT

Table 4.8 (continued)

Panel B: Influence of center-based regulations on reading scores

Variables	(1) Reading	(2) Reading	(3) Reading	(4) Reading	(5) Reading	(6) Reading	(7) Reading
overall center	−0.03						
	(0.02)						
development center		−0.02					
		(0.02)					
health center			−0.06*				
			(0.04)				
staff center				−0.02			
				(0.02)			
environment center					0.13***		
					(0.02)		
ratio center						−0.00	
						(0.04)	
education center							0.16***
							(0.05)
Observations	4,768	5,762	8,749	5,808	8,633	9,368	8,542
R^2	0.245	0.248	0.242	0.251	0.240	0.240	0.244

NOTE: Columns show the influence of regulation on reading scores, according to the type of preschool program the child attended. The ECLS-K and ECLS-B provide detailed information by type of preschool program. Standard errors in parentheses. Estimates include set of year and state dummies and individual and family controls. Sample includes only children attending center care in the year prior to kindergarten. Standard errors are robust to clustering at the state level. * significant at the 0.01 level; ** significant at the 0.05 level; *** significant at the 0.01 level.
SOURCE: ECLS-K, ECLS-B.

reading scores using the same test. Unlike many other standardized tests, the ages at which children were tested in math and reading varies significantly. For example, children were tested anywhere between the ages of two and 11. Consequently, there is a control for the age at which the children took the test.[4]

In the NLSY, specifications used controls that were similar to those used in the other analysis in the chapter. These approaches include a full set of year and state dummies to estimate state fixed effects and year effects. Some of the individual controls include the child's age, race, and gender. The family controls include the mother's and father's education levels, mother's aptitude as measured by the Armed Forces

Table 4.9 Influence of Center-Based Regulation on Math Scores, Using the NLSY

	Panel A						
	(1)	(2)	(3)	(4)	(5)	(6)	(7)
Variables	Math	Math	Math	Math	Math	Math	Math
overall center	0.18						
	(0.23)						
development center		0.21					
		(0.29)					
health center			1.54***				
			(0.53)				
staff center				0.00			
				(0.26)			
environment center					0.48		
					(1.09)		
ratio center						0.89	
						(1.29)	
education center							1.37
							(1.98)
Observations	604	625	670	632	669	671	659
R^2	0.237	0.238	0.251	0.242	0.246	0.247	0.251

NOTE: Columns show the influence of regulation on math scores, according to the type of preschool program the child attended. The ECLS-K and ECLS-B provide detailed information by type of preschool program. Robust standard errors in parentheses. Regressions include year and state dummies and individual and family controls. Sample includes only children attending center care at age three. Standard errors are robust to clustering at the state level. * significant at the 0.10 level; ** significant at the 0.05 level; *** significant at the 0.01 level.
SOURCE: NLSY.

Qualifying Test (AFQT), and family arrangement. When all of these factors are accounted for, it is evident that regulation has no effect for the overall measure of regulation, but that some of the individual factors, such as regulating the environment of center-based preschool education and regulating health and safety, matter for some of the measures of student achievement.

Table 4.9 (continued)

	Panel B						
	(1)	(2)	(3)	(4)	(5)	(6)	(7)
Variables	Reading	Reading	Reading	Reading	Reading	Reading	Reading
overall center	−0.02						
	(0.19)						
development		−0.08					
center		(0.22)					
health center			1.24***				
			(0.31)				
staff center				−0.07			
				(0.22)			
environment					0.25		
center					(0.85)		
ratio center						−0.59	
						(1.02)	
education							2.20**
center							(0.82)
Observations	595	616	660	622	659	661	649
R^2	0.331	0.319	0.328	0.320	0.324	0.325	0.332

NOTE: Columns show the influence of regulation on reading scores, according to the type of preschool program the child attended. The ECLS-K and ECLS-B provide detailed information by type of preschool program. Robust standard errors in parentheses. Regressions include year and state dummies and individual and family controls. Sample includes only children attending center care at age 3. Standard errors are robust to clustering at the state level. * significant at the 0.10 level; ** significant at the 0.05 level; *** significant at the 0.01 level.
SOURCE: NLSY.

SUMMARY AND CONCLUSIONS

This chapter attempted to measure many of the key elements of the costs and benefits of government regulation of child care, with a focus on occupational licensing. The regulation of child care is at an early stage of development, in terms of both the number of states that require it and the standards to be licensed. The estimates fail to find any evidence that the wages of preschool teachers or child care workers are affected by government regulation. This finding is not surprising, since the requirements are both relatively new and at low levels. However, there is some evidence, albeit not conclusive, that government regulation appears to affect child care enrollment in center-based care by making it more difficult to find teachers and support staff, thereby reducing enrollment. Unfortunately, no reliable price data are available to examine this issue in more detail. One potential benefit of increased regulation is an increase in the quality of child care. This effect could be measured by improved child development and early childhood academic achievement scores. The results for the overall index variable fail to show evidence of benefits related to increased early childhood academic achievement in math and reading scores across two major government databases—the ECLS-K and the NLSY—but several individual factors such as environment, health, and education-based regulations are significant in some of the estimates for both reading and math scores.

At these levels of regulation and in this industry, the regulation of child care is unlikely to show much influence. The estimates in this chapter confirm this prediction. If regulation does little to change costs through wages or only modestly affects costs through changes in enrollment patterns, there are few reasons to enact the kinds of low levels of licensing that are considered in this chapter. This is especially true if these regulations result in governmental monitoring or fees that do not seem to generate major benefits to either workers or children. Furthermore, the estimates show that occupational regulations have no measurable influence on test scores.

The remainder of the book examines occupations and industries at much higher levels of regulation, where licensing laws have been in effect for much longer time periods. The expectation is that regulations that are more rigorous and have been in force for a longer time are more likely to have an influence on the compensation of members of the occupation and on consumers of their services.

Notes

1. I thank Matthew Hendricks for his contributions to this chapter. He is an assistant professor of economics at the University of Tulsa.
2. Similar estimates of wage determination for other day care workers and for all day care workers showed similarly inconclusive results.
3. Estimates were also developed for the role of overall regulation in family-based care, and the results are similar, in that some individual factors have an influence on preschool children's test scores.
4. Additional robustness tests were conducted for family- and center-based care using various specifications and controls, and none found consistently significant results. Overall, these regulation indices did not show any influence on children's cognitive test scores using the NLSY.

5

Of Life, Limbs, and Licensing: Electricians and Plumbers

With Kyoung Won Park

Possession of any of these licenses gives the holder enormous economic advantage, for he is protected from competition from nonholders. Indeed, so important has the license become that outsiders wishing to compete for business in an area where they do not have a license may seek out a license holder who is no longer actively engaged in the business and arrange to rent his master's license.
—Shimberg, Esser, and Kruger (1973, p. 67)

Opposition to statewide licensing had come from plumbers who feel that such licensing makes it easier for outsiders to compete with them for local jobs. (Ibid., p. 69)

Every job must be passed and approved by the "city's electrical inspectors." Should the work be unsatisfactory, the contractor must bear the expense of making all necessary changes. It is this potential monetary penalty, say the proponents of licensing only contractors, that motivates the contractor to hire competent workers and to provide them with high-quality supervision. (Ibid., p. 70)

INTRODUCTION

Most of this book is devoted to the analysis of regulated white-collar occupations; however, this chapter examines electricians and plumbers, two of the most highly skilled blue-collar occupations in the construction industry.[1] The chapter goes beyond merely looking at the traditional wage effects of occupational regulation to examine whether the training and monitoring of the work that is associated with occupational regulation contributes to the enhanced safety of the workers in the occupation. Although firm-related factors, such as financial leverage, may influence health and safety, the evaluation of the issue represents a first attempt to go beyond traditional economic measures to examine some of the potential benefits of regulation—benefits not only for consumers but also for workers using measures of nonmonetary outcomes (Cohn and Wardlaw 2013).

Analysts of government policies in the labor market have long held that licensing laws that restrict the supply of labor cause an increase in wages, but there has been little analysis of the influence of regulation on the conditions of work. We examine the influence of occupational licensing on the wages and workplace safety of electricians and plumbers, among the most regulated and skilled occupations directly involved in the construction industry.

A focus of this chapter is on the role of occupational licensing and other forms of government regulation for electricians, a heavily regulated occupation in the construction industry. The material in the chapter also examines plumbers, but given data constraints and the lack of variation in the laws governing this occupation, the analysis is in much less depth. Unlike previous chapters, which examine the role of occupational licensing on wages, prices, access, or quality to consumers, this chapter extends the analysis of regulation on the likelihood of occupational licensing reducing work-related deaths and serious job-related injuries, using new methods and data (Shepard 1978; Bond et al. 1980; Cox and Foster 1990; Kleiner and Todd 2007).

The central findings show that certain occupational licensing requirements, such as minimum age, education, and exam requirements, raise the wages of electricians by about 6 to 8 percent. These results are robust for several alternative specifications for electricians. However, the results for plumbers are murky. Furthermore, the estimates suggest a modest but significant trade-off between wages and work-related injuries for electricians, a result that agrees with economic theory on compensating differentials of trade-offs of pay for safety. Local licensing of electricians is associated with approximately a 12 percent wage premium beyond state regulations. This is consistent with the quotation at the beginning of the chapter that local licensing of the construction trades is often seen as a major economic benefit to the members of the trade. Neither the estimates for electricians nor those for plumbers show much evidence of a systematic influence of occupational licensing on the injury rates, severity of injuries, or death rates. As with the other chapters in this book, we first describe the institutional environment of the occupations and then describe the data and analysis used to examine the labor market and health and safety effects of occupational regulation by government.

PUBLIC POLICY APPROACHES TO OCCUPATIONAL HEALTH AND SAFETY

Public policies on health and safety have generally taken two approaches: the regulation and setting of standards, and the implementation of social insurance through worker compensation. Illustrations of the regulation approach are the passage of the Coal Mine Safety Act in 1969 and the Occupational Safety and Health Act (OSHA) in 1970.

The federal government has played a major role in protecting the health and safety of the workforce. For example, miners have been at the forefront of occupational health and safety legislation, largely because they have the highest rate of injury and death, and also because they have gathered the most attention through the media. Media attention has occurred in part because many of the deaths and injuries involve large groups of miners who are affected in one incident, usually in dramatic fashion. In contrast, deaths and injuries in construction tend to occur to a much greater extent in small groups, away from the spotlight of public attention. The focus on miners develops even though construction workers are likely to have multiple times as many overall deaths and injuries annually. Recent data provided by the Bureau of Labor Statistics show that construction workers have by far the greatest number of deaths and injuries of any industry, and that they rank high in rates of injury and death (BLS 2011). The analysis provided in this chapter adds to the literature on occupational health and safety by examining whether occupational regulation complements current regulatory policies to promote workplace health and safety by reducing the occurrence and severity of occupational injuries. If occupational regulation matters in improving health and safety in this sector, then it could potentially influence other sectors of the economy such as agriculture, mining, or manufacturing, which also have high levels of workplace injuries.

Furthermore, occupational licensing gives a standard method of providing a service to include the health and safety of the workers that are involved in the industry. For example, in the case of electricians, about 10 percent of their class time is spent in discussions of health and safety, and numerous teaching units in apprenticeship programs are explicitly devoted to health and safety (Center for Construction Research and Training 2009); see Box 5.1 for examples of these requirements. The expectation is that workers who have this background on safety from both the classroom and the on-the-job training would incur fewer workplace injuries and deaths. One of the objectives of this chapter is to examine training requirements in more detail with respect to electricians and plumbers, two regulated occupations in the industry.

Electrician Labor Market

Electricians were chosen to be examined in this section of the book because they are the most government-regulated craft in construction. Further reasons to focus the analysis on electricians are because they form a key element in the construction workforce, they are numerous in the industry, and they contribute much value to the industry. About 80 percent of all electricians work in the construction industry, and about 695,000 were employed in the industry in 2008. About 32 percent of all electricians are members of a union, with the largest portion belonging to the International Brotherhood of Electrical Workers. In comparison, about 13.8 percent of all construction workers are represented by a union (BLS 2012c; Hirsch and Macpherson 2011). As with other prevalent occupations in construction (e.g., plumbers and laborers), electricians' high level of unionization may raise wages, and the influence of unions on work rules is expected to be especially important within this occupation. As a consequence, unions may also contribute to reductions in occupational injuries. All states that have licensing for the occupation require electricians to take classes on safety. Michigan, for example, requires electrician apprentices to present a training course plan on health and safety in order to become licensed.

Until the Great Recession, the construction industry had been growing over time, and Figure 5.1 shows the increase by billions of dollars

Box 5.1 Training and Qualifications for Becoming an Electrician

Each year of training includes at least 144 hours of classroom instruction and 2,000 hours of on-the-job training. In the classroom, apprentices learn electrical theory, blueprint reading, mathematics, electrical code requirements, and safety and first aid practices. They also may receive specialized training in soldering, communications, fire alarm systems, and cranes and elevators.

On the job, apprentices work under the supervision of experienced electricians. At first, they drill holes, set anchors, and attach conduits. Later, they measure, fabricate, and install conduits and install, connect, and test wiring, outlets, and switches. They also learn to set up and draw diagrams for entire electrical systems. Eventually, they practice and master all of an electrician's main tasks.

Some people start their classroom training before seeking an apprenticeship. A number of public and private vocational-technical schools and training academies offer training to become an electrician. Employers often hire students who complete these programs and usually start them at a more advanced level than those without this training. A few people become electricians by first working as helpers—assisting electricians by setting up job sites, gathering materials, and doing other nonelectrical work—before entering an apprenticeship program. All apprentices need a high school diploma or a general equivalency diploma (GED). Electricians also may need additional classes in mathematics because they solve mathematical problems on the job.

Education continues throughout an electrician's career. Electricians may need to take classes to learn about changes to the National Electrical Code, and they often complete regular safety programs, manufacturer-specific training, and management training courses. Classes on such topics as low-voltage voice and data systems, telephone systems, video systems, and alternative energy systems such as solar energy and wind energy increasingly are being given as these systems become more prevalent. Other courses teach electricians how to become contractors.

(continued)

Box 5.1 (continued)

Licensure. Most states and localities require electricians to be licensed. Although licensing requirements vary from state to state, electricians usually must pass an examination that tests their knowledge of electrical theory, the National Electrical Code, and local and state electrical and building codes.

Electrical contractors who do electrical work for the public, as opposed to electricians who work for electrical contractors, often need a special license. In some states, electrical contractors need certification as master electricians. Most states require master electricians to have at least seven years of experience as an electrician or a bachelor's degree in electrical engineering or a related field.

SOURCE: BLS (2012b).

from 1990 to 2010 (BLS 2012a). Although the construction industry is highly cyclical and suffered a precipitous decline in output starting in 2006 and continuing through 2010, the figure shows the steady growth in output until the dramatic decline that began just before the recession of 2008. Figure 5.1 includes major sectors such as construction of buildings, heavy civil engineering construction, and specialty contractors over time (Center for Construction Research and Training 2009). Since employment grows and then declines based on business activity, we are careful to adjust for employment in the construction industry when showing the level of workplace deaths and injuries in subsequent tables and figures such as Figure 5.2.

The deaths and injuries of electricians rank among the highest in the construction industry (BLS 2011). However, deaths and injuries at the workplace have been in decline. Figure 5.2 shows the extent to which the death and injury rates for electricians have declined. A large decline took place in 1996, and the period following that steep fall has seen a steady decline in both deaths and injuries for electricians. According to the Center for Construction Research and Training, the secular decline occurred for a number of reasons. From a public policy perspective, in 1993 OSHA set standards that were implemented from 1993 through

Figure 5.1   Construction Sector Output in Constant 2005 Dollars from 1990 to 2010

SOURCE: Bureau of Labor Statistics, Office of Occupational Statistics and Employment Projections.

1996. These changes required electricians to reduce their work with live circuits, increased the use of aerial lifts as opposed to step ladders, and introduced underground utility mapping and verification requirements (Dong, Wang, and Herleikson 2010).

Figure 5.3 shows the growth in the number of states that require licensing for electricians and the percentage of electricians who are union members, which has declined in the occupation over time. Similar to national trends, the decline in the number and percentage of union members is related to the number of workers covered by state licensing (Kleiner and Krueger 2010). Specifically, the number of states that license electricians grew from 40 to 45 from 2000 to 2007, whereas the percentage of electricians in unions declined from 39.0 percent to 34.2 percent during the same period.

Not only has the level of licensing increased, but the intensity of the process of becoming licensed has become more difficult. Key officials at the Center for Construction Research and Training, as well as focus

Figure 5.2 Injury and Death Rates for Electricians, 1992–2007

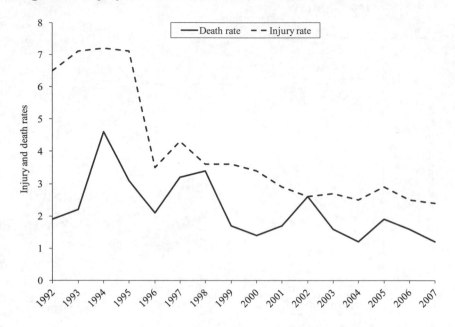

NOTE: Injury and death rates were computed as follows: Injury Rate = (Sum of the weight for the national estimate from the SOII / Estimated employment of electricians from the CPS MORG) × 100; and Death Rate = (Actual number of deaths from the CFOI / Estimated number of employed electricians from the CPS MORG) × 10,000.
SOURCE: Census of Fatal Occupational Injuries (CFOI) and Survey of Occupational Injuries and Illnesses (SOII).

groups comprising practitioners from the construction industry, collectively identified the following five components as important in becoming licensed: 1) a general age/education requirement, 2) an apprenticeship, 3) a written exam, 4) a practical performance exam, and 5) a continuing education requirement. These elements form the foundation of an index of the rigor of the licensing process, in addition to the type of licensing (i.e., state or local). This index makes it possible to trace the evolution of the intensity of the licensing index from 1992 through 2007. This evolution is shown in Figure 5.4 using a box-and-whisker graph of the sum of the five key elements of the licensing regulations for electricians. The results show a modest upward movement in the mean values, and the variance declines over time as the licensing pro-

Figure 5.3 Growth of State Occupational Licensing and Decline of Unions for Electricians, 2000–2007

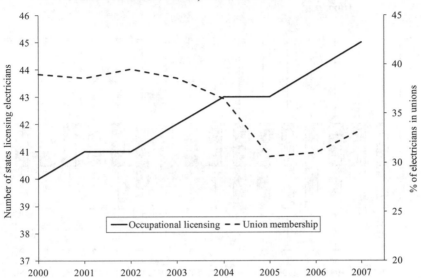

SOURCE: Current Population Survey (CPS) Outgoing Rotation Group (ORG) data, 2000–2007, and the authors' survey of licensing statutes for electricians by state from 1992 to 2007.

visions become more standardized. Occupational licensing is growing among states, and its provisions for an electrician to enter and maintain good standing as a licensed professional are becoming more stringent.

The path to becoming a licensed electrician generally involves four years of training and includes being an apprentice, a journeyman, and then a master electrician. The path usually includes full-time work plus attending classes several nights a week. Pass rates vary by region and often include local licensing beyond state-level regulations for each of the stages toward becoming a licensed electrician. About 10 percent of electricians then become contractors and open their own businesses. For states that license individuals, only licensed electricians can certify the quality of electrical work on a construction project, and only licensed individuals are allowed to perform wiring procedures on construction sites. Given this institutional background on the labor market for electricians, related factors might lead workers to earn more, work under safer conditions, and reduce job-related injuries.

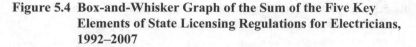

Figure 5.4 Box-and-Whisker Graph of the Sum of the Five Key Elements of State Licensing Regulations for Electricians, 1992–2007

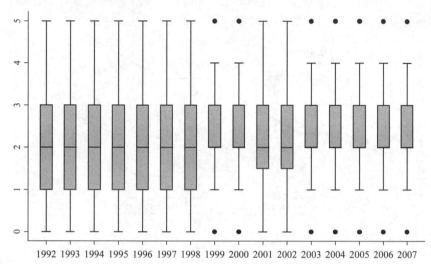

SOURCE: The authors' survey of licensing statutes for electricians by state, from 1992 to 2007.

Plumber Labor Market

The licensing of plumbers has followed a trajectory similar to that of electricians. Traditionally, the licensing of plumbers has been a local issue, since building codes have usually varied by city or county. Shimberg, Esser, and Kruger (1973) contend that the public health and safety argument for local licensing is "little more than a smoke-screen to obscure self-interest" (p. 69). Some states such as California preempt local licensing, and all regulation is at the state level. Others have state minimum requirements but have additional regulations based on unique local characteristics.

Figure 5.5 presents a box-and-whisker graph of the sum of the five key elements for state licensing regulations for plumbers from 1992 through 2007. There are no major changes in the figure to denote an increase in the toughness of those regulations or changes in the variance of the regulations. The major changes in the regulations governing

**Figure 5.5 Box-and-Whisker Graph of the Sum of the Five Key Elements
of State Licensing Regulations for Plumbers, 1992–2007**

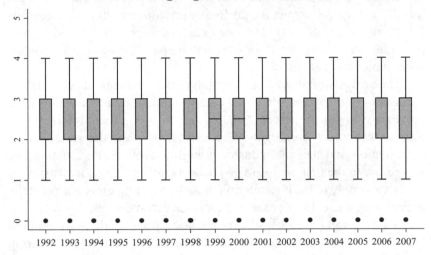

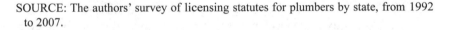

SOURCE: The authors' survey of licensing statutes for plumbers by state, from 1992
to 2007.

licensing took place prior to 1992—the year in which the data analysis in this chapter begins. As is the case with electricians, regulations
appear to be getting modestly more stringent for plumbers, according
to measures of education and training.[2] The data in Tables 5.4 and 5.5
also show there is a movement toward state licensing and away from
local licensing, which broadens the geographic market for plumbers
at the expense of local regulations. Perhaps unions and their members
prefer a wider geographic market with more potential jobs to a market
with higher wages and fewer job opportunities, which are the likely
outcomes of local licensing.

THEORIES OF THE EFFECTS OF REGULATION
ON WAGES AND SAFETY

This section first focuses on the theory of wage determination and
then examines the role of occupational regulation on reducing work-

related deaths and injuries. A starting point for the examination of wages and work injuries can be found in the comments of the eighteenth century economist Adam Smith on compensating differentials for various types of work. He noted that workers will demand a compensating wage differential for jobs that are perceived as risky or otherwise unpleasant (Smith 1937).

The analysis of wage determination under licensing in construction builds on work by Perloff (1980) on the influence of licensing laws on wage changes in the construction industry. The basic model posits that market forces are largely responsible for wage determination in construction and that the industry is highly cyclical. Perloff presents two cases. In the first, there are no costs to shifting across industries, so the labor supply to the construction industry is completely elastic at the opportunity wage. In this case, the increase in the demand for construction work would have little effect on wages, since workers would flow between the construction industry and other industries. (Manufacturing would be the most likely substitute in the model and would appear to be a plausible substitute for the skills of construction workers.)

In the other extreme case, a licensing law renders the supply of construction labor inelastic. Here, labor cannot flow between the sectors, so variations in construction demand would be reflected in the construction wage. In his empirical work, Perloff (1980) shows that for electricians, more so than for either laborers or plumbers, state regulations make the supply curve highly inelastic. Consequently, the ability of a state to limit entry or impose major costs on entry through licensing would enhance the occupation's ability to raise wages.

The institutional labor market literature has developed one additional issue that has been an important focus in construction: the determination of the geography of markets (Dickens and Lang 1992). These researchers argue that institutions in the labor market, such as unions or occupational associations, attempt to capture a geographic area. In the case of both electricians and plumbers, limiting the geographic area would result in greater control of the labor market and higher wages. Therefore, there is an incentive to limit the area to local licensing rather than expand the market to the state level. To the extent that the market has been expanded, it has been done to increase employment, but that may have come at the expense of higher wages.

The issue of the role of occupational regulation on the reduction of deaths and injuries is less developed. In general, a model developed by Viscusi, Harrington, and Vernon (2005) of the risk of injury or death can be presented as follows:

(5.1) $Risk_t = \alpha + \beta_1 Occupational\ Regulation_{t-1}$

$+\ \beta_2 Cyclical\ Effects_t + \beta_3 Industry\ Characteristics_t$

$+\ \beta_4 Worker\ Characteristics_t + \varepsilon,$

where occupational regulation includes the training, selection, and standardization effects of occupational licensing, cyclical effects in construction include the boom of the early 2000s, and industry controls include whether the person was in the construction industry and the human capital characteristics of the individuals that are covered in the sample.

An important issue in the occupational health and safety literature is whether regulations or standards for work are more effective than litigation such as worker compensation laws in reducing the incidence and severity of injury and the incidence of death. Most of the analyses on standards such as OSHA legislation find that occupational regulations or standards are not more effective (Smith 1976; Viscusi, Harrington, and Vernon 2005). In contrast, many of the studies on worker compensation and its influence on the incidence and severity of injury and the incidence of death show much larger influences. For example, Moore and Viscusi (1990) show that worker compensation laws reduce job fatality rates by about one-third, and that this legislation is much more effective than setting standards. Based on these findings, the expectation is that there are modest effects of occupational regulation standards in reducing injuries, and that the influence of these policies would be similar to the effects of legislation such as OSHA, where the influence of the policies appears to have diminished (Gray and Mendeloff 2005).

To the extent that licensing introduces standardization of procedures in electrical work or plumbing that take health and safety concerns into effect, the expectation is that regulation would reduce injuries and deaths. Specific programs such as apprenticeships, required classes on health and safety, and continuing education would all serve to reduce the likelihood of injuries at the workplace. Furthermore, licensing eliminates the lower part of the quality distribution within the occupation through time-intensive classes and the costs of occupation-specific education, and consequently would diminish the likelihood of death and injury by keeping more careless individuals from working in the occupation. Only those individuals who are willing to take on the time and money costs of continuing education, are committed to the occupation, and are willing to pay annual fees and attend seminars to stay in the occupation would be likely to know the appropriate procedures to stay safe at the workplace. Practitioners could also benefit from technological innovations learned in the workplace or at construction sites. Although these innovations could reduce injuries or deaths, they may be overlooked in assessments because they do not fit into the standard method of doing things. In addition, attempts at implementing unorthodox methods in response to technological change may result in the loss of a license.[3]

One final issue that helps define the role of occupational regulation in construction is the state or local political jurisdiction in place. In most jurisdictions, licensing for electricians and plumbers is done at the state level. However, some states have local licensing for electricians, and these local licensing regulations are sometimes more difficult for workers to complete than state-level regulations. Cook County, which includes the city of Chicago, is often given as an example of a jurisdiction having more and tougher requirements than the ones at the state level. Given the pervasiveness of local licenses that may, in some cases, be more rigorous than the ones at the state level, the analysis will examine the influence of local licenses to regulate electricians. Consequently, the issue of whether the regulation of occupations matters in raising wages or reducing the injuries and deaths of electricians is an empirical issue. The chapter now turns to that empirical issue. The data to estimate the models described above are detailed in the following section.

DATA ON LICENSING STATUTES, WAGE DETERMINATION, AND HEALTH AND SAFETY

Regulation Data

A group of researchers working with funding from the Department of Labor were among the first to examine the role of occupational regulation in construction. In a study that was commissioned by the department's Office of Research and mentioned at the beginning of this chapter, Shimberg, Esser, and Kruger (1973) discussed the role of occupational regulation in construction and also mentioned the difficulties of health and safety issues in the industry. The researchers also focused on the variations in occupational licensing in the industry for several occupations. The key elements of their findings were on the process of licensing and not on the outcomes. Their work focused on who is on the licensing boards for the occupation and whether state and local boards are or should be regulating the occupation. Their study also examined whether the boards were composed of political appointees, whether the pay was low, whether the boards were dominated by members of the occupation, and whether they had public members. Other analysis, also funded by the Department of Labor, focused on the quality of work under occupational licensing (Carroll and Gaston 1981).

In order to examine which of these occupational issues dominates the determination of health and safety for electricians, a regulatory index was developed based on the focus group responses that capture the major elements of the statutes across states. Table 5.1 displays the key elements (and their operational definition) of the licensing provisions in the statutes and administrative regulations that were examined for each of the states in the sample for electricians. Table 5.2 presents information on the changes in the various licensing statutes regulating the occupation by states over time.[4] It tabulates only the changes in occupational regulations in state statutes. For example, electricians in Alaska were licensed at the state level, and the five key elements of the licensing provisions did not change between 1992 and 2007.

Table 5.2 presents these values over the period from 1992 through 2007. The details of the provisions and the states and years in which they were passed are presented in Appendix Table B.1. The results indi-

Table 5.1 Key Elements and Definitions of Regulatory Variables

Variable	Definition
license	1 if either license is required by state statute or local statute; otherwise 0.
state license	1 if license is required by state statute; otherwise 0.
local license	1 if license is required by statute of local municipality; otherwise 0.
Five major components	
general requirements	1 if either a minimum level of education or of age is required to be licensed; otherwise 0.
apprentice codes	1 if occupation-specific experience as apprentice (or equivalent years of education) is required to be licensed; otherwise 0.
written exam	1 if a written exam is required to be licensed; otherwise 0.
performance exam	1 if a performance exam is required to be licensed; otherwise 0.
continuing education	1 if state has any requirement for license renewal; otherwise 0.

SOURCE: The authors' survey of licensing statutes for electricians and plumbers by state, from 1992 to 2007.

cate that the occupation experienced growth in regulations governing the entry and training requirements. The level of the index, or the number of items included in the measure, grew from 2.11 in 1992 to 2.38 in 2007, or almost 13 percent. This reflects the intensity of the growth of requirements to enter the occupation of electrician and maintain membership in that occupation.

In order to fully implement the empirical estimation strategy, we show in Panel A of Table 5.3 the states that changed licensing policies. For example, Iowa switched to state licensing from local regulations, and Louisiana changed from no licensing to state regulation of the occupation. A number of states allow electricians to be regulated at the local level, including populous states such as Illinois and New York. In Panel B of the table, we list the states that ranked highest and lowest using our index of regulation.

Table 5.4 gives the changes in the statutes for the period 1992 through 2007 for plumbers, the other occupation that is the subject of the analysis. The results show that a number of states had local regulation of the construction occupation. However, both South Dakota and

**Table 5.2 Changes in the Index of State Licensing Regulation for
Electricians, 1992–2007**

Year	No. of changes in occupational regulations in state statutes	Mean	sd
1992	38	2.11	0.98
1993	38	2.11	0.98
1994	38	2.18	1.04
1995	38	2.24	1.02
1996	38	2.24	1.02
1997	38	2.24	1.02
1998	38	2.29	1.01
1999	38	2.34	0.94
2000	40	2.33	0.94
2001	41	2.29	0.96
2002	41	2.32	0.96
2003	42	2.38	0.88
2004	43	2.35	0.90
2005	43	2.35	0.90
2006	43	2.35	0.90
2007	45	2.38	0.91
Total	642	2.28	0.95

SOURCE: The authors' survey of licensing statutes for electricians by state from 1992 to 2007.

Virginia moved to state licensing from local regulations, and Idaho moved to state certification from local regulations. Nebraska remained as the only state with no regulations for the occupation; Alaska, North Dakota, and Tennessee all moved from not having any regulation to state licensing during the period that was examined.

Table 5.5 shows the growth in the level of licensing for plumbers using the index developed earlier. For example, from 1992 until 2007, the mean of the index grew by 17 percent, and the standard deviation declined over the same time period. Over the period there was a standardization of state licensing beyond the clear growth shown in the table. Nevertheless, the changes in the index of statutes for plumbers were much smaller than those for electricians.

Table 5.3 States Staying with or Switching Their Level of Licensing, and State Rankings of Occupational Regulation of Electricians, 1992–2007

Panel A: Stayers and switchers of occupational regulation of electricians, 1992–2007

	State licensing	Local licensing	No licensing
Stayers	All other states	Illinois, Kansas, Missouri, New York, Pennsylvania	Indiana
Switchers		Delaware (to state licensing in 2000), Iowa (to state licensing in 2007), Kentucky (to state licensing in 2001), Texas (to state licensing in 2003)	Louisiana (to state licensing in 2004), Massachusetts (to state licensing in 2007), Tennessee (to state licensing in 2000)

Panel B: Regulation rankings of the top and bottom groupings of states for electricians, 2007

Top States	Sum of the five requirements	Bottom states	Sum of the five requirements
Arizona	5	Alaska	1
Massachusetts	4	Kentucky	1
Wyoming	4	Louisiana	1
Alabama and 17 other states	3	Mississippi	1

SOURCE: Authors' survey of licensing statutes for electricians by state, 1992 to 2007.

Workplace Safety Data

The analysis of information comes from two sources of confidential data: the Survey of Occupational Injuries and Illnesses (SOII) and the Census of Fatal Occupational Injuries (CFOI), with Bureau of Labor Statistics (BLS) supervision over the handling of the data for public dissemination (for detailed information, see BLS [2013a]). To examine the role of occupational licensing in potentially reducing serious nonfatal injuries, we use the SOII, which is a confidential establishment-level survey for nonfatal injury data administered by the BLS and stored at its Washington, D.C., offices. The SOII lists nonfatal injuries reported by establishments in the private sector for 39 states between 1992 and 2007. Although the injuries are divided into three categories,[5] the focus

Table 5.4 Stayers and Switchers in Occupational Regulation of Plumbers, 1992–2007

	State licensing	Local licensing	Certification	No licensing
Stayers	All other states	Iowa, Kansas, Massachusetts, Mississippi, New York, Pennsylvania, Wyoming		Nebraska, West Virginia
Switchers		South Dakota (to state licensing in 1999), Virginia (to state licensing in 1995)	Idaho (to state licensing in 1996)	Alaska (to state licensing in 2005), North Dakota (to state licensing in 1993), Tennessee (to state licensing in 2006)

SOURCE: Authors' survey of licensing statutes for plumbers by state, 1992 to 2007.

Table 5.5 Changes in the Index of State Licensing Regulation for Plumbers, 1992–2007

Year	No. of changes in occupational regulations in state statutes	Mean	sd
1992	42	2.24	1.21
1993	42	2.33	1.18
1994	42	2.33	1.18
1995	43	2.35	1.17
1996	43	2.42	1.18
1997	43	2.42	1.18
1998	43	2.42	1.18
1999	44	2.36	1.22
2000	44	2.39	1.20
2001	44	2.41	1.23
2002	44	2.43	1.23
2003	44	2.50	1.17
2004	44	2.50	1.17
2005	44	2.55	1.11
2006	44	2.61	1.06
2007	44	2.61	1.06
Total	694	2.43	1.16

SOURCE: Authors' survey of licensing statutes for plumbers by state, 1992 to 2007.

is on cases involving injuries of workers from the age of 16 to 64 that resulted in an absence from work, as measured by "days away from work."[6]

Table 5.6 shows the main events resulting in workplace nonfatal injuries for electricians and plumbers from 1992 through 2007. The industry rate for both occupations is about the same—namely 15 percent for electricians and 13 percent for plumbers. For both regulated occupations, overexertion in lifting resulted in the highest number of nonfatal injuries. For electricians, injuries such as falling and bending were also important types of injuries. Similarly, bending and falls were major forms of nonfatal injuries for plumbers.

To maintain consistency in the analysis, much of the data is restricted to fatal injuries among workers ages 16 to 64 in the private sector, but including 50 states and the District of Columbia. The data are from the CFOI, another confidential fatal injury data source that is administered and stored at the BLS offices in Washington, D.C.

Because the SOII and CFOI do not have the employment information, one important issue in building an uninterrupted time series for the empirical analysis is to estimate the denominator (i.e., the employment within states in a given year) for computing both the injury rates and death rates at the workplace. Using the Current Population Survey (CPS) Merged Outgoing Rotation Group (MORG) data from 1992 to 2007 (downloaded from http://www.nber.org/morg/annual/), an estimate was developed for employment of electricians in a state in a given year, and then the injury rates and death rates by state and year were computed.[7] Finally, the sample selection rules for this study (e.g., persons from the age of 16 to 64 and in the private sector) would necessarily produce death and injury rates that are different from those publicly available through the BLS.

Table 5.7 summarizes the five most frequent events that led to fatal injuries for electricians. Not surprisingly, the results show that four of the frequent events were related to electrocutions and explained about 55 percent of electrician deaths. Figure 5.6 compares the days away from work (a measure of the severity of the injury) for electricians, a regulated occupation, and for laborers, an unregulated construction occupation. The figure highlights two findings. First, there are relatively small differences in the days away from work for the two occupations, which do very different tasks, but both are involved in difficult con-

Table 5.6 Five Main Events Causing Workplace Non-Fatal Injuries, 1992–2007

Electricians			Plumbers		
Events (code)	Estimated occurrences	% of estimated occurrences	Events (code)	Estimated occurrences	% of estimated occurrences
Overexertion in lifting (221)	12,400	9.05	Overexertion in lifting (221)	17,100	14.05
Fall from ladder (113)	11,625	8.48	Bending, climbing, crawling, reaching, twisting (211)	7,742	6.36
Bending, climbing, crawling, reaching, twisting (211)	8,608	6.28	Struck by falling object (021)	6,406	5.26
Struck against stationary object (012)	7,405	5.40	Fall to floor, walkway, or other surface (131)	6,858	5.63
Struck by slipping handheld object (0232)	7,267	5.30	Fall from ladder (113)	6,061	4.98
Others	89,788	65.49	Others	77,552	63.71
Total	137,093	15	Total	121,719	13

SOURCE: The SOII and CFOI from 1992 to 2007.

Table 5.7 Five Main Events Causing Workplace Deaths for Electricians, 1992–2007

Events (code)	% of actual occurrences
Contact with wiring, transformers, or other electrical components (3120)	26.0
Contact with overhead power lines (3130)	18.2
Fall from ladder (1130)	5.8
Contact with electric current of machine, tool, appliance, or light fixture (3110)	5.0
Contact with electric current, unspecified (3100)	4.5
Others	40.4
Total	99.9

NOTE: Column does not sum to 100.0 because of rounding.
SOURCE: The CFOI from 1992 to 2007.

Figure 5.6 Severity of Injuries Due to Nonfatal Injuries for Electricians and Laborers, by the Percentage Who Lost Days of Work

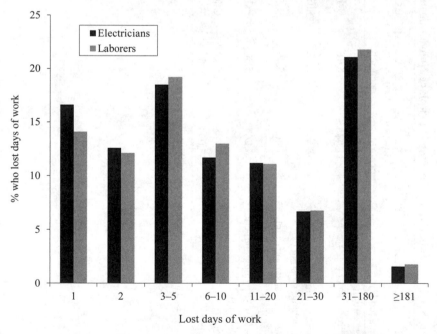

SOURCE: The SOII from 1992 to 2007.

struction tasks at work. Second, most of the injuries were relatively minor: 47.7 percent of injured electricians returned to work within five days, and 77 percent returned to work within a month. Injuries causing absence from work for more than 180 days made up only 1.6 percent of the total.

Economic Data

As a key part of the examination of the influence of regulation on the labor market, the analysis uses data from the CPS MORG. Table 5.8 presents the basic information that was used for the analysis. The standard variables from the MORG include human capital variables for electricians such as gender, age, experience, education, race, part-time employment, union membership, and sector. The estimates for the wage models, using information from the American Community Survey (ACS) from 2000 through 2007, show that the results are similar to those in the CPS. Since the ACS has no information on unionization—an important element for occupational licensing in wage and safety determination—the results only present estimates from the CPS.

The empirical strategy was to initially estimate the role of regulation on wage determination for workers in construction, with an emphasis on electricians.[8] These models will update and refine the work by Perloff (1980). Next, estimates were developed of the influence of occupational licensing on the incidence, severity, and death of construction workers, with a focus on electricians. The estimates provide several tests of the robustness of the estimates with various specifications and across databases and occupations.

Wage Determination

Initially, there is an examination and estimate of an earnings model with licensing regulations. The basic model is specified as follows:

$$(5.2) \quad \ln(Earnings_{ist}) = \alpha + \beta R_{st} + \gamma X_{ist} + \delta_s + \theta_t + \varepsilon_{ist},$$

where $Earnings_{ist}$ represents the hourly earnings of electricians i in state s in year t; R_{st} stands for the licensing occupational regulations and components of the regulation in person i's state s in year t; X_{ist} is

Table 5.8 Basic Statistics from the CPS MORG, 1992–2007, for Electricians

Variable	n	Mean	sd
Hourly earnings	9,747	21.13	9.85
Gender (1: male; 0: female)	11,050	0.98	0.13
Age (years)	11,050	37.09	10.91
Experience (age − years of school − 6)	11,050	18.46	10.95
Experience squared (÷ 1,000)	11,050	4.61	4.68
High school graduate	11,050	0.46	0.50
Some college experience	11,050	0.24	0.43
College diploma or more	11,050	0.23	0.42
Marriage	11,050	0.63	0.48
White	11,050	0.92	0.27
Hispanic origin	11,050	0.83	0.28
Part-time	11,050	0.02	0.15
Government	11,050	0.02	0.14
Union member	9,748	0.37	0.48

SOURCE: The Current Population Survey's Merged Outgoing Rotation Group (MORG) files, from 1992 to 2007.

the vector that includes covariates measuring the characteristics of each person; δ and θ are state and year fixed effects, respectively; and ε_{ist} is the error term in the panel data.

Table 5.9 shows the estimates from the above model of the influence of licensing on wages for electricians. The model also includes estimates of the influence of unions on wage determination, since it is also an important labor market institution in the construction industry. The results show no statistically significant impact of the measure of the overall index of licensing on earnings. However, the additional estimates suggest that licensing matters in most of the specifications in the model. For example, the summated rating scale of licensing at the state-level variable is statistically significant, but the magnitude of the coefficient is small. In contrast to the overall effects of licensing in the economy, the value for local licensing is significant and positive for almost all the specifications (Kleiner and Krueger 2013). The range of significant coefficients is from 8 to 13 percent. Several of the specific entry requirements are significant. Local licensing regulations, such as ones that are quite difficult (e.g., those that exist in Cook County, Illinois), can serve to raise the wages of electricians. In addition, the coefficients for the general requirements of age and education are significant, as are the provisions for taking an exam and having an apprenticeship. This is also consistent with the institutional industrial-relations approach that holds that occupations can gain economic advantages by limiting the geographic market (Perlman 1928). Further analysis of licensing at the local level and for other construction-related occupations could add more detailed geographical data to the basic results for electricians.

In order to probe the basic wage estimate further, Table 5.10 presents the role of potential compensating wage differentials within the context of occupational licensing, injury rates, and worker compensation insurance controls. The estimates suggest a small influence of approximately 1 percent on the logarithm of hourly wages for a 1-percentage-point increase in the injury rate. Most of the other licensing variables maintain similar magnitudes and significance, with the inclusion of both a measure of workers' compensation insurance premiums and the rate of injury. These findings are consistent with other estimates, dating to the original work by Adam Smith (see the 1937 edition of the original 1776 volume) on the trade-off of higher wages for more risk, and appear to hold for the model and the use of the CPS data (Smith 1937).

In contrast to the estimates for electricians, the wage effects for plumbers were not nearly as robust or as clear, and consequently are not shown in a separate table, since the estimates are not stable or significant.[9] As with electricians, the influence of the overall index for licensing is not statistically significant. Moreover, there is no clear pattern of regulation having an influence at the state or local level or having an impact on wage determination. Unlike the influence of apprenticeships, exam requirements, and continuing education requirements for electricians, there was, if anything, a small, negative influence of these required policies on the wage determination for plumbers. In other words, low-quality plumbers may be substituted for those who do have these requirements, and they are the ones who are getting more work in the construction industry. Moreover, given the lack of variation in the data for plumbers, there may be more noise in the wage data for this occupation. Nevertheless, these results can serve as a starting point for further research into the puzzle as to why regulations matter so little for this highly skilled and regulated occupation.

Table 5.9 The Influence of Occupational Licensing on Hourly Earnings for Electricians, 1992–2007

	(1)	(2)	(3)	(4)	(5)	(6)	(7)	(8)	(9)	(10)	(11)	(12)
	Hourly earnings											
Union membership		0.270*** (0.013)		0.270*** (0.013)		0.270*** (0.013)	0.270*** (0.013)	0.270*** (0.013)	0.270*** (0.013)	0.270*** (0.013)	0.270*** (0.013)	0.270*** (0.013)
State license	−0.056** (0.025)	−0.045* (0.024)	−0.007 (0.045)	0.013 (0.041)								
Local license			0.069 (0.052)	0.083* (0.048)	0.124*** (0.032)	0.128*** (0.029)	0.065** (0.029)	0.130*** (0.038)	0.125*** (0.030)	0.070** (0.029)	0.072** (0.030)	0.086* (0.043)
Summated measures					0.028*** (0.009)	0.033*** (0.008)						
General requirements							0.087*** (0.021)					0.077** (0.036)
Apprenticeship code								0.064** (0.029)				−0.018 (0.028)
Written exam									0.070** (0.027)			0.044 (0.028)
Performance exam										0.004 (0.009)		−0.055 (0.038)
Continuing education											0.054 (0.037)	0.035 (0.023)
Constant	1.745*** (0.121)	1.743*** (0.106)	1.696*** (0.129)	1.683*** (0.116)	1.597*** (0.124)	1.588*** (0.106)	1.691*** (0.098)	1.631*** (0.111)	1.619*** (0.107)	1.694*** (0.099)	1.695*** (0.099)	1.715*** (0.110)
Basic controls[a]	Y	Y	Y	Y	Y	Y	Y	Y	Y	Y	Y	Y
State controls[b]	Y	Y	Y	Y	Y	Y	Y	Y	Y	Y	Y	Y
Year fixed	Y	Y	Y	Y	Y	Y	Y	Y	Y	Y	Y	Y
State fixed	Y	Y	Y	Y	Y	Y	Y	Y	Y	Y	Y	Y

N	9,724	9,724	9,724	9,724	9,724	9,724	9,724	9,724	9,724	9,724	9,724	9,724
R-squared	0.29	0.35	0.29	0.35	0.29	0.36	0.36	0.36	0.36	0.36	0.36	0.36

NOTE: Columns show the influence of each measure of regulation on hourly earnings of electricians with the control variables listed below. *significant at the 0.10 level; **significant at the 0.05 level; ***significant at the 0.01 level. Standard errors, shown in parentheses, are clustered by state. Y = yes.

[a] "Basic controls" include gender; age; experience and experience squared; dummy variables indicating high school graduates, some college experience, and college graduates and more levels of education; marital status; white, Hispanic origin; part-time; and governmental workers.

[b] "State controls" include employment growth rate, unemployment rate, and rate of union coverage in the construction industry.

SOURCE: CPS data.

Table 5.10 Compensating Differentials for Injuries with Licensing Effects on Hourly Earnings for Electricians, 1992–2007

	Hourly earnings								
	(1)	(2)	(3)	(4)	(5)	(6)	(7)	(8)	(9)
Wc premium rate[a]	−0.010	−0.010	−0.011	−0.011	−0.011	−0.010	−0.010	−0.010	−0.011
	(0.007)	(0.007)	(0.007)	(0.007)	(0.007)	(0.007)	(0.007)	(0.007)	(0.007)
Injury rate	0.008**	0.008**	0.008**	0.008**	0.008**	0.008**	0.008**	0.008**	0.008**
	(0.003)	(0.003)	(0.003)	(0.003)	(0.003)	(0.003)	(0.003)	(0.003)	(0.003)
Union membership	0.261***	0.261***	0.261***	0.261***	0.261***	0.261***	0.261***	0.261***	0.261***
	(0.017)	(0.017)	(0.017)	(0.017)	(0.017)	(0.017)	(0.017)	(0.017)	(0.017)
State license	−0.056**	0.021							
	(0.024)	(0.040)							
Local license		0.107**	0.140***	0.083***	0.152***	0.136***	0.087***	0.088***	0.074**
		(0.041)	(0.021)	(0.019)	(0.043)	(0.027)	(0.019)	(0.020)	(0.032)
Summated measures			0.031***						
			(0.009)						
General requirements				0.111***					0.016
				(0.030)					(0.037)
Apprenticeship code					0.069***				−0.030*
					(0.041)				(0.016)
Written exam						0.063**			0.026
						(0.030)			(0.030)
Performance exam							−0.012		−0.014
							(0.016)		(0.016)

155

	(1)	(2)	(3)	(4)	(5)	(6)	(7)	(8)	(9)
Continuing education								0.024	−0.000
								(0.071)	(0.049)
Constant	1.752***	1.679***	1.605***	1.702***	1.634***	1.631***	1.712***	1.698***	1.716
	(0.099)	(0.108)	(0.102)	(0.096)	(0.110)	(0.106)	(0.096)	(0.095)	(0.105)
Basic controls[b]	Y	Y	Y	Y	Y	Y	Y	Y	Y
State controls[c]	Y	Y	Y	Y	Y	Y	Y	Y	Y
Year fixed	Y	Y	Y	Y	Y	Y	Y	Y	Y
State fixed	Y	Y	Y	Y	Y	Y	Y	Y	Y
R-squared	0.33	0.33	0.33	0.33	0.33	0.33	0.33	0.33	0.033
N	5,975	5,975	5,975	5,975	5,975	5,975	5,975	5,975	5,975

NOTE: *significant at the 0.10 level; **significant at the 0.05 level; ***significant at the 0.01 level. Standard errors, shown in parentheses, are clustered by state. Y = yes.

[a] "Wc premium rate" is the compensating differential—how much extra workers get paid for doing more dangerous work.

[b] "Basic controls" include gender; age; experience and experience squared; dummy variables indicating high school graduates, some college graduates, and college graduates and more levels of education; marital status; white, Hispanic origin; part-time; and governmental workers.

[c] "State controls" include employment growth rate, unemployment rate, and rate of union coverage in the construction industry.

SOURCE: CPS data.

IMPLEMENTING THE HEALTH AND SAFETY MODELS WITH LICENSING REGULATIONS

The main part of the analysis focuses on the incidence of injuries at the state level. This approach is then expanded by including two more stringent measures of safety outcomes in the model. The methods of developing the data for our analysis are shown in Appendix Table B.2. These measures include the severity of injuries, as measured by days away from work due to injury or illness and by the death incidence rates at the state level. The basic model for the injury incidence rate can be stated as follows:

$$(5.3) \quad Injury\ Rates_{st} = \alpha + \beta R_{st} + \gamma X_{st} + \delta_s + \eta_t + \varepsilon_{st},$$

where *Injury Rates$_{st}$* stands for the injury incidence rates of electricians in state s in year t; R_{st} represents the licensing occupational regulations and components of the regulation in state s in year t; X_{st} is the vector that includes covariates measuring characteristics of each state s; δ and η are state and year fixed effects, respectively; and ε_{st} is the error term.[10]

Table 5.11 shows the influence of licensing on the reporting of injuries for electricians. The overall summated rating scale shows a positive influence, and several of the elements of the index, such as general age and education requirements, apprenticeships, and continuing education, are all positively related to the incidence or reporting of workplace injuries. However, the existence of a performance exam, which provides direct evidence of the skills an electrician must exhibit in order to become licensed, is negatively related to the reporting of workplace injuries. One reason for the increase in the reporting and documentation of injuries may be that licensing requires more incidence reporting and documentation of any type of work-related injury. The implementation of a licensing regime requires the more technical types of regulatory requirements, but they are not necessarily related to serious types of injuries.[11]

Table 5.12 provides information on the role of state licensing on the state injury rate for plumbers. The results show that the regulations have no influence on the injury rates. The injury rate for plumbers is low, and there is little variation in the injury rates for the members of the occupation across states. Similar to the licensing of electricians, licensing of plumbers does not seem to improve the injury rate in the occupation.

The next section of the analysis of injuries and occupational regulation examines the severity of injuries at the individual level using information on the duration of time away from work because of injuries, as recorded in the SOII. The severity of injury model can be stated as follows:

$$(5.4) \quad Severity\ of\ Injury_{ist} = \alpha + \beta R_{st} + \gamma X_{ist} + \delta_s + \eta_t + \varepsilon_{ist},$$

where *Severity of Injury*$_{ist}$ is measured by the days away from work because of injury/illness of individual electricians i in state s in year t; R_{st} is the licensing measure of occupational regulation and its components in person i's state s in year t; X_{ist} is the vector that includes covariates measuring the characteristics of each injured/ill person as well as of the state where the person was injured; δ and η are state and year fixed effects, respectively; and ε_{ist} is the error term.

Specifically, we estimate Equation (5.4) using a Weibull survival model, a commonly used estimation method in the unemployment and workers' compensation literature (e.g., Butler and Worrall 1983). This statistical model estimates the time it takes to return to work based on the characteristics of occupational licensing and state and year of the injury. It should be noted that some of the information on these individuals from the SOII that was needed to create the control variables is different from those in the wage equations. From the survival analysis, the estimates for the severity of injuries based on the time needed to return to work for electricians are presented in Table 5.13. In contrast to the positive estimates presented in the previous table, in Table 5.13 the estimates show that licensing has no significant impact on the time it takes to return to work following an injury. The coefficient for a performance exam reduces the duration of being away from work, which is consistent with the results in Table 5.11. In Table 5.13, the only other licensing provision that increases the duration of the days to return to work from an injury for electricians is the continuing education variable. The estimates show no general influence of the role for licensing on the days away from work in the fixed-effects models.

Table 5.11 Influence of Occupational Licensing on Workplace Injury Rates for Electricians, 1992–2007

	(1)	(2)	(3)	(4)	(5)	(6)	(7)	(8)	(9)
State license	-0.443	-0.182							
	(0.952)	(0.943)							
Local license		0.420	2.625	0.420	3.121	1.359	0.592	1.171	1.982
		(1.754)	(1.579)	(1.451)	(1.853)	(1.598)	(1.456)	(1.516)	(2.076)
Summated measures			1.105**						
			(0.478)						
General requirements				3.329**					2.045
				(1.305)					(1.445)
Apprenticeship code					2.749**				1.123*
					(1.077)				(0.641)
Written exam						1.244			0.124
						(1.227)			(1.245)
Performance exam							-4.579***		0.241
							(0.948)		(2.371)
Continuing education								1.629*	1.086
								(0.885)	(0.848)
Constant	3.743	2.240	-2.080	1.415	-1.789	0.483	6.593	2.157	-0.205
	(4.373)	(4.671)	(4.793)	(4.177)	(4.560)	(4.854)	(4.427)	(4.104)	(4.523)
Basic controls[a]	Y	Y	Y	Y	Y	Y	Y	Y	Y
State controls[b]	Y	Y	Y	Y	Y	Y	Y	Y	Y
Year fixed	Y	Y	Y	Y	Y	Y	Y	Y	Y
State fixed	Y	Y	Y	Y	Y	Y	Y	Y	Y

159

| N | 620 | 620 | 620 | 620 | 620 | 620 | 620 | 620 |
| R | 0.41 | 0.42 | 0.41 | 0.41 | 0.41 | 0.41 | 0.41 | 0.42 |

NOTE: *significant at the 0.10 level; **significant at the 0.05 level; ***significant at the 0.01 level. Standard errors, shown in parentheses, are clustered by state. Y = yes.

[a] "Basic controls" include proportions of the population ages 20–24, 25–34, 35–44, 45–54, and 55–64; proportion of married; white and other nonwhite; and proportions of high school graduates, some college experience, and college graduates and more levels of education.
[b] "State controls" include laborers' injury rate, employment growth rate, unemployment rate, and rate of union coverage in the construction industry.

SOURCE: CPS, SOIL, and CFOI.

Table 5.12 The Effects of Occupational Licensing on the State Workplace Injury Rates for Plumbers, 1992–2007

	Workplace injury rates						
	(1)	(2)	(3)	(4)	(5)	(6)	(7)
Licensed	0.073	0.481					
	(0.304)	(1.213)					
State license			0.090	0.492			
			(0.324)	(1.220)			
Local license			−0.042	−2.113			
			(0.561)	(1.386)			
Apprenticeship					0.237		
					(0.564)		
Exam requirement						0.274	
						(0.846)	
Continuing education							0.088
							(0.645)
Year fixed	Y	Y	Y	Y	Y	Y	Y
Other state controls	N	Y	N	Y	Y	Y	Y
State fixed	N	Y	N	Y	Y	Y	Y
Observations	578	578	578	578	514	514	514
R-squared	0.16	0.28	0.16	0.28	0.27	0.27	0.27

NOTE: Standard errors, shown in parentheses, are clustered by state. Other state controls include the percentages of the following variables: the six age groups 20–24, 25–34, 35–44, 45–54, 55–64, and 65 and greater (age group 16–19 is used as a reference); marriage status; white and nonwhite (the portion of African American is used as a reference); Hispanic origin; high school diploma, some college, college diploma and more (high school dropouts used as a reference); part-time; unemployment rate, employment growth, and union coverage in the construction industry. Y = yes; N = no.
SOURCE: CPS, SOII, and CFOI.

The final model that is estimated tests for the role of occupational regulation in the incidence of death rates for electricians. The basic specification follows the earlier models and is presented as follows:

$$(5.5) \quad Death\ Rates_{stE} = \alpha + \beta R_{st} + \gamma X_{st} + \delta_s + \theta_t + \varepsilon_{st} ,$$

where $Death\ Rates_{st}$ represents the death incidence rates of Electricians (E) in state s in year t; R_{st} stands for the licensing occupational regulations and components of the regulation in state s in year t; X_{st} is the vector that includes covariates measuring the characteristics of each state s; δ and θ are state and year fixed effects, respectively; and ε_{st} is the error term.

Table 5.14 shows that measures of occupational regulation have little influence on the death rates of electricians in construction. The overall measure of regulation is negative but does not rise to the level of statistical significance. Although the coefficient on the performance exam is statistically significant and positive only at the 0.10 level, in contrast to the previous findings in the other tables, the other components of the government regulations are not significant in reducing the death rates of electricians. The performance exam result for workplace deaths may be due to the small number of these events relative to the larger number of injuries that are more frequent and can be evaluated more carefully. We found that the results for regulations were similar to those of OSHA, which also found that regulations seem to have small effects on outcomes for safety and health (Weil 2001).

In order to be consistent with reporting the earlier estimates for electricians, we include Table 5.15, which shows similar results for plumbers. The model is the same basic one that was used for electricians. The results suggest that local licensing is associated with somewhat reduced death rates, but that state regulations do not have much statistical influence on the death rates for plumbers for the period 1992 through 2007. Regulations at the state level do not appear to influence either wage determination or death and injury rates for plumbers.

A final set of estimates, presented in Table 5.16, illustrates the potential effect of endogeneity, which may present an issue to the extent that high levels of deaths and injuries in a previous period may have influenced the passage of state or locally based occupational licensing laws for electricians. Table 5.16 shows the hazard ratios from a Weibull survival model. The estimates on prior deaths and injuries or prior workers' compensation rates are not statistically significant, indicating an absence of this form of simultaneity bias.[12] Although there may be unobservables that are not accounted for in the model, such as unique political factors in a state that contributed to the passage of licensing laws, there are no variables in standard data sets that show that these factors are obviously associated with the passage of laws regulating electricians.

162

Table 5.13 Hazard Model Estimates of the Influence of Occupational Licensing on Duration of the Days to Return to Work for Electricians (using a Weibull distribution of duration), 1992–2007

	Days to return to work								
	(1)	(2)	(3)	(4)	(5)	(6)	(7)	(8)	(9)
State license	-0.018 (0.075)	-0.229 (0.184)							
Local license		-0.149 (0.188)	0.106 (0.081)	0.070 (0.055)	0.210* (0.116)	-0.019 (0.110)	0.072 (0.054)	0.083 (0.053)	0.411*** (0.116)
Summated measures			0.020 (0.030)						
General requirements				0.028 (0.062)					-0.366*** (0.136)
Apprenticeship code					0.137 (0.112)				0.469*** (0.050)
Written exam						-0.118 (0.125)			-0.171 (0.124)
Performance exam							-0.139* (0.094)		-0.135 (0.091)
Continuing education								0.158*** (0.045)	0.168*** (0.056)
Constant	-0.748*** (0.272)	-0.637* (0.310)	-0.916*** (0.316)	-0.857*** (0.271)	-0.991*** (0.313)	-0.735*** (0.307)	-0.716** (0.306)	-0.863*** (0.273)	-0.991*** (0.318)
Basic controls[a]	Y	Y	Y	Y	Y	Y	Y	Y	Y
State controls[b]	Y	Y	Y	Y	Y	Y	Y	Y	Y
Year fixed	Y	Y	Y	Y	Y	Y	Y	Y	Y

State fixed	Y	Y	Y	Y	Y	Y	Y	Y	Y
Log Likelihood	−266,510	−266,502	−266,526	−266,528	−266,509	−266,514	−266,529	−266,510	−266,426
N	20,745	20,745	20,745	20,745	20,745	20,745	20,745	20,745	20,745

NOTE: *significant at the 0.10 level; **significant at the 0.05 level; ***significant at the 0.01 level. Unstandardized coefficients are shown; standard errors, shown in parentheses, are clustered by state. Y = yes.

[a] "Basic controls" include age, age squared, gender, and dummy variables, indicating four different groupings of length of services and four different groupings of races.

[b] "State controls" include laborers' injury rate, employment growth rate, unemployment rate, and rate of union coverage in the construction industry.

SOURCE: CPS, SOII, and CFOI.

164

Table 5.14 Influence of Occupational Licensing on Workplace Death Rates for Electricians, 1992–2007

	Workplace death rates								
	(1)	(2)	(3)	(4)	(5)	(6)	(7)	(8)	(9)
State license	-0.848	0.045							
	(0.882)	(0.533)							
Local license		1.478	1.333	1.408	0.578	1.524	1.435	1.377	-0.267
		(1.495)	(1.704)	(1.348)	(1.685)	(1.671)	(1.348)	(1.531)	(2.031)
Summated measures			-0.056						
			(0.312)						
General requirements				0.482					1.519
				(1.024)					(1.567)
Apprenticeship code					-0.931				-2.025*
					(0.812)				(1.094)
Written exam						0.144			0.687
						(0.997)			(1.005)
Performance exam							5.806*		1.918
							(3.160)		(2.318)
Continuing education								-0.170	-0.521
								(0.830)	(1.093)
Constant	0.354	-0.662	-0.388	-0.716	0.753	-0.796	-6.414	-0.614	-0.814
	(4.431)	(4.442)	(4.145)	(4.002)	(4.198)	(4.446)	(5.372)	(4.057)	(4.012)
Basic controls[a]	Y	Y	Y	Y	Y	Y	Y	Y	Y
State controls[b]	Y	Y	Y	Y	Y	Y	Y	Y	Y
Year fixed	Y	Y	Y	Y	Y	Y	Y	Y	Y
State fixed	Y	Y	Y	Y	Y	Y	Y	Y	Y

R-squared	0.21	0.21	0.21	0.21	0.21	0.21	0.21	0.21
N	809	809	809	809	809	809	809	809

NOTE: *significant at the 0.10 level; ** significant at the 0.05 level; *** significant at the 0.01 level. Standard errors, shown in parentheses, are clustered by state. Y = yes.

[a] "Basic controls" include proportions of the population ages 20–24, 25–34, 35–44, 45–54, and 55–64; proportion of married; white and other nonwhite; and proportions of high school graduates, some college experience, and college graduates and more levels of education.

[b] "State controls" include laborers' injury rate, employment growth rate, unemployment rate, and rate of union coverage in the construction industry.

SOURCE: CPS, SOII, and CFOI.

Table 5.15 The Effects of Occupational Licensing on the State Death Rates for Plumbers, 1992–2007

	Death rates						
	(1)	(2)	(3)	(4)	(5)	(6)	(7)
Licensed	−0.002	0.003					
	(0.003)	(0.009)					
State license			−0.003	0.004			
			(0.002)	(0.006)			
Local license			−0.007***	−0.016***			
			(0.002)	(0.007)			
Apprenticeship					0.005*		
					(0.003)		
Exam requirement						−0.001	
						(0.005)	
Continuing education							−0.003
							(0.004)
Year fixed	Y	Y	Y	Y	Y	Y	Y
Other state controls	N	Y	N	Y	Y	Y	Y
State fixed	N	Y	N	Y	Y	Y	Y
Observations	787	787	787	787	666	666	666
R-squared	0.11	0.21	0.11	0.21	0.24	0.24	0.24

NOTE: *significant at the 0.10 level; ** significant at the 0.05 level; ***significant at the 0.01 level. Standard errors, shown in parentheses, are clustered by state. Other state controls include the percentages of the following variables: the six age groups 20–24, 25–34, 35–44, 45–54, 55–64, and 65 and greater (using the age group 16–19 as a reference); marriage status; white and nonwhite (using the portion of African American as a reference); Hispanic origin; high school diploma, some college, college diploma and more levels of education (using high school dropouts as a reference); part-time; and the unemployment rate, employment growth, and union coverage in the construction industry. Y = yes; N = no.
SOURCE: CPS, SOII, and CFOI.

SUMMARY AND CONCLUSIONS

The general issue of occupational regulation has particular relevance to the potential health and safety of electricians and plumbers, whose rates of occupational injuries and deaths are among the highest of any blue-collar occupation. The main focus of this chapter has been the development of the first analysis in a modeling framework of how licensing influences both wage determination and health and safety in the workplace. The chapter provides multivariate estimates linking various levels of state or local occupational regulation to levels of and changes in occupational injuries and deaths of electricians and plumbers.

There has been significant growth of licensing for both occupations at the state level from 1992 to 2007. First, the chapter documents the growth of regulation by states in the occupations. Next, the results show estimates of the impact of occupational regulation on wages. The results suggest that the influence of occupational regulation has generally been significant for wage determination at both the state and local levels. Furthermore, estimates find that there is a small but statistically significant wage premium for the incidence of work-related injuries, which is consistent with much of the literature on compensating wage differentials for dangerous or unpleasant work. A potentially more effective policy seems to be the use of a social insurance such as workers' compensation to reduce the most severe occupational injuries and deaths at the workplace.

Finally, the results for the incidence and severity of injury and death rates show that the impact of occupational regulation on deaths and injuries is statistically insignificant or murky in the multivariate analysis for both electricians and plumbers. The estimates presented in this chapter provide a first approximation and new data for the relationship between occupational licensing, wages, and deaths and injuries for important occupations in the construction industry. Although regulation may have an influence through the monopoly effect on wage determination for electricians, licensing does not appear to be influential in reducing either life-threatening injuries or the risk of injuring limbs— two hazards that workers in these two essential occupations face in the construction industry.

Table 5.16 Hazard Model Estimates of Time to Adoption of a State Occupational Licensing Statute for Electricians (using a Weibull distribution of duration), 2009

Variables	No licensing to state licensing			Local licensing to state licensing		
	(1)	(2)	(3)	(1)	(2)	(3)
injury rate $_t$	1.315		1.250	0.846		0.816
	(0.240)		(0.227)	(0.100)		(0.102)
injury rate $_{t-1}$		1.047	0.941		1.129	1.084
		(0.309)	(0.241)		(0.268)	(0.141)
work comp premium rate $_t$	1.049		1.930	0.874		1.930
	(0.316)		(3.704)	(0.246)		(3.704)
work comp premium rate $_{t-1}$		1.015	0.551		0.910	0.551
		(0.274)	(1.077)		(0.198)	(1.077)
union coverage rate $_t$	0.851*		0.778	0.807*		0.778
	(0.833)		(0.213)	(0.100)		(0.213)
union coverage rate $_{t-1}$		0.899*	1.098		0.883***	1.098
		(0.538)	(0.246)		(0.039)	(0.246)
χ^2	4.22	19.72	–	6.82	10.66	249.23
prob > χ^2	0.23	0.00	–	0.08	0.01	0.00
log pseudo—likelihood	19.01	17.77	19.33	18.49	17.32	18.89
N	67	60	60	91	82	82

NOTE: *significant at the 0.10 level; ** significant at the 0.05 level; ***significant at the 0.01 level. Hazard ratios are shown. Standard errors, shown in parentheses, are clustered by state. χ^2 and its p-value in column 3 with no licensing to state licensing are not shown, because these estimates were regarded as not reliable under the parameters set by StataCorp Data Analysis and Statistical Software.
SOURCE: CPS, SOII, and CFOI.

Notes

1. The research in the chapter was partially funded by the Center for Construction Research and Training through a grant from the U.S. Department of Health and Human Services. I thank Kyoung Won Park for his assistance with this chapter. Park is an assistant professor in the School of Economics and Business Administration at Hanyang University in the Republic of Korea.
2. Table 5.5 shows the changes in the index of regulation from 1992 through 2007.
3. One example of such an innovation is plastic wiring, which may demand a different safety protocol than copper wiring, but the licensing authority may still require the older procedures. The delays in implementation of official protocol may lead to workplace injuries for electricians.
4. Although there is an ability to track the changes in the licensing provisions in the statutes and administrative regulations when these occupations are licensed at the state level, the ability to track local statutes is limited by both data availability and costs, and there is a lessened ability to obtain those changes when these occupations are licensed at the local level, such as with city and county regulations. As a consequence, the data contain only information on whether these occupations are licensed at the state or local level, and have only partial information on specific provisions of some key elements of the occupational regulations for plumbers and electricians at the substate level.
5. The three categories are 1) injuries that cause an absence from work, 2) injuries that cause a restriction of work or job transfer, and 3) injuries that do not affect working capacity (BLS 2013a).
6. Starting with the 2002 data, the SOII does not report injuries separate from illnesses. We expect that the change in the measure should not have affected our analysis because illnesses account for less than 2 percent of nonfatal injuries and illness in BLS reports (Center for Construction Research and Training 2009).
7. Specifically, we computed the injury rate and death rate as follows: Injury rate = (Sum of the weight for the national estimate from the SOII / Estimated employment of electricians from the CPS MORG) × 100; and Death rate = (Actual number of deaths from the CFOI / Estimated number of employed electricians from the CPS MORG) × 10,000.
8. The estimates for plumbers showed murky results both for the issue of wage determination and for health and safety. The results for health and safety show that there was a decline in deaths and injuries, but that decline stopped in the early 2000s and held steady following that period.
9. Wage estimates for plumbers using state and year fixed effects can be found in Kleiner and Park (2010b).
10. The state-level control variables were aggregated using the individual variables from the CPS MORG data. The same state-level control variables are also included in empirical analyses for the state death rates.
11. Another rationale for these findings is that the use of state fixed effects may serve

to inflate the coefficient values. When we estimate the models without state fixed effects, none of the licensing coefficients are significant.

12. Estimates were also developed using the same models for death rates and injury rates for plumbers, and the results were qualitatively similar.

6
Battles among Universally Licensed Occupations

with Kyoung Won Park

Whether or not a dental hygiene clinic can be a successful business model is none of a dentist's business. The free market system will determine that, not a dentist. Most dentists are notoriously very poor businessmen/women.

—Reader comment made to a blog post about a California law allowing hygienists to open independent clinics (Frey 2008)

The American Dental Association has taken a strong stance against dental therapists in Minnesota and nationally, arguing that only a dentist has the skills to pull teeth or engage in other permanent or invasive procedures.

—Jackie Crosby (2012), *Minneapolis Star Tribune* writer

What are the policy issues among universally licensed occupations? This chapter focuses on occupations that are licensed in all states and focuses on one of the policy issues that may arise when two related occupations are not only complementary to each other but also able to be substituted for one another.[1] The broad growth of occupational regulations over the past 60 years has resulted in some situations in which licensing regulations create overlap between occupational groups, and in these situations occupations may compete for the same type of work. Unlike the previous chapters, which examine occupations that are not universally licensed, this chapter looks at occupations that are regulated in all 50 states and at some of the unintended consequences resulting from the policy of universal licensure. The issue of who gets to do the work and whether government should decide on these jurisdictional disputes is growing as the number of occupations that are licensed continues to expand. Furthermore, occupational subfields such as dental hygienists have developed to the point where they are now licensed in all states. Examples of occupations that are both complementary and competitive are doctors and nurses, physical therapists and occupational therapists, dentists and hygienists, architects and interior designers, engineers and architects, and electricians and electrical engineers. The public policy consequences can be substantial. In health care, for example, in states where licensing laws allow only doctors to provide certain common procedures related to well-baby exams, these procedures cost as much as 8 to 10 percent more than in states where nurse practitioners can perform the same procedures (Kleiner et al. 2012).

This chapter focuses on two occupations—dentists and dental hygienists—that are universally licensed and provide complementary services to patients, but that also, as service providers, can act as substitutes for certain tasks. However, for key services the states determine who can do the work, the market structure, and what is required for the patient. The chapter examines the labor market implications of these governmental requirements. With the growth in the number of individuals who are regulated or are seeking regulation by the states, this case study is able to illuminate the potential economic issues of the increased regulation of occupations in the U.S. labor market, especially where the work of the regulated occupations overlaps. It also gives an illustration of the kinds of issues that arise as more occupations become regulated and turf battles arise over who is legally allowed to do work for pay.

In order to examine the relationships between dentists and hygienists, the chapter initially explores the evolution of state regulation for both occupations, and what battle lines have evolved for the occupations. Next, it shows the anatomy of state regulations for dental hygienists over time. The chapter further develops an approach that describes the basic production function in dentistry, with dentists fulfilling an essential role and hygienists providing additional key elements. The results show how a potential monopsony relationship between dentists and hygienists can develop—i.e., a relationship where there is only one feasible employer, where there are frictions in the market and employers have the ability to collude to set wages, and which then influences the earnings and employment of hygienists and dentists. In an empirical section, the influence on hygienists' earnings of state regulations that grant hygienists the ability to be self-employed is shown to be associated with an earnings increase of approximately 10 percent. Furthermore, when hygienists are able to work without the supervision of a dentist, there is an associated increase in the state-level employment growth of hygienists, but a decrease in the employment growth and earnings for dentists. This suggests that for some tasks they are substitutes for one another. These results are robust to sensitivity tests for similar partially licensed occupations and other health-related occupations that are regulated. To the extent that these results suggest inefficiencies due to licensing and monopsonistic deadweight loss, the chapter provides estimates of these losses.

A BRIEF HISTORY OF THE EVOLUTION OF THE REGULATION OF DENTISTS AND DENTAL HYGIENISTS

This part of the chapter presents the evolution of state licensing of dentists and hygienists and shows how state policies have changed from fostering a situation in which dentists had almost exclusive control of the hygienist labor market activities to creating a situation that favors greater autonomy for dental hygienists (Adams 2004).

The state licensing of dentists initially started in South Carolina in 1876; Pennsylvania followed suit the next year. The last state to fully license dentists was North Carolina in 1935. As of 2011, most members of licensing boards are appointed by the governor through a list provided by the state dental association. Generally, dentists dominate membership on the state licensing boards. However, other licensed professionals such as hygienists or dental assistants may also be on licensing boards in states where they are regulated, and they generally have a minor role in the process. In 2010, 17 states had separate hygienist committees that provided recommendations to the board and, in some cases, to the legislature (Wanchek 2010). As recently as 1994, nine states forbid the employment of more than two hygienists per dentist in a dental office, fixing the ratio for these two occupations (ADHA 1994). One of the functions of the licensing board is to deal with disciplinary issues involving dentists, which vary from sexual harassment of patients to incompetent delivery of dental services. However, the licensing board function that deals with the allocation of work among various service providers and that gives services to clients is of direct interest for the analysis. For example, the licensing board makes recommendations to the legislature on regulations governing which occupation provides certain dental services. Furthermore, it provides legal services to defend regulatory practices in state courts. In addition, the board can issue statements on appropriate regulations for continuing education, such as which classes count toward the completion of the requirement. Finally, the licensing board usually has the ability to determine which procedures, such as dental sealants, are appropriate for each occupational category, from dentist to dental assistant.

The Regulation of Hygienists

The state licensing of dental hygienists began with the regulation of hygienists by New York in 1868. Over 50 years passed before other state governments followed suit, when five additional states licensed this occupation between 1919 and 1921. By 1952, 29 states had full licensing of dental hygienists, and by the early 1950s all of the other states started to license dental hygienists (Council of State Governments 1952). A relatively unique part of the regulation of dental hygienists is that hygienists are regulated by dentists, rather than self-regulated, in most states (Wanchek 2010)—exceptions are Washington, Connecticut, and New Mexico. In Washington, dental hygienists are regulated by the director of the state health department in consultation with a committee of three dental hygienists and a consumer. In Connecticut, dental hygienists are regulated directly by the health department. In New Mexico, hygienists are regulated by a committee of five dental hygienists, one dentist, and a consumer. In all the other states, dentists dominate the decision-making process of who gets to do the work.

Initially, dental hygiene programs lasted for one year, but they have since been expanded. In 2010, depending on the state, it took between two and four years to complete the education requirements. A particularly illustrative example of regulatory oversight of the occupation occurred when military dental hygienists who returned to the civilian workforce requested permission to sit for the hygienist's exam. The civilian hygienists protested, saying that the military hygienists needed the same number of years of dental hygiene training as the civilian hygienists in order to take the licensing exam.

One of the key issues for the licensing boards of dental services was the work that dentists could do relative to hygienists and the supervision of dental hygienists by dentists (Helm 1993). Traditionally, dentists are required to be physically present when hygienists are doing their work. The licensing board would determine the precise meaning of the requirement, but it would generally mean that dentists had to be physically present somewhere in the building. Since dentists can either engage in leisure or see other patients while hygienists are seeing patients, this practice could be perceived as a form of featherbedding, where services are paid for without any clearly defined work being provided.

As early as 1932, the issue of determining the proper tasks of hygienists relative to dentists was raised at national meetings of hygienists, with a view that hygienists should have greater autonomy. Specifically, this meant the ability to work independently of dentists and to conduct more sophisticated dental procedures. A key part of the history of the profession has focused on the importance of hygienists playing a more important role in the policy process, particularly with respect to legislative issues. Until 1988, when Colorado first allowed hygienists to practice without the direct supervision of a dentist, hygienists had been required to work for or be under the direction of a dentist. Since that time, seven states have allowed hygienists to be self-employed without the direct oversight of a dentist. Hygienists also have attempted to limit the supply of practitioners. For example, as of 2007, no state permitted reciprocity, or the movement of dental hygienists from other states. Dental hygienists must meet the requirements of the state they are moving to in order to be granted a license.

As of 2007, seven states (California, Colorado, Montana, Nebraska, New Mexico, Oregon, and Washington) allowed hygienists to be self-employed other than as independent contractors to dentists, and only three states (California, Colorado, and New Mexico) permitted a dental hygienist to own a dental hygiene practice (Beach et. al. 2007). Montana and Nebraska adopted the provision allowing hygienists to be self-employed other than as independent contractors in 2003 and 2007, respectively. The work by dental hygienists who are self-employed is restricted to specific dental practices that vary across these states. For example, in Colorado hygienists are allowed to clean teeth and do simple restorative work, independently of dentists.

In the late 1970s, the American Dental Hygienists' Association (ADHA) supported alternative practice methods that would allow the dental hygienist to become the primary provider of initial services, in accordance with state dental and dental hygiene practice acts (Motley 1988). In response to these policy changes, the American Dental Association (ADA) passed a resolution stating that dental hygienists are auxiliaries who must work under the supervision of a dentist, who also would retain ownership and managerial authority (Beach et al. 2007). Over time, hygienists have been able to gain greater authority in certain states (as granted by the legislatures) as their numbers have increased in overall dental practice and consequently their influence in crafting licensing laws has grown. As of 2008 there were more than 174,000 dental hygienists in the United States (BLS 2012a). These policy provisions by the two dental service organizations set the battleground for conflicts in state legislatures, licensing boards, and the courts.

State-Level Examination of Dental Hygienists' Legally Permitted Job Characteristics

As noted earlier, the number of tasks that dental hygienists have been permitted to do over the past several years has grown. Table 6.1 provides a full listing of the provisions that are graphed in Figure 6.1; some of the key components of the tasks include prophylaxis (cleaning), fluoride treatment, sealant application, x-rays, amalgam restorations, local anesthesia, nitrous oxide, initial screening, and patient referral (National Center for Health Workforce Analysis 2004). In order to show the growth in hygienists' autonomy over time, Figure 6.1 uses a box-and-whisker graphic analysis of state regulation, which gives the mean and spread of the regulation of hygienists over the period 2001–2007. Panel A shows the overall ranking of the dental hygienists' professional practice environment that is allowed by statute or legal rulings. Panel B shows the number of dental tasks that hygienists are permitted to do, independently of dentists, by state law or administrative or court rulings in the state.

A report funded by the Kellogg Foundation, the Rasmuson Foundation, and the Bethel Community Services Foundation showed that dental hygienists did as well as dentists in performing routine tasks such as the ones listed here (Wetterhall et al. 2010). The results in Panels A and B of Figure 6.1 show a movement toward greater autonomy for hygienists in dental practice from 2001 to 2007. The mean value of the summated rating scale for all states was 43.67 (sd = 19.84) in 2001 and increased to 49.10 (sd = 20.54) by 2007 (out of 100 possible points). Most of the changes in state regulations occurred between 2002 and 2007, a period during which more states allowed hygienists to perform additional procedures. Panel A shows the overall results, which suggest that in spite of generally greater control of the regulatory process by dentists, hygienists have been able to gain more autonomy over the delivery of dental services, including the ability to control their own offices without the supervision of a dentist. Moreover, even within states that have full control over the delivery of dental services, there has been growth in the independence of hygienists from monitoring by dentists with respect to

Figure 6.1 Box-and-Whisker Graph Showing the Growth and Spread of State Regulations on the Professional Practice Environment of Dental Hygienists, by State over Time

Panel A: Dental Hygiene Professional Practice Index (DHPPI), 2001–2007

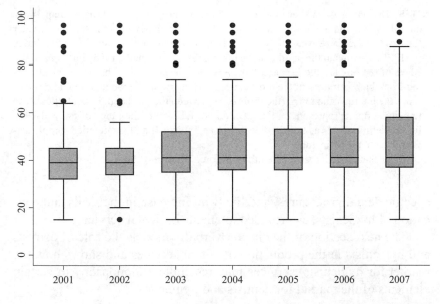

(continued)

Figure 6.1 (continued)

Panel B: Number of tasks permitted over 2001–2007

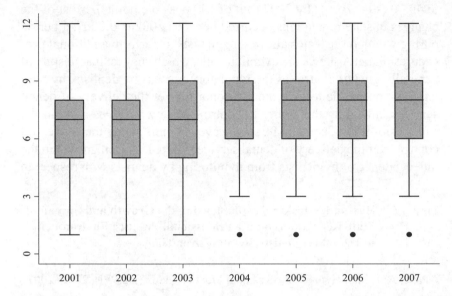

NOTE: The box-and-whisker plot shows annual values, by year, of the median, interquartile range, and outliers of the summated rating scale based on the National Center
for Health Workforce Analysis's (2004) Dental Hygiene Professional Practice Index
(DHPPI). The line in the middle of the box represents the median. The bottom and top
edges of the box are the first and third quartiles, respectively. The whiskers extending from the box represent the most extreme point within the range of one-and-a-half
times the interquartile range (the difference between the third and first quartiles). The
remaining points represent outliers that do not fall within the range of the whiskers;
for the definition of each of the variables, see Table 6.1, and for detailed sample statistics, see Panel B in Table 6.3.
SOURCE: National Center for Health Workforce Analysis (2004).

specific dental procedures, and likely an increase in the skills and education of hygienists, as provided to clients of dental services.

The next section of the chapter verbally models the role of dentists
and hygienists in the production of dental services and shows how the
market for hygienists' services may resemble a monopsony in certain
elements of the market for dentists and hygienists.

Table 6.1 Definitions of Regulatory Variables

Variables	Definitions
DHPPI	A simple sum of all the components of the DHPPI, ranging from 0 to 100.
tasks permitted (summated)	A simple sum of whether hygienists are permitted to perform the following practices: prophylaxis, fluoride treatment, sealant application, x-rays, amalgam restorations, local anesthesia, nitrous oxide, initial screening/assessment, refer patients, and other expanded functions. We coded each practice as 1 if hygienists are allowed to perform; otherwise coded as 0.
tasks permitted (Rasch)	A Rasch scale of tasks permitted that is used to form the summated measure of tasks permitted.
independence from dentists (summated)	A simple sum of whether hygienists are able to perform dental hygiene practices without supervision of dentists at the following locations: dentist's office, long-term care facilities, schools, public health agencies, correctional facilities, mental health facilities, hospitals/rehabilitation hospitals or convalescent settings, and personal residences. We coded each location as 1 if hygienists are able to perform dental hygiene practices without supervision of dentists; otherwise 0.
independence from dentists (Rasch)	A Rasch scale of independence from dentists that is used to form the summated measure of independence from dentists.
self-employment allowed	We coded 1 when the provision allows hygienist to be self-employed other than as independent contractor; otherwise 0.

SOURCE: National Center for Health Workforce Analysis (2004).

A MODEL OF DENTAL SERVICES PRODUCTION

This section initially develops the basic production function for dental services and then expands it to include government regulation of work practices, where dentists are required to supervise hygienists. The model serves as a basis to inform the empirical work, rather than as a fully specified general equilibrium model of dental production under regulation. The unit of analysis for the model is the office-based dental practice. Following Reinhardt (1972), this entity can be treated as a firm of which the dentist is the owner/manager who faces a profit maximization decision. Within this context, the dentist makes decisions regarding her own effort to maximize income, subject to constraints including the technical production relationship between her labor and other inputs. These inputs include capital and the use of hygienists and other somewhat less knowledgeable workers, such as dental technicians, aides, and clerical and administrative assistants.

As was noted earlier in this book, Shapiro (1986) provides a guide for analyzing occupations that are universally licensed. In his model of licensing he envisions a labor market where service output has two types of workers: high-skilled and lower-skilled. In order to adapt the model to a production function and the market for dentists and hygienists, one can think of a stylized version of production and output. If labor services can be provided only by a dentist and hygienists can work only for a dentist, then dental services can be provided only when a dentist is present. Hygienists' income and work are therefore tied to the success of a dentist.

Within this profit relationship for the dentists, the hygienist's wage is determined by the decisions of the dentist as to the use of the hygienist's labor input and technology mix by the high-skilled provider, the dentist. Assuming profits are constant, as the hygienist's wage goes down, the dentist's wage will go up. Also implied is that the hygienist's employment will go up and the dentist's employment will go down. These conditions, which are a modified production function, can therefore lead to conditions that are consistent with elements of a monopsony market for hygienists who are controlled by dentists.

CAN REGULATION RESULT IN CONDITIONS CONSISTENT WITH MONOPSONY IN THE LABOR MARKET?

Milton Friedman noted that under occupational licensing, all regulated occupations are often assumed to attempt to capture the rents of licensing and reallocate resources from the consumer to the regulated practitioners (Friedman 1962). The application to this case study assumes that the relatively low-skilled (hygienist) workers can by law do only low-skilled work and are allowed to work only under the supervision of relatively high-skilled workers. With favorable regulation for dentists, the high-skilled workers that control low-skilled workers' tasks and their ability to do work only for certain types of employers have the monopsonistic characteristics of employing lower-skilled workers and capturing rents. When regulation of employment by high-skilled workers of low-skilled workers ceases, low-skilled workers can open their own establishments and capture the licensing rents for themselves (Groshen 1991). For monopsony to exist, the labor market must generally have two key assumptions (Manning 2003). First, important frictions are assumed to be present. In the case of two universally licensed occupations, with one dominant, this requires the supervision of the other, and the assumption of frictions in the labor market is established. In this case, state law requires that hygienists work under the supervision of a dentist; they are not allowed to work on their own or open an office in competition with a dentist.

Second, employers have some ability to set wages. Since dental hygienists have no major options for employment other than working for or under the supervision of a dentist, dentists can have significant market power to collude to set wages in a local market. This is consistent with one of the elements of monopsony (Lipscomb and Douglass 1982). Even if there are many dentists bidding for their services, the market for hygienists is less than it would be without either the legal constraints established through law or the administrative rules established by the dental board. Although not an ideal case of monopsony, such as the textbook cases of mine operators in a small town or a large manufacturer in a small isolated town, the general conditions established by Manning are present in the case of dentists and hygienists.

A simple model of monopsony in the context of occupational licensing is shown in Figure 6.2, where a monopsonist employer maximizes profits with employment L, which equates demand (given by the marginal revenue product of labor [MRPL] curve) to marginal cost MC at point A. With licensing, both occupations are able to restrict the supply of labor and raise wages within their occupation. The model informs the empirical work in the next section of the study.

In the case where dentists are making positive profits on the marginal hygienists, there is no incentive to increase employment because doing so would require increasing the wage to attract the extra worker, and this higher wage must be paid to all existing workers. The gap between the wage and the marginal revenue product in Figure 6.2 is referred to as the rate of exploitation (Manning 2003). In the case of hygienists,

Figure 6.2 A Graphical Representation on Monopsony and Licensing

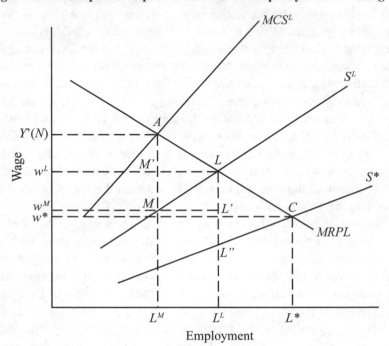

NOTE: A monopsonist employer maximizes profits with employment L^M, which equates demand, given by the marginal revenue product of labor ($MRPL$) curve, to marginal cost MC at point A. Supply curve S^L is the result of licensing. The wage is then determined on the supply curve of licensed workers S^L, at point M, and is equal to w^M. By contrast, a competitive labor market would reach equilibrium at point C, where supply S^* equals demand. This would lead to employment L^* and wage w^*. Triangle AMC is deadweight loss, the part that has been lost by society as a result of the monopsonistic restriction of employment; and rectangle $w^L w^M M M'$ is the part that the monopsonist licensed employer has exploited from the other licensed workers. Triangle $LL''C$ is deadweight loss, the part of the competitive social surplus that has been lost by society because of the licensing of workers.

SOURCE: Developed by the authors.

the model predicts that laws that require hygienists to work for or be supervised by dentists would result in lower wages and employment for hygienists. In addition, if the laws were relaxed, there would likely be lower earnings and employment for dentists, since the level of exploitation would be reduced. Furthermore, the lower employment and wage caused by the monopsony power has two distinct effects on the economic welfare of the occupations. First, the law favors dentists' control over the market structure and, as a consequence, it redistributes welfare away from workers (hygienists) to their employers (dentists). Second, the market structure established by these two occupations reduces the aggregate (or social) welfare enjoyed by both groups taken together, since the employers' net gain is smaller than the loss inflicted on workers. It is a net social loss or deadweight loss. As such, it is a measure of the market failure caused by monopsony power, through a misallocation of resources to employer dentists and away from worker hygienists.

Figure 6.2 also shows that a monopsonist employer in the face of licensing maximizes profits with employment L^M in a way that equates demand (given by the marginal revenue product of labor [$MRPL$] curve) to marginal cost MC at point A. The supply curve S^L is the result of licensing. The wage (w) is then determined on the supply curve of licensed workers S^L, at point M, and is equal to w^M. By contrast, a competitive labor market would reach equilibrium at point C, where supply S^* equals demand. This would lead to employment L^* and wage w^*. Triangle AMC is deadweight loss, the part that has been lost by society as a result of the monopsonistic restriction of employment by both occupations; and rectangle $w^L w^M MM'$ is the part that the monopsonist licensed employer has exploited from the other licensed workers. Triangle $LL''C$ is deadweight loss, the part of the competitive social surplus that has been lost by society because of the licensing of workers.

The estimates of the empirical influence of monopsony without licensing have been mixed. For example, the results for specific industries range from major league baseball, where the impact has been large (100 to 600 percent), to teachers, nurses, and nursing assistants, where the influence has been 5 percent or less (Scully 1974; Zimbalist 1992; Kahn 2000; Matsudaira 2010). For the overall labor market, the impact of monopsony has been estimated at less than 3 percent (Brown and Medoff 1989). This analysis is the first attempt to estimate monopsony for both workers and their primary occupational employer as a result of variations in occupational licensing statutes, specifically related to the ability of hygienists to open their own dental-practice offices or do work independently of dentists, which is a weak form of monopsony (Boal and Ransom 1997).

HOW TO MEASURE DENTAL HYGIENE
PROFESSIONAL PRACTICES

The Dental Hygiene Professional Practice Index (DHPPI) is used to assess state government regulations on the professional practice environments of dental hygienists. The National Center for Health Workforce Analysis (2004) originally compiled this index, which consists of state government regulations in the 50 states and the District of Columbia for 2001, and the index is extended and updated to 2007 (Table 6.1 gives the main regulatory components that have changed since 2001). These major professional regulatory components include the following:

- **Legal and regulatory environment.** This includes governance of the profession through the state regulatory board of dental hygiene or through a dental hygiene committee empowered by a dental board with a mandate to regulate the profession, licensure by credential/endorsement with no new clinical exam required, scope of practice defined in law or regulations, and restriction to patient of record of the primary employing dentist.

- **Supervision in different practice settings.** This includes dental supervision requirements across a variety of health settings including private dental offices, long-term care facilities, schools, public health agencies, correctional facilities, and similar institutional facilities. The supervision requirements vary from direct supervision to general and collaborator supervision, to complete autonomy.

- **Tasks permitted under varying levels of supervision.** This includes tasks allowed for dental hygienists to provide basic services such as prophylaxis (dental cleaning), sealants, fluoride treatments, x-rays, and hygiene screening and assessment, as well as expanded functions such as placing amalgam restorations (tooth fillings), administration of local anesthesia, and administration of nitrous oxide.[2]

- **Reimbursement.** Direct Medicaid reimbursement and direct payment to hygienists by other third-party insurers or patients.

The raw score of the DHPPI is a 100-point scale with different weights attached to subitems under the four major components, indicating that a higher score means a less restrictive practice environment for dental hygienists.

For empirical analysis, a DHPPI index is an overall index to capture the spread in each state's regulatory system for the professional practice environment, as coded by the National Center for Health Workforce Analysis (2004). Because certain regulatory components are more important to wage determination and employment outcomes than other components, we also examine each individual component in two ways. In particular, we focus on two major components: 1) tasks permitted and 2) supervision requirements. Because the weights to the subitems of these components of the DHPPI are assigned in somewhat arbitrary fashion, we develop both the summated rating scale and the statistically weighted index (Rasch index) for each component. Therefore, we examine how each state's regulatory system for the professional practice environments affects the market outcomes of the professions by using both linear (summated rating scale) and nonlinear (Rasch index) measures of the regulatory system. Finally, we analyze whether the provision that permits hygienists to be self-employed other than as independent contractors affects the market outcomes. Table 6.1 gives the key values of the indices.[3]

Table 6.2 shows the top and bottom five states ranked by their summated DHPPI. Although the rankings of the top five states have remained the same, with only a minor change in the DHPPI for the years 2001–2007, the rankings of the bottom five states have changed, with a relatively larger growth in the DHPPI. In particular, Kentucky, the second-lowest state in the DHPPI, went through a substantial change during the period. The state with the largest growth was Montana, with an increase of 43 points. Not only has the DHPPI been increasing, but there also has been considerable variation across states and over time.

Table 6.2 Rankings of the Top and Bottom Five Regulated States and Changes in Their Dental Hygiene Professional Practice Index (DHPPI)

	Top five states		Bottom five states	
Year	State	DHPPI	State	DHPPI
2001	Colorado	97	Mississippi	15
	Washington	94	Alabama	18
	Oregon	88	Kentucky	18
	California	86	West Virginia	20
	New Mexico	86	Virginia	21
2007	Colorado	97	Mississippi	15
	Washington	94	Alabama	20
	Oregon	90	Georgia	23
	California	88	West Virginia	26
	New Mexico	87	Arkansas	28

	Top five states by change in DHPPI 2001–2007		
	2001	2007	Change
Montana	43	86	43
Oklahoma	28	52	24
Nebraska	44	68	24
Kentucky	18	40	22
Arizona	42	62	20

SOURCE: Author survey of occupational regulation among states, tabulated using DHPPI.

LABOR MARKET ANALYSIS FOR DENTISTS AND HYGIENISTS WITH OCCUPATIONAL LICENSING REGULATIONS

Table 6.3 provides descriptive statistics from the American Community Survey (ACS) for key labor market variables as well as other market and regulatory variables used in our analysis.[4] The values show that the average age of dentists is about six years higher than that of hygienists, and that dentists have six more years of schooling. Furthermore, the dentistry profession tends to be male-dominated, whereas 97 percent of hygienists are females. The average hourly earnings of dentists are more than three times higher than those of hygienists. One important distinction gleaned from the data is that 71 percent of dentists are self-employed, but only 2 percent of hygienists work for themselves. Part of this difference may be due to state laws that require dentists to directly supervise the work of hygienists. The data for dentists were derived from the ACS, and the methods are shown in Appendix C, with the sample selection criteria in Appendix Table C.1.

The estimates in Tables 6.4 and 6.5 demonstrate the association between DHPPI and hourly earnings for dental hygienists and dentists, using individual-level data in the ACS. The basic general earnings equation can be stated as follows:

$$(6.1) \quad \ln\left(Earnings_{ist}^{\frac{D}{H}}\right) = \alpha + \beta R_{st} + \gamma X_{ist} + \theta Z_{st} + \delta_s + \eta_t + \mu_{ist},$$

where $Earnings_{ist}$ is the hourly earnings of the dentist (D) or dental hygienist (H) i in state s in time period t; R_{st} represents the DHPPI and its components in person i's state s in time period t; the vector X_{ist} includes covariates measuring the characteristics of each person; the vector Z_{st} includes time-varying state-level controls such as the state median household income and the percentage of uninsured in the state; δ_s and η_t are state and year fixed effects, respectively; and μ_{ist} is the error term.[5]

Table 6.4 shows the influence of the overall DHPPI index on the logarithm of hourly earnings of hygienists, using all the controls for individual characteristics shown in Table 6.3, which were extracted from the ACS. These estimates show that the DHPPI level is not a significant factor in determining hourly earnings. However, the legal ability either to be self-employed or to have tasks unsupervised is a key factor influencing wage determination. For example, having the legal ability to be self-employed raises hygienists' hourly earnings by approximately a statistically significant 10 percent. Similarly, working unsupervised, measured by the summated score and the Rasch score, is associated with a 1.2 and 0.7 percent increase in earnings for hygienists, respectively. These additional measures of legal restrictions are used to provide additional sensitivity analysis for the measures of legal restrictions on the practice of dentistry. The issue of whether hygienists were directly reimbursed under the state government regulations with the same specifications was also examined. Although we do not report the

188

Table 6.3 Summary Statistics for the Labor Market Variables Using the ACS, 2001–2007

Panel A: Individual sample statistics

	Dental hygienists (n = 5,886)		Dentists (n = 7,220)	
	Mean	sd	Mean	sd
Age	40.55	10.11	46.98	10.02
Schooling (in years)	14.65	1.25	20.30	1.05
Experience (in years)	19.90	10.07	20.67	10.09
Gender (male: 1; female: 0)	0.03	0.17	0.80	0.40
Married (married: 1; not married: 0)	0.74	0.44	0.84	0.37
Experience squared (/1,000)	0.50	0.42	0.53	0.41
White (white: 1; others: 0)	0.92	0.26	0.84	0.36
Black (black: 1; others: 0)	0.02	0.14	0.02	0.15
Others (others: 1; otherwise: 0)	0.05	0.23	0.13	0.34
Citizen (U.S. citizen: 1; others: 0)	0.98	0.13	0.96	0.19
Work for-profit (yes: 1; no: 0)	0.94	0.24	0.22	0.41
Work for not-for-profit (yes: 1; no: 0)	0.02	0.13	0.02	0.14
Work for government (yes: 1; no: 0)	0.02	0.15	0.05	0.22
Self-employment (yes: 1; no: 0)	0.02	0.14	0.71	0.45
Hourly earnings (in 2007 dollars)	28.81	11.93	95.46	67.66

Panel B: State sample statistics

	n	Mean	sd	Source
DHPPI	357	46.80	20.02	Nat. Ctr. for Health Workforce Analysis (2004)
Tasks permitted (summated)	357	7.19	2.55	"
Tasks permitted (Rasch)	357	1.44	1.76	"
Independence from dentists (summated)	357	1.12	2.56	"
Independence from dentists (Rasch)	357	−8.19	4.27	"
Self-employment allowed	357	0.11	0.32	"
Growth in the number of dental hygienists	298	0.04	0.15	Occupational Employment Survey
Growth in the number of dentists	272	0.02	0.21	"
State median household income ($)	357	44,984.93	7,597.42	Current Population Survey
Percentage of uninsured	357	13.67	3.76	"
State median price of amalgam restoration ($)	336	112.66	19.73	Survey of Dental Fees (American Dental
State median price of prophylaxis ($)	343	49.47	8.54	Association 2001, 2003, 2005, 2007)

SOURCE: American Community Survey (ACS) and Dental Hygiene Professional Practice Index (DHPPI).

190

Table 6.4 Pooled OLS Model of Log Hourly Earnings for Dental Hygienists Using the ACS, 2001–2007

	(1)	(2)	(3)	(4)	(5)	(6)
DHPPI	0.000					
	(0.002)					
Tasks permitted (summated)		0.005				
		(0.007)				
Tasks permitted (Rasch)			0.005			
			(0.010)			
Independence from dentists (summated)				0.012**		
				(0.006)		
Independence from dentists (Rasch)					0.007*	
					(0.004)	
Self-employment allowed						0.100**
						(0.041)
Experience	0.017****	0.017****	0.017****	0.017****	0.017****	0.017****
	(0.003)	(0.003)	(0.003)	(0.003)	(0.003)	(0.003)
Experience squared (/1,000)	-0.345****	-0.345****	-0.345****	-0.344****	-0.344****	-0.344****
	(0.061)	(0.061)	(0.061)	(0.061)	(0.061)	(0.061)
Schooling (in years)	0.043****	0.043****	0.043****	0.043****	0.043****	0.043****
	(0.007)	(0.007)	(0.007)	(0.007)	(0.007)	(0.007)
Gender	-0.065*	-0.064*	-0.064*	-0.064*	-0.065*	-0.064*
	(0.034)	(0.034)	(0.034)	(0.034)	(0.034)	(0.034)
Marital status	0.008	0.008	0.008	0.008	0.008	0.008
	(0.014)	(0.014)	(0.014)	(0.014)	(0.014)	(0.014)

	(1)	(2)	(3)	(4)	(5)	(6)
White	0.002	0.002	0.002	0.002	0.002	0.002
	(0.032)	(0.032)	(0.032)	(0.032)	(0.032)	(0.032)
Black	−0.080	−0.080	−0.080	−0.080	−0.080	−0.080
	(0.048)	(0.048)	(0.048)	(0.048)	(0.048)	(0.048)
Citizen	0.142***	0.142***	0.142***	0.143***	0.143***	0.143***
	(0.044)	(0.044)	(0.044)	(0.048)	(0.048)	(0.048)
Work for for-profit	0.168****	0.168****	0.168****	0.167****	0.167****	0.167****
	(0.034)	(0.033)	(0.033)	(0.044)	(0.044)	(0.044)
Work for not-for-profit	0.093*	0.093*	0.093*	0.093*	0.093*	0.093*
	(0.048)	(0.048)	(0.048)	(0.048)	(0.048)	(0.048)
Self-employment	0.137*	0.137*	0.137*	0.137*	0.137*	0.137*
	(0.069)	(0.069)	(0.069)	(0.069)	(0.069)	(0.069)
Constant	−3.087	−3.106	−3.256	−2.793	−2.981	−3.036
	(3.048)	(2.998)	(2.963)	(3.078)	(2.980)	(2.968)
State controls with state fixed effects	Y	Y	Y	Y	Y	Y
Year fixed effects	Y	Y	Y	Y	Y	Y
R-squared	0.171	0.171	0.171	0.172	0.172	0.172
N	5,886	5,886	5,886	5,886	5,886	5,886

NOTE: Robust standard errors clustered at the state level are reported in parentheses. * significant at the 0.10 level; ** significant at the 0.05 level; *** significant at the 0.01 level; **** significant at the 0.001 level. State controls include state median household income and the percentage of uninsured in the state. For this and the following tables, the six columns show different specifications—i.e., different independent variables used or different control variables to show how the alternative specifications influenced wage determination. These varying estimates provide a guide for the sensitivity of the model to alternative specifications. Y = yes.
SOURCE: Developed by the authors using ACS data.

Table 6.5 Pooled OLS Model of Log Hourly Earnings for Dentists Using the ACS, 2001–2007

	(1)	(2)	(3)	(4)	(5)	(6)
DHPPI	-0.002					
	(0.003)					
Tasks permitted (summated)		-0.005				
		(0.020)				
Tasks permitted (Rasch)			-0.014			
			(0.023)			
Independence from dentists (summated)				-0.005		
Independence from dentists (Rasch)					-0.014*	(0.008)
					(0.017)	
Self-employment allowed						-0.162**
						(0.077)
Experience	0.031****	0.031****	0.031****	0.031****	0.031****	0.031****
	(0.005)	(0.005)	(0.005)	(0.005)	(0.005)	(0.005)
Experience squared (/1,000)	-0.610****	-0.609****	-0.609****	-0.610****	-0.610****	-0.611****
	(0.112)	(0.112)	(0.112)	(0.112)	(0.112)	(0.112)
Schooling (in years)	-0.015	-0.015	-0.015	-0.015	-0.015	-0.015
	(0.011)	(0.011)	(0.011)	(0.011)	(0.011)	(0.011)
Gender	0.244****	0.244****	0.244****	0.244****	0.244****	0.244****
	(0.018)	(0.018)	(0.018)	(0.018)	(0.018)	(0.018)
Marital status	0.115****	0.115****	0.114****	0.115****	0.115****	0.115****
	(0.020)	(0.020)	(0.020)	(0.020)	(0.020)	(0.020)

	(1)	(2)	(3)	(4)	(5)	(6)
White	0.097****	0.097****	0.097****	0.097****	0.097****	0.097****
	(0.017)	(0.017)	(0.017)	(0.017)	(0.017)	(0.017)
Black	−0.036	−0.036	−0.036	−0.037	−0.037	−0.037
	(0.058)	(0.059)	(0.059)	(0.058)	(0.058)	(0.058)
Citizen	0.067	0.067	0.067	0.067	0.067	0.067
	(0.041)	(0.041)	(0.041)	(0.041)	(0.041)	(0.041)
Work for for-profit	0.387****	0.387****	0.387****	0.387****	0.387****	0.387****
	(0.032)	(0.032)	(0.032)	(0.032)	(0.032)	(0.032)
Work for not-for-profit	0.111*	0.111*	0.111*	0.111*	0.110*	0.110*
	(0.057)	(0.057)	(0.057)	(0.057)	(0.057)	(0.057)
Self-employment	0.500****	0.500****	0.501****	0.500****	0.500****	0.500****
	(0.037)	(0.037)	(0.037)	(0.037)	(0.037)	(0.037)
Constant	11.574*	11.848*	12.090*	11.727*	11.365*	11.511*
	(6.138)	(6.065)	(6.144)	(6.095)	(6.142)	(6.046)
State controls with state fixed effects	Y	Y	Y	Y	Y	Y
Year fixed effects	Y	Y	Y	Y	Y	Y
R-squared	0.122	0.122	0.122	0.122	0.122	0.122
N	7,220	7,220	7,220	7,220	7,220	7,220

NOTE: Robust standard errors clustered at the state level are reported in parentheses. * significant at the 0.10 level; ** significant at the 0.05 level; *** significant at the 0.01 level; **** significant at the 0.001 level. State controls include state median household income and the percentage of uninsured in the state. Y = yes.
SOURCE: Developed by the authors using ACS data.

results in the table, we find that the direct reimbursement was associated with approximately 5.1 percent higher earnings for hygienists and 8.4 percent lower earnings for dentists, and that it was statistically significant at the 0.01 level only for hygienists. However, the direct reimbursement was not statistically significant in the employment growth models in Tables 6.6 and 6.7. In order to test for the robustness of the results, a further analysis also examined whether state provisions that allow for hygienists to be self-employed are associated with earnings dispersions for the two occupations. These further tests were estimated in Appendix Table C.2 and were consistent with the results presented in Tables 6.4 and 6.5.

In contrast, for dentists in Table 6.5, the estimates from the model using the same set of controls from the ACS as in Table 6.4 indicate that having state provisions that allow for hygienists to be self-employed is associated with approximately 16 percent lower hourly earnings for the dentists in that state. It appears that dentists lose more, perhaps because they are no longer able to require hygienists to work only for them in order to provide dental services. The consequence of the legal provision may result in higher costs due to higher wages for hygienists. In addition, there may be lost income because hygienists may be taking patients away from full-service dentists and recommending fewer costly dental procedures. For example, the assumption is that independent dental hygienists are more likely to recommend lower-cost dental sealants, but that a hygienist who works in a full-service office may have incentives to recommend a higher-cost dental filling because of bonuses or promotion opportunities. To further illustrate, there are strong incentive effects for dentists to recommend more costly procedures. On average, sealants cost $37, but most fillings cost more than $100 and also need to be replaced periodically (Simonsen 1991). Once fillings are installed, there is a greater likelihood for both crowns and root canal procedures, both of which cost more than $1,000 each. Since hygienists can only work with sealants, having independent hygienists can have a major impact on dental incomes by changing the service and product mix. There is some evidence that sealants provide protection from further tooth decay that is as good as or better than the protection from fillings (Gooch et al. 2009). Furthermore, the signs of the coefficients for the ability of hygienists to engage in broader work assignments are negative in the remainder of the specifications for dentists' wage determinations.

The analysis also examined whether state provisions that allow for hygienists to be self-employed are associated with earnings dispersions for the two occupations. The employment effects of variations in state statutes for dental hygienists and dentists are given in Tables 6.6 and 6.7, respectively.[6] The general employment equation can be stated as follows:

$$(6.2) \quad Employment_{st}^{\frac{D}{H}} = \alpha + \beta R_{st} + \gamma X_{st} + \delta_s + \eta_t + \mu_{st},$$

where $Employment_{st}$ is the employment growth of dentists (D) or hygienists (H) in state s in time period t; R_{st} is the DHPPI and its components in state s in time period t; the vector X_{st} includes covariates measuring economic and dental characteristics within each state; δ_s and η_t are state and year fixed effects, respectively; and μ_{st} is the error term.

The estimates from the reduced form model in Tables 6.6 and 6.7 use the Occupational Employment Statistics (OES) from the Bureau of Labor Statistics (BLS 2013b). One advantage of the data is that it is collected at the state level and gives information on an aggregate state level, as opposed to the individual-level information provided in the ACS. Since almost all hygienists are required to work for a dentist, the estimates from the database have few errors in the values for employment change that might be present if hygienists worked independently. Although the ACS has individual-level data, the estimates for small states may have large errors. The estimates show that the overall index is not significantly associated with the employment growth of hygienists in equations that include state-level controls, such as the growth in the number of dentists in the state, the state median household income, the percentage of uninsured in the state, and the state median prices of amalgam restoration and prophylaxis in each specification in the table. However, as shown in Table 6.6, whether hygienists can be self-employed is positively and statistically significant at the 0.10 level in its association with employment growth of hygienists by about 6 percent. Furthermore, enhancing the ability of hygienists to do various tasks without the supervision of dentists is also associated with positive employment growth for their occupation.

Table 6.6 Models of Employment Growth for Dental Hygienists by State, Using the OES Data, 2001–2007

	(1)	(2)	(3)	(4)	(5)	(6)
DHPPI	0.004 (0.003)					
Tasks permitted (summated)		-0.020 (0.034)				
Tasks permitted (Rasch)			-0.037 (0.045)			
Independence from dentists (summated)				0.009*		
Independence from dentists (Rasch)					0.006** (0.005)	
Self-employment allowed						0.061* (0.034)
Dental hygienist's employment growth rate	-0.146** (0.064)	-0.155** (0.061)	-0.151** (0.063)	-0.150** (0.064)	-0.150** (0.064)	-0.151** (0.064)
State median household income (/1,000)	-0.015 (0.012)	-0.013 (0.013)	-0.014 (0.013)	-0.014 (0.012)	-0.014 (0.012)	-0.014 (0.012)
Rate of uninsured	-0.004 (0.008)	-0.001 (0.009)	-0.002 (0.008)	-0.004 (0.008)	-0.004 (0.008)	-0.003 (0.008)
State median price of prophylaxis	0.008 (0.009)	0.009 (0.010)	0.010 (0.010)	0.008 (0.009)	0.008 (0.009)	0.008 (0.009)
State median price of amalgam restoration	0.000 (0.004)	0.000 (0.004)	0.000 (0.004)	0.000 (0.004)	0.001 (0.004)	0.001 (0.004)

Constant	1.399	1.381	1.245	1.421	1.472	1.409
	(1.102)	(1.108)	(1.140)	(1.111)	(1.104)	(1.112)
State fixed effects	Y	Y	Y	Y	Y	Y
Year fixed effects	Y	Y	Y	Y	Y	Y
R-squared	0.221	0.216	0.219	0.215	0.215	0.215
N	250	250	250	250	250	250

NOTE: Robust standard errors clustered at the state level are reported in parentheses. * significant at the 0.10 level; ** significant at the 0.05 level; *** significant at the 0.01 level; **** significant at the 0.001 level. Y = yes.

SOURCE: Developed by the authors using ACS data.

Table 6.7 Models of Employment Growth for Dentists by State, Using the OES Data, 2001–2007

	(1)	(2)	(3)	(4)	(5)	(6)
DHPPI	-0.005 (0.003)					
Tasks permitted (summated)		-0.022 (0.042)				
Tasks permitted (Rasch)			0.022 (0.050)			
Independence from dentists (summated)				-0.036**** (0.005)		
Independence from dentists (Rasch)					-0.024**** (0.005)	
Self-employment allowed						-0.255**** (0.039)
Dentists' employment growth rate	-0.282 (0.192)	-0.300 (0.189)	-0.293 (0.189)	-0.287 (0.189)	-0.287 (0.189)	-0.288 (0.189)
State median household income (/1,000)	-0.002 (0.013)	-0.004 (0.013)	-0.004 (0.013)	-0.003 (0.013)	-0.003 (0.013)	-0.003 (0.013)
Rate of uninsured	-0.002 (0.010)	-0.003 (0.010)	-0.005 (0.011)	0.000 (0.010)	-0.001 (0.010)	-0.001 (0.010)
State median price of prophylaxis	0.007 (0.015)	0.010 (0.013)	0.006 (0.013)	0.006 (0.014)	0.006 (0.014)	0.006 (0.014)
State median price of amalgam restoration	0.002 (0.003)	0.001 (0.003)	0.002 (0.002)	0.002 (0.003)	0.001 (0.003)	0.001 (0.003)

Constant	0.817	0.772	0.911	0.792	0.607	0.847
	(1.774)	(1.762)	(1.688)	(1.738)	(1.736)	(1.748)
State fixed effects	Y	Y	Y	Y	Y	Y
Year fixed effects	Y	Y	Y	Y	Y	Y
R-squared	0.243	0.239	0.238	0.247	0.246	0.246
N	250	250	250	250	250	250

NOTE: Robust standard errors clustered at the state level are reported in parentheses. * significant at the 0.10 level; ** significant at the 0.05 level; *** significant at the 0.01 level; **** significant at the 0.001 level. Y = yes.
SOURCE: Developed by the authors using ACS data.

Table 6.7 shows the relationship between the statutes and the growth of employment for dentists in the state. The estimates show that giving greater autonomy to hygienists is associated with a significantly negative 26 percent employment growth of dentists. Since the average growth rate of dentists' employment is 2 percent, having a law that allows hygienists to have an independent business would reduce dentists' growth rate to about 1.5 percent. This is a small absolute amount. Since hygienists and dentists are often substitutes for each other in the production of dental services, the state provisions favoring hygienists may reduce the need for dentists in the state. In order to test for the robustness and sensitivity of the results, estimates show two cases involving the role of the DHPPI in the earnings of dental assistants who are not universally licensed and have different requirements from dental hygienists, and they found no influence on their earnings in the ACS of the index to include market structure. In another test case, estimates were performed for another robustness check using data from the ACS for registered nurses, who have another set of statutes influencing the market structure for their occupation. The estimates showed that the DHPPI had no influence on the earnings of registered nurses. These results suggest that the estimates were not a consequence of other factors that were not captured by the state fixed effects.

Since the results suggest elements of monopsony as shown in the theory, there are also potential redistribution effects and economic losses within the context of both occupations being licensed. If there is no reduction in the quality of services that are provided to patients with fewer regulations in dentistry, then an application of a deadweight loss analysis can give the basic parameters to estimate potential losses to society from monopsony in the market (Kleiner and Kudrle 2000). Using the parameters developed from the results in the earlier tables, Box 6.1 shows that the reallocation from hygienists to dentists is approximately $1.34 billion per year. The output loss due to the monopsonistic restriction of employment is approximately $0.08 billion per year. The output loss due to licensing is between $0.54 and $0.68 billion per year. Therefore, the total losses associated with overall occupational licensing and within-occupation regulation are between $0.62 and $0.76 billion annually. This results in approximately a 1 percent annual reduction in the output of dental services for those states that required dentists' supervision of dental hygienists, using a basic deadweight loss analysis (Car-

Box 6.1 A Static Simulation of the Effects of State Regulations on U.S. Dental Service Costs

Estimates of U.S. dental service expenditures:
- U.S. dental service expenditures are approximately $96.36 billion (Centers for Medicare and Medicaid Services 2008).
- Labor costs account for 60 percent of health care spending (Schwieters and Harper 2007).
- Dental hygienists account for approximately 23.2 percent of the total labor costs (from the ratio of the average hourly earnings of dentists and hygienists in Table 6.3).
- Therefore, labor costs for hygienists are approximately $13.40 billion (= $96.36 billion × 0.60 × 0.232), which is rectangle $w^M O L^M M$ (= $w^M \times L^M$) in Figure 6.2.

Analysis of monopsonistic exploitation and deadweight loss using basic demand analysis:
- Monopsonistic exploitation (rectangle $w^L w^M M M'$ in Figure 6.2).
- ° We substitute the estimates of 0.100 for $(W^L - W^M)/W^M$ and 0.061 for $(L^L - L^M)/L^M$ (from Tables 6.4 and 6.6).
- ° Then, we are able to compute the reallocation from hygienists to dentists (rectangle $w^M w^L M' M$) as follows: $(w^L - w^M) \times L^M = 0.100\ w^M \times L^M = 0.100 \times \$13.40$ billion = $1.34 billion.
- ° Although we cannot compute a deadweight loss because of the restrictions (i.e., triangle AML as a whole), we can approximate it with triangle $M'ML$ by multiplying by two. Then, the deadweight loss due to the monopsonistic employment restriction is $(w^L - w^M) \times (L^L - L^M) = 0.100\ w^M \times 0.061\ L^M = 0.100 \times 0.061 \times \$13.40$ billion = $0.08 billion.

- Licensing effect
- ° To compute the licensing effect, we compute hygienists' total revenue (rectangle $w^L O L^L L$ in Figure 6.2). For this, we only need to compute rectangle $M L^M L^L L'$ as follows: $(L^L - L^M) \times w^M = 0.061\ L^M \times w^M = 0.061 \times \$13.40$ billion = $0.82 billion.
- ° Then, hygienists' total revenue is $15.64 billion (= $13.40 billion + $1.34 billion + $0.08 billion + $0.82 billion).

(continued)

Box 6.1 (continued)

○   Given that the licensing premium is 15 percent economy-wide
   (Kleiner and Krueger 2010), then the reallocation from consumers
   to hygienists' services is $2.35 billion (= 0.15 × $15.64 billion).
○   Also, given that the mean value of demand elasticity of labor is 0.3
   (Hamermesh 1993), the deadweight loss due to licensing (i.e., triangle *LL"C* in Figure 6.2) should be about $0.70 billion. If only 80
   percent is deadweight (Carneiro, Heckman, and Vytlacil 2009), then
   it would be more like $0.56 billion.

•   The total output losses would be $0.56 to $0.70 billion because of
   licensing plus the monopsony effect of $0.08 billion, which equals
   $0.64 to $0.78 billion.

SOURCE: Authors' calculations.

neiro, Heckman, and Vytlacil 2009). This analysis does not include the misallocation of resources within production or the losses to consumers who allocated their resources toward dentistry and away from other purchases (Schmidt 2012).

REVIEW AND SUMMARY

The licensing of occupations is most pervasive among health care occupations. This chapter has examined two occupations—dentists and dental hygienists—that are universally licensed in all 50 states in the United States. Initially the chapter explored the evolution of licensing for these two occupations, as well as the legal conditions governing per-missible tasks for hygienists that affect both occupations. Conflict has arisen over the allocation of work and the supervision of tasks. Next the chapter developed the anatomy and timing, by state, of the implemen-tation of regulations that guide the work that each of the occupations can legally do according to state statutes and administrative decisions. Given this institutional background, we developed a basic model of dental production that has elements of occupational licensing favoring dentists in the production of services for patients. The results from the model show that regulations requiring dentists to supervise hygienists result in higher earnings for dentists and lower earnings and employment for dental hygienists. The model is extended to show that it has elements of monopsony that can result in potential deadweight losses to society if licensing and these monopsony rents are pervasive.

The estimates from the empirical models show the influence of regulations that favor tasks that hygienists can perform on the wages and employment of dentists and hygienists for the period 2001–2007. During this time period, hygienists were allowed to do more tasks, and in seven states they were allowed to work without the supervision of a dentist. The time and state fixed-effects models for both dentists and hygienists show that fostering greater autonomy by legally allowing hygienists to work independently of dentists is associated with an approximately 10 percent higher wage and a 6 percent increase in the employment growth of dental hygienists. Conversely, these state provisions are associated with approximately a 16 percent reduction in dentists' hourly earnings and a 26 percent reduction in dentists' employment growth in the states that have adopted them. In part, this larger loss by dentists is a result of the change in the service and product mix that is delivered by hygienists as compared to full-service dental offices. In a simple deadweight loss analysis consistent with a monopsony model, the typical state would lose approximately 1 percent of dental expenditures because of licensing and by not allowing hygienists to practice on their own. These estimates are lower-bound estimates, and the loss to society is likely higher.

Overall, the results suggest that state laws on permissible tasks matter in wage and employment determination for both dentists and hygienists. With occupational licensing, the final arbiter of who gets to do the work is the responsibility of the state legislature and the courts. The decisions by these policymakers appear to influence wage and employment outcomes for practitioners in the occupations. One could also examine, in the manner outlined in this chapter, additional potential conflicts for licensed occupations, such as architects and interior designers or doctors and nurses, arising from the issue of who can legally do certain tasks.

Notes

1. I thank Kyoung Won Park for his assistance with this chapter, which is based on and uses material from Kleiner and Park (2010a).
2. We note that this component also includes other provisions, such as whether a hygienist may be self-employed other than as an independent contractor. We separated this provision from the other components and treat it as a qualitatively different variable in our empirical analysis.
3. The correlations among the major components of the original DHPPI range from 0.56 to 0.96, and their intercorrelation (i.e., Cronbach's alpha) is 0.77. Although the correlations among the two summated ratings of task permitted and self-employment range from 0.50 to 0.75 and their intercorrelation is 0.67, the correlations among the two Rasch indices and self-employment range from 0.41 to 0.73, and their intercorrelation is 0.51.
4. We choose to analyze the ACS as our main data set over alternative data sets such as the CPS, because the use of the ACS over time allows us to have enough observations by state to fully implement the empirical model, which requires state and year controls. For a detailed sampling framework of the ACS, see U.S. Census Bureau (2013).
5. Although an alternative specification might be a difference-in-difference approach, the data available do not track the same individuals over time by state. However, our ability to control for time and state fixed effects suggests that our policy variables influence wages for each occupation beyond state- or time-varying characteristics.
6. As a further test of the reliability of our employment data, we correlated the data from the Occupational Employment Statistics (OES) with membership data from the ADHA by state for 2002–2006 and with the number of active dentists in 2006 from the ADA. Their correlation was 0.92 and 0.96, respectively. This suggests that the OES is an appropriate measure of dentists' and hygienists' employment by state and year.

7
Lessons from Studies on the Stages of Occupational Regulation

The essential task of democratic society is to establish a proper balance between freedom and order. A danger in modern democracy is the threat of overthrowing the equilibrium either by excessive emphasis on governmental regulation on the one hand or by the irresponsibility and inequalities of completely unregulated freedom on the other hand.

Flowing directly from this major concern of democratic government and more immediately pertinent to the problems involved in state licensing of occupations is the role of government in reconciling public and special interests. Ours is a society in which organized special groups are in conflict with each other not only in serving their own private interests but over the very definition of what constitutes the public interest. Much of the business of state administration therefore consists in reconciling the demands of special groups upon government. These interest groups compete with one another in attempting to bring public policy into conformity with their own particular objectives.

—Council of State Governments (1952, p. 1)

INTRODUCTION

The purpose of the book has been to examine several occupations that are at different stages of government regulation and determine to what extent licensing has influenced the individuals in the occupation, consumers, or other closely related occupational practitioners. Since governments at the local, state, and national levels are confronted with the interests of the members of the occupations and, in rare cases, consumers of the services seeking more regulation, the goal of this book is to provide new analysis and evidence on how these labor markets work in the face of government regulations. With the decline of union membership and the growth of employment in the service sector, workers and their agents (unions or professional associations) have attempted to establish a "web of rules" to regularize work and reduce competition in the field (Dunlop 1958). The book has provided a number of case studies that examine how licensing has affected interior designers, mortgage brokers, preschool teachers, electricians and plumbers, and dentists and hygienists. Along a continuum moving from less to more regulation, the book has traced the regulatory development of interior designers, the least-regulated occupation, and that of dentists and hygienists, both universally licensed occupations.

As stated in Chapter 1 as part of the introduction to this volume, the stages of regulation are an arbitrary and, in some ways, a limited way of looking at the sequence of regulation. The approach utilizes not merely the uniformities in the sequence of regulation but also the uniqueness of each occupation's experience with regulation (Rostow 1960). The volume also examined the tension that exists between the occupations over the "span of control" of job tasks that are regulated by the state. Occupations that have been regulated for a relatively short period of time and have minimal requirements for entry are usually unable to achieve their economic goals of better compensation and less competition. For the other selected occupations, the more heavily regulated occupations have been licensed for a longer time and have attained more rigorous entry requirements, which have led to higher earnings and more voice in the economic conditions of the tasks.

A common thread throughout the volume included showing the growth of regulation and its variations over time across a wide variety of occupations. Each chapter depicted the influence of increased regulation on the wages of the occupations and, where the data were available, its employment effects. The research also showed several unique aspects, including outcomes for consumers in the case of regulation of mortgage brokers and outcomes for children whose preschool teachers and their assistants were licensed. Another unique aspect of the analysis is the examination of occupations such as those of dentists and hygienists, who battle with regulators over who gets to do the regulated work. A further innovation is the examination of how regulations may influence the number of injuries and deaths of plumbers and electricians, two occupations that have among the highest work-related injuries. Overall, there is a common theme throughout the volume, yet each chapter delves into the unique aspects of a particular occupation, how it is regulated, and the economic consequences of the corresponding regulations.

OVERARCHING FINDINGS

This section summarizes the key findings for each of the occupations studied in this volume, starting with the least regulated and progressing to the most regulated ones. Initially, this section examines the role of regulation in influencing the wages and employment for interior designers (the subject of Chapter 2), who are licensed in three states and the District of Columbia. For occupations at this initial stage of regulation, where certification rather than licensing dominates, there is conflicting evidence as to whether regulation raises wages or does much to improve quality. National data from the American Community Survey (ACS) from 2000 to 2009 show that regulation and the licensing of interior designers had a small and insignificant influence on overall wage determination. An examination of the employment growth of interior designers during the same time period shows that regulation had a small influence on employment growth, once state economic characteristics were taken into account. Furthermore, the economic factors available for our analysis were not important in determining whether a law was passed. Perhaps the organizational or political skills of the leaders of the profession were the more important factors in determining whether interior designers were licensed.

In Chapter 3, the occupation of mortgage broker was examined. The evaluation of the occupation introduces and summarizes a compilation of mortgage broker licensing requirements from the 50 states and the District of Columbia for the period 1996–2006. The data are used to analyze whether mortgage broker licensing or any of its components have significant relationships with labor or service market outcomes. Investigation of the index constructed to measure the difficulty of entering the profession shows that regulations in general do not significantly affect labor market or consumer market outcomes.

One regulation common in many states—that mortgage brokers maintain a surety bond or a minimum net worth—has a significant and

fairly consistent statistical association with higher wages, fewer brokers, fewer subprime mortgages, higher foreclosure rates on subprime
mortgages, and a higher percentage of mortgages carrying high interest rates. This result is often viewed as a counterintuitive finding by
those who suggest that occupational regulation either does not matter
or can have positive influences on labor markets and consumer financial
well-being.

The analysis of preschool education regulation takes on an industry
that is in both the public and private sectors. The regulation of child
care services is at an early stage of development in terms of both the
number of states that require it and the standards to be licensed. In addition, enforcement is lax. The estimates presented in Chapter 4 fail to
find any evidence that the wages of child care workers are affected by
government regulation. This finding is not surprising, since the requirements are both relatively new and at low levels. However, there is some,
albeit not conclusive, evidence of the cost effects of regulation on child
care enrollment. Unfortunately, no reliable price data were available in
the surveys examined to evaluate this issue in more detail. One potential benefit of increased regulation is an increase in the educational
attainment quality of child care, which was measured by child development and early childhood academic achievement scores. Data from the
Early Childhood Longitudinal Study–Birth and Kindergarten cohorts
(ECLS-B and ECLS-K) as well as the National Longitudinal Survey of
Youth (NLSY), three major government databases, show some effect of
center-based regulation, but no effect of occupational regulation on any
improvement in early childhood academic achievement scores—that
is, math and reading scores—due to occupational regulations. At these
levels of regulation and in this industry, the regulation of child care is
unlikely to show much influence. If regulation does little to change costs
through wages or change enrollment patterns or educational attainment,
there are few reasons to enact the low levels of licensing that were measured and used in this segment of the book. This is especially the case
if these regulations result in governmental monitoring or in fees that
do not seem to generate many benefits to either workers or children.
Furthermore, the estimates show that occupational regulations have no
measurable influence on national test scores. The additional costs may
be more regulatory agencies, with few observable benefits.

Chapter 5 presented an analysis and a discussion of the role of regulation for two blue-collar occupations in the construction industry—namely, plumbers and electricians. The central findings of the chapter show that certain occupational licensing requirements, such as minimum age, education, and exam requirements, raise the wages of electricians by about 6 to 8 percent. However, the results for plumbers are murky and not consistent. Beyond that, the estimates suggest a modest trade-off between wages and work-related injuries for electricians, a result that is consistent with economic theory that dates back to Adam Smith's work from the late 1700s, which states that employers needed to compensate workers for unpleasant or dangerous tasks (Smith 1937). Local licensing of electricians is associated with approximately a 12 percent wage premium beyond state regulations, suggesting a further influence of local regulations on the occupation. Neither the estimates for electricians nor those for plumbers show much evidence of a systematic influence of occupational licensing on the injury rates, severity of injuries, or death rates. Overall, regulation is shown to have a significant impact on wages for electricians but no discernible effect on increasing safety in this occupation.

Chapter 6 examined the potential conflict between two universally licensed occupations—namely, dental hygienists and dentists. The discussion and analysis initially explored the evolution of state regulation for both occupations and the battle lines that have evolved between the two fields. Next, the chapter showed the anatomy of state regulations for dental hygienists over time. The empirical section examined the influence of state regulations on hygienists' earnings and specifically on the ability of hygienists to be self-employed. This change in regulations is shown to be associated with an earnings increase of approximately 10 percent. Furthermore, when hygienists are able to work without the supervision of a dentist, there is an associated increase in the state-level employment growth of hygienists, but a decrease in the employment growth and earnings for dentists. Estimated economic costs were developed that showed the potential overall losses to society of these legislative and internal administrative battles for control of regulatory decisions on markets.

In order to succinctly summarize the findings presented in this book, Table 7.1 gives the level of occupational regulation of each of the occupations examined. Next, the table shows the results for the labor market, and if applicable the effects for consumers or other outcome measures. The overarching results show that as an occupation increases its coverage and the time it has been regulated, it enhances its ability to raise wages and reduce employment growth. This is because occupational licensing boards, which are usually controlled by members of the occupation, can limit supply and capture jobs for the licensed occupation. Also, as with previous studies of the influence of occupational regulation, there appears to be little to no influence on outcomes as measured by consumer welfare or the safety of workers on the job.

Regulation of Other Occupations

Since the publication of my previous book, *Licensing Occupations: Ensuring Quality or Restricting Competition?* (Kleiner 2006), other researchers have implemented studies for a number of occupations. This section will report on many of them. With the growth of licensing to almost 30 percent of the U.S. workforce, the number of occupations that have become licensed and the requirements for both initial entry and migration from other states have increased (Kleiner and Krueger 2010; U.S. Department of the Treasury and U.S. Department of Defense 2012; Bielick et al. 2013). For the most part, the examination of these occupations has been limited to those that are universally licensed. For example, studies of the labor market effects have been implemented on engineers, barbers, lawyers, real estate agents, nurses and doctors, and teachers. The results suggest that the impact on training and labor supply of occupational licensing may be fairly small (Klee 2010). Consequently, any workforce development benefits of occupational licensing may be small in comparison to the overall costs in other areas. Fewer studies have examined occupations that are licensed in some states and not in others. For example, massage therapists and radiologic technologists are licensed in some states and show variations in regulations on a state-by-state basis.

The policy issue of the restriction of geographic mobility because of licensing has been a long-standing topic of interest to academics and policymakers, because it raises wages and also can influence labor supply in states (Kleiner, Gay, and Greene 1982). More recently, top policymakers have noted that restrictions of geographic mobility can

Table 7.1 Summary of Key Findings in the Volume

Occupation	Level of occupational regulation	Labor market effects	Other
Interior designers	Low	None to modest wage and employment effects	Efforts at the state level to become universally licensed
Mortgage brokers	Low to moderate	Modest wage and employment effects	Recent moves to gain universal licensing; more regulation has murky effects on consumers
Preschool instructors and related assistants	Moderate	Modest to no wage effects	Movement to universal licensing; little evidence of major influence on academic performance
Electricians and plumbers	High	Moderate wage effects	Movement to make regulations more stringent; little evidence of any influence on worker safety
Dentists and dental hygienists	Universal	Moderate to high wage effects	Relaxed regulations result in gains for hygienists at the expense of dentists

have a particularly severe impact on military families (U.S. Department of the Treasury and U.S. Department of Defense 2012). The same set of restrictions can also limit individuals from moving to accept jobs and can contribute to higher structural unemployment levels. To the extent that mobility is restricted across states through occupational licensing, access is reduced and labor market outcomes are potentially affected. Furthermore, as the stages of regulation advance, the ability of regulators to limit geographic mobility is likely to grow.

Universally Licensed Occupations

Included in the list of universally licensed occupations that have been analyzed in some detail are lawyers, teachers, and nurses. These occupations are at the highest stage of occupational regulation. A body of evidence is developing on the impact of occupational licensing similar to the work on the influence of unions on relative wages that was pioneered by H. Gregg Lewis at the University of Chicago over several decades (Lewis 1986). For example, the influence of tougher licensing statutes on lawyers—an occupation that is among the most visible universally licensed occupations—occurs upon entry. Mario Pagliero shows that the difficulty of the law exam or the passage rate significantly affects the number of new lawyers that enter a state. Furthermore, the ability for state bar exams to set tougher standards (and hence affect outcomes) influences the number of potential new entrants into the legal profession. As was found in earlier analysis by Maurizi, attorneys respond to labor market fluctuations by varying the bar exam pass rate (Maurizi 1974; Kleiner 1990; Pagliero 2010).

Another universally licensed occupation that has recently received attention is that of public school teachers. Some studies on the licensing of teachers have examined the influence of licensing on wages, whereas others have focused on the educational attainment of students (Kleiner and Petree 1988; Angrist and Guryan 2003; Kleiner 2011; Larsen 2012). Overall, in the public sector, licensing generally shows modest effects on the wages of teachers and no influence on average student achievement (Goldhaber and Brewer 2000). Larsen examines the distributional effects across wealthy and lower-income school districts. He finds no influence of tougher licensing for lower-income school districts, but some positive effects of tougher regulation from higher test scores for higher-income school districts. At least for public school teachers, the influence of more rigorous licensing results in somewhat higher wages and little effect on quality, both of which tend to favor more wealthy districts.

Nurses make up a universally licensed occupation that has had to work under the supervision of physicians. Nurses became regulated much later than physicians. By 1923, all 48 states had certification legislation that required practitioners to meet certain qualifications in order to use the title of nurse (Comer 2007). New York enacted the first mandatory licensure legislation for nurses in 1947. Marks and Law (2012) ask whether, during the transition from certification, which the last state had adopted in 1923, to licensing, which occurred largely after 1950, there were any wage and employment effects for the occupation. To examine the issue, they use individual-level census data on registered and practical nurses in the United States from 1950 to 1970. As part of their analysis, they take advantage of a quasi experiment made possible by the fact that, by the beginning of the sample period, all states already had certification in place and some states already required a license. During the subsequent decade, several states switched from certification to a mandatory licensing regime, while others did not. Accordingly, Marks and Law infer the effect of licensure in a difference-in-differences framework that uses states that did not change their regulatory regime as a control. They find that the shift from certification to mandatory licensing had no effect on the wages or the participation rate of practical and registered nurses. Since they only examine the period immediately after the switch, it may be that it takes some time for the full effect of the transition to take place. Moreover, the grandfathering in of the incumbent practitioners may also have played a role in the lack of a finding of wage effects in the transition to more rigorous regulations.

A within-state analysis of a universally licensed occupation was implemented by Powell and Vorotnikov (2012). In their study within Massachusetts, they examined the effects of a continuing education requirement that was added to real estate licensing laws in 1999. According to the authors, the Massachusetts Association of Realtors lobbied for the change, stating that it would enhance the quality of service for the public. Powell and Vorotnikov's estimates do not find any improvement in the quality of service as measured by complaints to the real estate licensing board. However, the adoption of continuing education requirements reduced the number of licensed active agents by between 39 and 58 percent and increased the incomes of those who remained by between 11 and 17 percent. These estimates are in line with other results of the influence of tougher licensing laws in other occupations (Kleiner and Todd 2007).

Among the longest-standing generally licensed occupations in all states is that of barbers (only the state of Alabama does not fund its licensing board, though the legislation to repeal licensing did not pass). Licensing of barbers began in the late 1800s, starting with the state of Minnesota in 1897 and then spreading to other states with the assistance of the barbers union. Although estimates of the positive impact of licensing on barbers' wages vary, the most current estimates suggest an impact on wages of between 11 and 22 percent (Kleiner 2006; Timmons and Thornton 2010).

Finally, a unique case is the regulated and universally licensed occupation of engineers. The regulation of the occupation is unique because only a small percentage, usually estimated at less than 20 percent, of the members of the occupation are licensed by states. Hur, Kleiner, and Wang (2013) present a comprehensive analysis of the role of occupational licensing on the labor market for civil, electrical, and industrial engineers. These three branches of engineering account for the largest number of engineers covered by occupational licensing statutes in the United States. The empirical section shows that licensing for these occupations grew more rigorous from 1995 to 2009. The estimates from the statistical models of the engineering labor market find that the more regulated engineers earn slightly higher wages but have modestly lower employment growth.

Although the regulation of engineers may provide a consistent set of guidelines for entering the occupation and potential economic rents for engineers, it may also reduce the variation in their numbers within and across states. Although the standards are clear, regulation may reduce innovation coming from engineers with new and different kinds of training that do not fit easily into the traditional ways that licensing requires tasks to be completed. In addition, it has the potential to result in higher wages for engineers and slower employment growth in the occupation. A possible consequence of the growth of regulation of the occupation may be to reduce access to engineers by their customers, as well as to slow down the ability of builders and manufacturers to use their vital services in the U.S. economy.

The influence of universally licensed occupations serves to drive up wages and reduce the new entrants into the occupation. Their effect is similar to the closed shop provisions that were outlawed under the Taft-Hartley Act (1947), which amended the National Labor Relations Act; these provisions had allowed only union members to apply for jobs. In other words, licensing limits employment opportunities. As has been shown in the union wage literature, the impact of "monopoly unions" is to raise wages and reduce employment (Lewis 1986). In the case of unions, these outcomes can be a direct influence of natural monopolies in the product market or private sector negotiation strategies that lead to market advantages for unions. On the other hand, occupational licensing can create government-sanctioned monopolies that may be granted for health and safety reasons, and that can also result in control over the labor market by the occupation. A goal of the policy planner is to maximize the health and safety component and minimize the monopoly aspect of regulation (Freeman and Medoff 1985). Whereas unions can restrict the supply of labor for a specific firm, licensing in the long run can limit the number of practitioners in an economy and thereby reduce the supply of practitioners, especially as the stages of regulation advance.

Partially Licensed Occupations

More recently, occupations that are licensed in some states and not in others have been analyzed. As an example, the economic effects of the regulation of massage therapists have been examined (Thornton and Timmons 2013). Governmental regulation of massage therapists has grown, but regulation also varies across states. As of 2010, of the 48 contiguous states—the states for which the authors could obtain data—36 require massage therapists to be licensed, five require certification, and only seven still have no form of state regulation of the profession. In some of these seven states, however, regulation exists at the local government level. States that license massage therapists mandate certain education requirements such as passing an examination, fulfilling a minimum number of continuing education credits, and the payment of licensing fees. Thornton and Timmons find that licensing massage therapists raises their hourly earnings by almost 16 percent and reduces the ratio of massage therapists per capita by state.

Timmons and Thornton (2008) also examine the occupation of radiologic technologists, another occupation that is licensed in some states. They evaluate the influence that state licensing has on radiologic technologists' wages with a unique data set that allows them to control for place of work and job specialization. The authors' estimates find that radiologic technologists working in states with licensing statutes earn from 3.3 to 6.9 percent more than radiologic technologists working in states without licensing. Their estimates provide further support for the effects of occupational licensing on the wages of practitioners.

Although the evidence is more limited as to the influence of licensing where only some states regulate the occupation, the evidence cited in this book suggests that licensing laws in a state raise the wages of the regulated practitioners relative to those in unregulated states. Not surprisingly, the estimates vary depending on the service market conditions for the occupations. Although the empirical evidence is not nearly as strong as in the case of universal licensing, the effects for occupations that are partially licensed suggest that conditions in the service market are critical in determination of any monopoly effects, and that there are occupation-specific conditions that largely dominate the economic outcomes. As occupations are able to cross the threshold to higher stages of regulation, they are more likely to be able to gain economic benefits.

INFLUENCE ON THE QUALITY OF THE SERVICE

Several recent studies have focused on the quality effects of occupational licensing. The subjects of these studies cover everything from floral arrangements to educational attainment to well-baby exams. In the first example, Carpenter (2011) conducted a field experiment on the influence of the licensing of florists on the quality of floral arrangements. "Floral experts" in Louisiana assessed the quality of floral arrangements and found that licensed florists in that state did not produce better-quality floral arrangements than their counterparts in Texas, where florists are not licensed. However, the flower arrangements in

Louisiana, regulated by the state, cost more for the same product and service than in Texas.

A study by Larsen (2012), discussed earlier in this chapter, obtains empirical results for public education that support the basic theoretical analysis of the Shapiro model, which says that licensing assists those who prefer higher-quality services and who usually have higher incomes, more than those who prefer lower-quality services and who on average have lower incomes. That is, students in lower-income but highly licensed school districts do not do better on test scores, but students in wealthier districts that are regulated obtain higher scores on the standardized tests that are used as outcome measures.

A final study by Kleiner et al. (2012) examines the role of relaxing occupational licensing requirements on both wage determination and the price of medical services. The researchers investigate how these regulations may affect wages and the cost of providing certain types of medical services using two methods. First, they use data from the 2002–2007 ACS to study how changes in state licensing regulations have influenced the wages of nurse practitioners and physicians. Second, analyzing a large database of private health insurance claims for "well-child" exams, they estimate the effect of the regulation changes on the prices of medical services included in the exam that insurance companies actually pay for. They find that the wages of nurses are increased by legally allowing nurse practitioners to do more tasks, and that prices of the service examined can be reduced by relaxing the licensing requirements. No evidence of a decline in quality of services was found using mortality or malpractice insurance rates.

WHEN DO REGULATIONS REALLY BITE?

Since many of the results in this book show that for occupations that are at early stages of regulation, such as interior designers and preschool teachers, regulation has either no or, at best, modest effects on wage determination, then at what stage does regulation matter? This section will show when influences of occupational regulation may affect wage determination. In my previous book, *Licensing Occupations: Ensuring*

Quality or Restricting Competition? (Kleiner 2006), I presented evidence that occupations that have been regulated for long time periods, such as those of dentists and lawyers, also have significant returns over occupations that are not regulated. In addition, Timmons and Thornton (2010) find large economic gains for lesser-educated occupations such as barbers that have been licensed for decades. The basic case study evidence in the United States suggests that licensing raises wages over time. Additional analysis of interior designers, discussed in Chapter 2, shows that there is a positive and significant effect of duration since the passage of more restrictive licensing laws on wage determination (Kleiner and Vorotnikov 2012).

Further economy-wide evidence of the influence of the longevity of licensure laws on wage determination is provided by a recent report for the British government that examines the role of occupational licensing on wage determination in the United Kingdom (Bryson et al. 2012). In general, the authors find that the overall wage effects of licensing in the UK are similar to those in the United States, but that for those occupations that were recently regulated, the impacts were minor. However, as shown in Table 7.2, the longer the occupations were able to reduce competition and limit the supply of practitioners, the more the influence of regulation increased. For example, the influence of licensing increased only slightly for those occupations that were licensed in the 1990s relative to ones that were regulated within the past 10 years, by a statistically insignificant 4 percent. However, occupations that were licensed prior to 1990, dating back to before 1950, were associated with wage increases from 17 percent to almost 30 percent relative to ones that were licensed during the past 10 years. Although it would be interesting to examine whether similar results hold for the United States, these results for Britain suggest that at initial stages of regulation, wage effects are minimal. Similarly, a quasi random assignment study in the Netherlands of those who got into medical school and became doctors, relative to those who passed the exam for medical school but lost the state-run lottery for admission and did not become doctors, shows a lifetime earnings effect of more than 20 percent. The researchers find that the influence of regulation grows over the lifetime of the physicians (Ketel et al. 2012). As licensing becomes more established and more individuals within the occupation are subject to the entry and continuing education aspects of regulations, then the wage effects are more

Table 7.2 Regression Estimates for Wage Determination among British Workers in Licensed Occupations, by Length of Time Licensed in the UK

Year became licensed[a]	Occupations with universal licensing ln(wage/hour)
Before 1950	0.261***
	[4.88]
1950–1979	0.297***
	[5.24]
1980–1989	0.169***
	[2.64]
1990–1999	0.042
	[0.83]
R-squared	0.41
Observations	10,466

NOTE: t statistics in brackets. * significant at the 0.10 level; ** significant at the 0.05 level; *** significant at the 0.01 level. The model includes standard human capital and other entry requirements.
[a] The reference group consists of those occupations that were licensed between 2000 and 2010.
SOURCE: Bryson et al. (2012).

likely to be pronounced. If these results hold when applied to the United States, then many of the occupations studied in this book will see even greater wage growth than they have experienced to date, and the costs of using their services will likely rise the longer they are licensed and the more the stages of regulation advance.

ARE LICENSING REQUIREMENTS COMPLEMENTS OR SUBSTITUTES FOR UNIONIZATION?

Recent evidence demonstrates that despite relatively favorable economic and political conditions during the 1990s, trade union membership and influence in the United States continued to remain low (Hirsch 2012). At the same time, different forms of occupational regulation such as registration, certification, and licensing are growing dramatically. Economists have long recognized the economic effects of occupational regulation and have commonly compared them to those of unionization (Kleiner and Krueger 2010).

Based on this analysis, the argument has been made that although both of those labor market institutions can be understood as mechanisms by which supply restrictions can be achieved, their relative success in rent extraction differs (Koumenta, Humphris, and Kleiner 2011). Although the wage effects of union membership and licensing attainment are similar in the United States, the market conditions within which these labor market institutions operate are more favorable for the growth of licensing than of unions (e.g., low employer dependency, coverage for the employee's work life). For example, employers generally are not dependent on a licensed workforce, and are not generally opposed if some members of their workforce have a license. In addition, once an individual becomes licensed, that employee is more likely to maintain that status throughout his or her work life. Koumenta, Humphris, and Kleiner suggest that because of the fall in societal collectivism, registration, certification, and licensing are "products" more employees want, and that employee membership is associated with a variety of desirable private goods with little scope for free riding (Olson 1965). Licensing is organized around "professional identities" and is often associated with professionalization and up-skilling, which makes it attractive to low-skilled occupational groups. Finally, state and employer attitudes toward licensing are much more favorable than toward unions. For example, the state receives more revenue relative to the cost of monitoring, and licensing is a potential source of hidden taxes, since the state can raise the cost of licensing permits with little public backlash.

For firms, licensing creates the perception of higher-quality services without the potential constraints that unions impose on the workplace. Furthermore, licensed engineers or accountants, although they may have high hourly earnings or costs, still make up a small percentage of the overall costs of labor to the firm, resulting in much less employer opposition to licensing than to unionization, where employers must pay a negotiated wage to all employees. For many occupations such as teachers and nurses, licensing and unionization are clearly complements. Moreover, being both licensed and in a union raises the wage premium to 22 percent, from about 15 percent for only being licensed (Kleiner and Krueger 2010). However, being covered by a collective bargaining agreement results in higher wage gains than being covered by a licensing law (Gittleman and Kleiner 2013). But here again, being covered by both collective bargaining and a licensing law, according to Gittleman and Kleiner, results in the largest wage gains. Nevertheless, against a backdrop of declining union influence and membership, occupational regulation largely serves as a labor market substitute rather than as a complement to unionization in a more service-oriented economy. Certainly, unions in certain occupations can use licensing to provide elements of a closed shop, where the individuals who are hired must be licensed in order to work there. Where these conditions exist, unions have been shown to raise wages. The same can be said for those who attain occupational licensing.

POLICY PERSPECTIVES

Although occupational licensing has been growing, several proposals have been made to slow the growth of occupational licensing in favor of certification. For example, in Minnesota, in both 2011 and 2012, the legislature passed a bill out of the Minnesota Senate Commerce and Consumer Protection Committee that explicitly favors certification over licensing. The bill states that "no government shall require an occupational license, certification, registration, or other occupational regulation that imposes a substantial burden on the person unless the government demonstrates that it has a compelling interest in protecting against present and recognizable harm to the public health and safety, and [that] the regulation is the least restrictive means to furthering that compelling government interest."[1] In addition, the proposed bill states that "an individual who brings an action or asserts a defense under this section has the initial burden of proof that the statute or administrative rule or a government practice related to the statute or rule substantially burdens the individual's right to engage in an occupation not prohibited by law. If the individual meets the burden of proof . . . the government must then demonstrate by clear and convincing evidence that the government has a compelling interest in protecting against present and recognizable harm to the public health and safety, and [that] the regulation is the least restrictive means for furthering that compelling governmental interest." Legislation covering similar issues has been introduced in the Utah Legislature (Goldstein 2012). This proposed Minnesota statute is an example of model legislation on occupational licensing and is currently being proposed by the Institute for Justice (IJ), a libertarian public interest law firm that has handled numerous cases for individuals who have challenged occupational licensing laws in the courts because they have not been allowed to work as a consequence of such laws. Appendix D presents the IJ model legislation that the proposed Minnesota statute largely follows.

The proposed Minnesota statute goes a long way toward favoring a policy of the least possible regulation of occupations by the government, and it allows the courts to determine whether an individual has been harmed, with the largest burden of proof being on the state to show that there are compelling health and safety issues for the members of the occupation to be licensed. In other words, the burden of proof falls on the state or local government to show that there are actual dangers to health and safety. One alleged drawback of the proposed licensing regulation in Minnesota would be the increased litigation costs if individuals who thought that they could do the work, and should be able to do the work, engaged the state in a significant number of lawsuits. The legal costs could be balanced by the reduction in economic rents to the members of the licensed occupations and the increased aggregate output for the services of the new members of the licensed occupations.

One illustration of the extent to which the research on occupational licensing has influenced policy comes from Iowa. In 2013, Governor Terry Branstad vetoed an act that would have licensed four occupations in the health sector. In his veto message to the Speaker of the Iowa House of Representatives, he noted the following: "Licenses serve to increase costs on licensees, increase consumer costs and options, and reduce opportunities for new workers. One of my goals is to grow jobs by eliminating impediments to economic growth imposed by burdensome administrative rules and regulations."[2] Further down his message to the Speaker, Branstad noted the following policy alternative: "Given that the certification process for substance abuse and addictive disorder counseling and prevention professionals is well-functioning and serves the interests of protecting health and public safety, there is no need to add an additional mandated layer of regulation and four new licenses."[3] In his view, certification provided a more cost-effective method of regulation.

Calls to reduce occupational licensing barriers to interstate mobility have come from the executive branch of the federal government, including the U.S. Department of the Treasury and U.S. Department of Defense (2012). These policy recommendations have been made because the families of military personnel have had a difficult time moving across states and pursuing their careers, because of variations in state licensing laws. The Department of Defense views this effect as a hardship on military families. At a minimum, the ability to recognize other states' licenses, similar to the recognition of driver's licenses across states, would serve to help military families as well as greatly assist the economy in general by reducing structural unemployment due to state regulation barriers. It would also allow licensed workers to maximize their incomes and productivity by enabling them to move across state lines without institutional constraints. These legislative efforts to reduce regulatory barriers across states may have increasing support from state or national policymakers.

PROSPECTS FOR FURTHER RESEARCH

Since the publication of my earlier volume on occupational licensing in 2006, the quality and quantity of research on occupational regulation have significantly increased (Kleiner 2006). Some of that work has been cited in this chapter. Nevertheless, many key questions remain unanswered. For example, can we identify whether or when the main monopoly effects of occupational licensing occur? Are there important "voice effects" of licensing for the members of the occupation, similar to those identified in the union literature?[4] To what extent are there estimated benefits of higher quality for consumers? Is innovation in services or products reduced as a consequence of occupational licensing?

To what extent are the personnel policies that apply to the firm applicable within licensed occupations (Lazear and Shaw 2007)? Are these benefits mainly for higher-income consumers, and are there distributional aspects of the allocation of the quality effects of occupational licensing? Do states raise licensing fees to supplement or substitute for other forms of taxation? How often do licensing boards revoke the occupational licenses of incompetent or unscrupulous individuals?

At least two nations in the European Union—Germany and Poland—are moving in a different direction in comparison to the United States and Britain. These two nations have entertained proposals to significantly reduce regulation in their occupational labor markets (Miller 2004; Sendrowicz 2012). In other European countries, such as Finland, Sweden, Denmark, and the Netherlands, an occupation that is usually licensed in the United States (e.g., that of attorneys) is instead certified (Pagliero and Timmons 2012).

In Israel, physicians who came from the former Soviet Union and faced an easier barrier to becoming licensed had substantially higher earnings than physicians from the former Soviet Union who faced a much stiffer barrier. The degree of difficulty in getting licensed was based on experience. Specifically, those with less than 20 years of experience had to take a difficult general medical knowledge licensing exam to become licensed in Israel. This exam had a fairly low pass rate. Consequently, many of these former Soviet physicians did not become practicing doctors in Israel and entered entirely different professions (Kugler and Sauer 2005). Conversely, the physicians with more than 20 years of experience in the Soviet Union were granted an exemption to the exam and issued a temporary general practitioner license for six months. During this period, they were allowed to practice medicine under the observation of native physicians. At the end of the six months, it was nearly certain that the immigrant physicians on the observation track would receive a permanent license.

Do the stages of regulation patterns outlined in this book apply to other certified or licensed occupations? Are there alternative methods that could be applied to the data analyzed in this volume that may result in different statistical or analytical outcomes? Australia is now reevaluating its occupational licensing policies in the context of workforce development to examine whether licensing enhances human capital growth (Cooney 2013). Can licensing influence greater human capital growth in a nation?

How are wages determined or how is quality assessed in geographic areas or political jurisdictions that are often free of state and local government licensing, such as on Native American tribal lands (Harrison et al. 2012)? Are there lessons to be learned in the United States from cross-national comparisons? What are the impacts on licensed and seemingly related unlicensed individuals in the occupation, as well as on consumers? What are the additional costs to the firm of hiring licensed workers (e.g., CPAs or engineers) relative to unlicensed workers over the course of their employment with the firm?

This type of analysis has already been implemented in the academic labor management literature (Lee and Mas 2009). In addition, the dynamics of the organizations involved in the licensing process, from unions to licensing boards, need more detailed examination. In less developed nations, such as in Southeast Asia or Africa, would the effect of occupational licensing for either consumers or licensed practitioners be greater than for consumers or practitioners in more developed nations in North America or Europe?

Although a number of studies examining the price effects of occupational licensing were completed in the 1970s and 1980s, few updates or further examinations of the influence of regulation on prices have occurred since that time (Bond et al. 1980; Cox and Foster 1990). Given the growth of health care costs in particular, what would prices be with less regulation?

An attempt to answer any of the questions just mentioned requires that more and better data be developed. Although detailed regulatory information for occupations is difficult to gather because it involves a detailed examination of local, state, and federal statutes, this work is necessary for a proper examination of the influence of licensing on labor market institutions. Governmental or private nonprofit organizations could serve as depositories of this type of information. Ideally, this would include administrative hearing information, decisions by administrative boards, and key state court decisions on the regulation of occupations. Moreover, data should be maintained by the states and made available to researchers and policy analysts on the number and characteristics of licensed individuals. This information should also be stored and made centrally available for basic research and replication.

The major governmental statistical agencies, such as the Bureau of Labor Statistics, the Bureau of Economic Analysis, and the Census Bureau, should keep administrative files of data on occupational regulation from both individuals and the states. Examples of questions for such data have been developed and tested as part of the Princeton Data

Improvement Initiative (PDII 2008). For example, Kleiner and Krueger (2013) would like to have the following questions included in national government surveys such as the Current Population Survey (CPS), the Survey of Income and Program Participation (SIPP), and the National Longitudinal Survey (Box 7.1).

Including these questions in national government surveys would enhance the ability of citizens and their state and national governments to determine the labor market and service market consequences of various forms of government regulation (Kleiner and Krueger 2013). Recent efforts toward getting some of the data on federal government surveys have been successful, because the SIPP plans to ask similar questions during the 2013 wave of surveys (Boivin 2012). During 2012, states such as Minnesota, New Hampshire, Utah, and Arizona were actively considering legislation that would place more of the burden for justifying licensing statutes on governmental entities rather than on the individuals who were seeking employment. If these states are successful in requiring governmental entities to justify regulations, then more survey

---

Box 7.1 Sample Questions from the Princeton Data Improvement Initiative for a National Government Survey on Occupational Regulation

Do you have a license or certification that is required by a federal, state, or local government agency to do your job?

YES 1

NO .... 2 (Go to Q25)

IN PROCESS/WORKING ON IT..3

Would someone who does not have a license or certificate be legally allowed to do your job?

YES 1

NO 2

Is everyone who does your job eventually required to have a license or certification by a federal, state, or local government agency?

YES 1

NO 2

SOURCE: Princeton Data Improvement Initiative (PDII).

and administrative information will be required on occupational regulation and its effect on consumers. The governmental agencies most able to supply the information are those statistical agencies at the federal level.

The chapter opened with a quotation from the 1952 Council of State Governments report stating that "the essential task of democratic society is to establish a proper balance between freedom and order." In the case of occupational licensing, the evaluation, policymaking, and implementation of this institution of licensing embodies the tension between these two laudable goals of order and freedom. Since licensing influences many more individuals in the United States than unions or the minimum wage, its evaluation should be important for social science researchers, policymakers, and citizens (Kleiner and Krueger 2013). Furthermore, occupational licensing influences the labor market for both licensed and unlicensed practitioners. It also affects the ability of consumers to obtain important services. Moreover, it determines the distribution of those services, both among the well-off and for those in or near poverty. Finally, it helps determine the structure of markets where service market monopolies are provided by government. As the politics of occupational licensing ebb and flow with economic and political trends, it is important to shine the light of data and analysis on the subject to determine both the equity and the efficiency aspects through the various stages of the evolution of occupational licensing.

Notes

1. For a detailed explanation of the statute, see Minnesota H.F. No. 2002, as introduced in the 87th Legislative Session (2011–2012), posted on the state Web site February 1, 2012 (Minnesota State Legislature 2012).
2. Terry E. Branstad to Kraig Paulsen, 26 April 2013, Office of the Governor of Iowa, Des Moines, Iowa. https://governor.iowa.gov/wp-content/uploads/2013/04/4-26-13-Veto-Message-for-HF-569.pdf.
3. Ibid.
4. The term "collective voice effects," as described in Freeman and Medoff (1985), refers to the ability of workers to influence the terms and conditions at work. Similarly, the professions can set standards and pay, as well as determine who can work within licensed jobs.

Appendix A

Details of the Characteristics of Preschool Center-Based and Family-Based Regulation Variables and Index Composition

Appendix Table A.1 Center-Based Regulation Variables and Index Composition

Variable name		Center-based regulation variable description	Index (besides overall)
ageadcdum	1	Min. age for assistant teacher at center = 1 if > 16; 0 otherwise	Development, staff
ageddcdum	2	Minimum age for director at center = 1 if > 18; 0 otherwise	Development, staff
agetdcdum	3	Minimum age for teacher at center = 1 if > 18; 0 otherwise	Development, staff
cdhrsadcdum	4	Min. hours of child development coursework required for aides in center = 1 if > 0	Development, staff
cdhrsddcdum	5	Min. hrs. of child devel. coursework required for director of center = 1 if $\geq$ 180	Development, staff
cdhrstdcdum	6	Min. hours of child develop. coursework req. for assis. teacher at center = 1 if > 0	Development, staff
edadcdum	7	Educ. req. for aide in center in years = 1 if > 8; 0 otherwise	Development, staff, educ
edddcdum	8	Educ. req. for director of center in years = 1 if $\geq$ 14	Development, staff, educ
edtdcdum	9	Educ. req. for teacher at center in years = 1 if > 12	Development, staff, educ
expadcdum	10	Childcare employment experience req. for aide in center in yrs. = 1 if > 0	Development, staff
expddcdum	11	Childcare employment experience required for dir. of center in years = 1 if $\geq$ 2	Development, staff
exptdcdum	12	Childcare employment experience req. for teacher at center in years = 1 if > 0	Development, staff
inftdcdum	13	Amount of indoor space req. per child at facil. (sq. ft.) = 1 if $\geq$ 35	Environment
ongohadcdum	14	Amt. of annual ongoing training req. for aides in center in hrs. = 1 if > 15	Development, staff
ongohddcdum	15	Annual ongoing training required for director of center in hrs. = 1 if > 8	Development, staff
ongohtdcdum	16	Ongoing annual training req. for asst. teacher at center in hrs. = 1 if > 15	Development, staff
outftdcdum	17	Amt. of outdoor space required per child at facil. (sq. ft.) = 1 if > 75	Environment
rat0dcdum	18	Max. child/caregiver for children age 0–11 months = 1 if < 4	Development, ratio
rat1dcdum	19	Max. child/caregiver for children age 12–23 months = 1 if < 5	Development, ratio
rat2dcdum	20	Max. child/caregiver ratio for children age 24–35 months = 1 if < 8	Development, ratio
rat3dcdum	21	Max. child/caregiver ratio for children age 36–47 months = 1 if < 12	Development, ratio
rat4dcdum	22	Max. child/caregiver ratio for children age 48–59 months = 1 if < 12	Development, ratio
rat5dcdum	23	Max. child/caregiver ratio for children age 60+ months = 1 if < 15	Development, ratio

231

size0dcdum	24	Max. group size for age 0–11 months in day care center = 1 if < 12	Development
size1dcdum	25	Max. group size for age 12–23 months in day care center = 1 if < 14	Development
size2dcdum	26	Max. group size for age 24–35 months in day care center = 1 if < 20	Development
size3dcdum	27	Max. group size for age 36–47 months in day care center = 1 if < 30	Development
size4dcdum	28	Max. group size for age 48–59 months in day care center = 1 if < 30	Development
size5dcdum	29	Max. group size for age 60 + months in day care center = 1 if < 32	Development
aiddc	30	Is first-aid certif. required for one or more staff members at day care center?	Health, staff
crimdc	31	Is a criminal background check required for any employees at day care center?	Health, staff
curricdc	32	Do regs. require a developmental program for day care centers?	Development
equipdc	33	Do regs. require developmentally appropriate equip. in day care centers?	Environment
finedc	34	Are fines imposed on day care centers that defy regs. and requirements?	Oversight
healdc	35	Is a health evaluation required for any employees at day care center?	Health
immundc	36	Are children who attend day care centers required to be immunized?	Health
insurdc	37	Is day care center facility required to carry liability insurance?	Health
ongoadc	38	Is annual ongoing training required for aides in day care center?	Development, staff
ongodadc	39	Is annual ongoing training required for director of day care center?	Development, staff
ongotdc	40	Is annual ongoing training required for teacher in day care center?	Development, staff
pickupdc	41	Do regs. indicate that centers may release children only to parents?	Health
preadc	42	Is prev. experience or training required of aide at day care center?	Development, staff
preddc	43	Is prev. experience or training required of director at day care center?	Development, staff
pretdc	44	Is prev. experience or training required of teacher at day care center?	Development, staff
punishdc	45	Is corporal punish. prohibited for all ages of children at day care center?	Health
sickdc	46	Do regs. require sick children to be excluded from child care center?	Health
visitdc	47	Do regs. allow parents free access to kids and facilities in day care center?	Oversight
revokedc	48	Does agency have authority to revoke day care center license?	Oversight

SOURCE: Hotz and Xiao (2011).

Appendix Table A.2 Family-Based Regulation Variables and Index Composition

Variable name		Family-based regulation variable	Index (besides overall)
agedfhdum	1	Min. age for a family daycare provider = 1 if > 18	Development, staff
cdhrsdfhdum	2	Min. hrs. of child devel. training required for family care provider = 1 if > 0	Development, staff
eddfhdum	3	Educ. req. for family day care provider in years = 1 if > 0	Development, staff, educ
inffhdum	4	Amt. of indoor space req. per child at family facility in (sq. ft.) = 1 if > 25	Environment
ongohdfhdum	5	Amt. of annual ongoing training req. for family provider in hrs. = 1 if > 0	Development, staff
outffhdum	6	Amt. of outdoor space req. per child at family facility in (sq. ft.) = 1 if > 0	Environment
rat0fhdum	7	Max. child/caregiver for children age 0–11 months in family based = 1 if < 3	Development, ratio
rat1fhdum	8	Max. child/caregiver for children age 12–23 months in family based = 1 if < 4	Development, ratio
rat2fhdum	9	Max. child/caregiver for children age 24–35 months in family based = 1 if < 6	Development, ratio
rat3fhdum	10	Max. child/caregiver for children age 36–47 months in family based = 1 if < 6	Development, ratio
rat4fhdum	11	Max. child/caregiver for children age 48–59 months in family based = 1 if < 6	Development, ratio
rat5fhdum	12	Max. child/caregiver for children age 60 + months in family based = 1 if < 6	Development, ratio
size0fhdum	13	Max. number of children age 0–11 months allowed in family home = 1 if < 4	Development
size1fhdum	14	Max. number of children age 12–23 months allowed in family home = 1 if < 4	Development
size2fhdum	15	Max. number of children age 24–35 months allowed in family home = 1 if < 6	Development
size3fhdum	16	Max. number of children age 36–47 months allowed in family home = 1 if < 6	Development
size4fhdum	17	Max. number of children age 48–59 months allowed in family home = 1 if < 6	Development
size5fhdum	18	Max. number of children age 60 + months allowed in family home = 1 if < 6	Development
sizetfhdum	19	Max. number of children allowed in family home = 1 if < 6	Development
aidfh	20	Is first-aid certif. required for family day care provider?	Health, staff
crimfh	21	Is a criminal background check required for a family day care provider?	Health, staff
curricfh	22	Do regs. require a developmental program for family homes?	Development

equipfh	23	Do regs. require developmentally appropriate equip. in family homes?	Environment
expdhdum	24	Childcare employment exper. req. for family day care provider in yrs. = 1 if > 0	Development, staff
fencefh	25	Do regs. indicate outdoor play area must be fenced in, family homes?	Health, environment
finefh	26	Are fines imposed on family homes that defy regs. and requirements?	Oversight
firefh	27	Do regs. require fire-health equip. in family homes?	Health
foodfh	28	Do regs. indicate nutritional requirements for meals and snacks, family homes?	Health
healfh	29	Is a health evaluation required for a family day care provider?	Health
immunfh	30	Are children who attend family homes required to be immunized?	Health
insurfh	31	Is family home facility required to carry liability insurance?	Oversight
ongodfh	32	Is annual ongoing training required for family day care provider?	Development, staff
predfh	33	Is training or orientation offered or required for family home providers?	Development, staff
punishfh	34	Is corporal punish. prohibited for all ages of children, family homes?	Health
revokefh	35	Does agency have authority to revoke family home license?	Oversight
sickfh	36	Do regs. require sick children be excluded from family homes?	Health
tranfh	37	Do regs. include spec. instructions for transporting children in family homes?	Health
unannfh	38	Is agency authorized to inspect family home without prior notice?	Oversight
visitfh	39	Do regs. allow parents free access to kids and facilities in family homes?	Oversight

SOURCE: Hotz and Xiao (2011).

Appendix B

Adoption of Occupational Regulations by State Statute for Electricians

Appendix Table B.1 Adoption of Occupational Regulations in State Statute, by State, for Electricians, 1992–2007

State	Year	Type of licensing	General requirement	Apprenticeship	Written exam	Performance exam	Continuous education
Alaska	1992	S	0	1	0	0	0
Alabama	1992	S	0	1	1	1	0
Arizona	1992	S	1	1	1	1	1
Arkansas	1992	S	0	1[a]	1	0	0
California	1992	S	1	1	1	0	0
Colorado	1992	S	0	1[a]	1	0	0
Connecticut	1992	S	1	1	1	0	0
Delaware	1992	L					
	2000	S	0	1	1	0	1
District of Columbia	1992	S	0	0	0	0	0
	1999	S	0	1	1	0	0
Florida	1992	S	1	1	1	0	0
Georgia	1992	S	1	1	1	0	0
Hawaii	1992	S	1	1	1	0	0
Idaho	1992	S	0	1	1	0	0
	1999	S	1	1	1	0	0
Illinois	1992	L					
Indiana	1992	N					
Iowa	1992	L					
	2007	S	0	1	1	0	0
Kansas	1992	L					
Kentucky	1992	L					
	2001	S	0	1[a]	0	0	0

State	Year	Type					
Louisiana	1992	N	0	0	1	0	0
	2004	S	0	1	1	0	0
Maine	1992	S	1	1[a]	1	0	0
Maryland	1992	S					
Massachusetts	1992	N					
	2007	S	1	1	1	0	1
Michigan	1992	S	1	1	1	0	0
Minnesota	1992	S	0	1	1	0	0
Mississippi	1992	S	0	0	1	0	0
Missouri	1992	L					
Montana	1992	S	0	1[a]	1	0	0
Nebraska	1992	S	0	1	0	0	0
Nevada	1992	S	1	1	1	0	0
New Hampshire	1992	S	0	1[a]	1	0	0
New Jersey	1992	S	0	0	0	0	0
	2003	S	1	1	1	0	0
New Mexico	1992	S	1	1	1	0	0
New York	1992	L					
North Carolina	1992	S	1	1[a]	0	0	0
North Dakota	1992	S	0	1[a]	1	0	0
Ohio	1992	S	1	1	1	0	0
Oklahoma	1992	S	1	0	1	0	0
	2002	S	1	1[a]	1	0	0
Oregon	1992	S	0	1	1	0	0
Pennsylvania	1992	L			0	0	0

Appendix Table B.1 (continued)

State	Year	Type of licensing	General requirement	Apprenticeship	Written exam	Performance exam	Continuous education
Rhode Island	1992	S	0	0	1	0	0
	1998	S	1	1[a]	1	0	0
South Carolina	1992	S	0	0	1	0	0
South Dakota	1992	S	0	1	1	0	0
Tennessee	1992	N					
	2000	S	0	0	1	0	0
Texas	1992	L					
	2003	S	0	1	1	0	0
Utah	1992	S	0	1	1	0	0
	2000	S	0	1[a]	1	0	0
Vermont	1992	S	0	1	1	0	0
Virginia	1992	S	0	0	1	0	0
	1995	S	1	1[a]	1	0	0
Washington	1992	S	0	1	1	0	1
	1999	S	0	1	1	0	0
West Virginia	1992	S	0	1	1	0	0
	1994	S	1	1[a]	1	0	0
Wisconsin	1992	S	0	1	1	0	0
Wyoming	1992	S	0	1[a]	1	0	0
	1994	S	1	1[a]	1	0	1

NOTE: S, L, C, and N in the column under heading "Type of licensing" refer to State, Local, Certification, and No license requirement, respectively; definitions of specific components and their values are shown in Table 5.1.

[a] In the "Apprenticeship" column, [a] indicates that higher occupation-specific experiences than apprenticeship (e.g., journeyman) are required.

SOURCE: Author's analysis of statutes.

Appendix Table B.2 Characteristics of the Data in the Analysis

	Panel A: Key descriptions of the SOII and CFOI	
	Survey of Occupational Injuries and Illnesses (SOII)	Census of Fatal Occupational Injuries (CFOI)
Sampling	• 39 states	• 50 states + DC
	• Nonfatal injuries and illnesses for private industry only	• Includes private and federal, state, and local government agencies
	• Excludes the self-employed, farms with fewer than 11 employees, private households, and federal government agencies	• Data on deaths compiled from death certificates, OSHA reports, workers' compensation reports, medical examiner reports, newspaper articles, other sources
Important changes	• Includes employees in state and local government agencies for national estimates only	• Change in the standard occupational classification (SOC) system and the standard industry codes (SIC) system in 2003
	• Change in the standard occupational classification (SOC) system and the standard industry codes (SIC) system in 2003	
	• No longer reports on injuries separate from illness starting with the 2002 data	

Panel B: Sample selection for electricians: industry and occupation codes		
	1992–2002	2003–2007
Industry codes	1500–1799 under 1987 SIC	23 (23600–23899) under 2003 NAICS
Occupation codes for electricians	555 Supervisors of electricians and power transmission installers	47-2111 Electricians;
		47-3013 Helpers of electricians
	575 Electricians	
	576 Electricians' apprentices	
	577 Electrical power-line installers and repairers	49-9051 Electrical power-line installers and repairers

Appendix C

Data Developed from the American Community Survey (ACS)

To generate the sample of dentists and dental hygienists, we started by dropping individuals who belong to the categories "Working without pay in family business or farm" and "Unemployed." Thus, the sample includes individuals who belong to the classes of 1) private wage and salary workers, 2) government workers (who may work in any local, state, or federal governmental unit), and 3) self-employed, both in their own not-incorporated business and in their own incorporated business.

Next, individuals whose education is "below associate" for dentists and individuals whose education is "below 12th grade without diploma" for dental hygienists were dropped. Also dropped were individuals whose age is greater than 65 and whose years of experience (= age − years of schooling − 6) are below zero and individuals whose usual working hours in the past 12 months were less than 20 hours or more than 60 hours.

Hourly earnings were determined by computing annual hours worked (i.e., from the ACS question, the usual working hours times the number of weeks for the past 12 months). Then we computed annual earnings by adding the wage and salary income (i.e., *wagp*) and the income from self-employment (i.e., *semp*), and then dividing the annual earnings by annual hours worked.

In computing the hourly earnings, however, the ACS has two potential measurement problems: 1) the presence of outliers and 2) the top-coding (or censoring) of both incomes (i.e., *wagp* and *semp*), particularly for dentists. First, a few individuals report implausibly high earnings relative to their hours of work, which would affect the estimated mean and variance of hourly earnings. There was a deletion of observations for the professionals whose hourly earnings were in the top 0.5 percent for each occupation. As a result, the highest hourly earnings were in the range of two times the top-coded hourly earnings. Next, we computed top-coded hourly earnings (we also top-coded hourly *wagp* and *semp*), assuming that the top-coded individuals worked for 40 hours and 52 weeks in a given year. For individuals who had *wagp* (*semp*) only, we assigned the top-coded hourly *wagp* (*semp*) as their hourly earnings. For individuals who had both *wagp* and *semp* and for whom the sum of hourly *wagp* and hourly *semp* was greater than the higher of the top-coded hourly *wagp* and the top-coded hourly *semp*, we assigned the higher of the top-coded hourly *wagp* and the top-coded hourly *semp* as their hourly earnings.

To deal with the top-codings, we followed the method used in much of the literature: we adjusted the top-coded incomes by a factor (typically, 1.33 or 1.40) that approximates the mean for those above the censoring point (Card and DiNardo 2002). In this paper, we present empirical results using hourly earnings adjusted by a factor of 1.40.

For individuals who reported implausibly low earnings, we deleted observations with measured hourly wages below the federal minimum wage of $5.15 during 2001–2007.

Appendix Table C.1 Sample Selection from the ACS

		Dental hygienists	Dentists
Initial observations		7,510	8,942
Selection rule 1:	Unemployed or working without pay in family business or farm	−20	−11
Selection rule 2:	Educational attainment	−48	−28
	Drop sample: Below associate for dentist; sample below 12th grade w/o diploma for dental hygienist		
Selection rule 3:	Age equal to or over 65	−142	−1,017
Selection rule 4:	Experience = Age − years of schooling − 6	−8	−36
Selection rule 5:	Less than 20 hours and more than 60 hours	−1,303	−534
Selection rule 6:	Drop individuals whose hourly earnings belong to the top 0.5%	−30	−37
Selection rule 7:	Hourly earnings less than the federal minimum of $5.15 during 2001–2007	−73	−59
Total observations		5,886	7,220

SOURCE: American Community Survey (ACS).

Appendix Table C.2 Models of State Median Hourly Earnings Gap between Hygienists and Dentists

	(1)	(2)	(3)	(4)	(5)	(6)
DHPPI	0.001					
	(0.008)					
Tasks permitted (summated)		−0.054				
		(0.043)				
Tasks permitted (Rasch)			−0.053			
			(0.057)			
Independence from dentists (summated)				−0.067****		
				(0.010)		
Independence from dentists (Rasch)					−0.049****	
					(0.010)	
Self-employment allowed						−0.534****
						(0.073)
Employment growth ratio	0.003	0.007	0.005	−0.005	−0.005	−0.005
	(0.037)	(0.038)	(0.038)	(0.036)	(0.036)	(0.036)
State median household income (/1,000)	−0.070***	−0.066***	−0.069***	−0.065***	−0.065***	−0.065***
	(0.022)	(0.022)	(0.022)	(0.022)	(0.022)	(0.022)
Rate of uninsured	−0.034	−0.029	−0.032	−0.024	−0.024	−0.024
	(0.026)	(0.025)	(0.025)	(0.026)	(0.026)	(0.026)
Constant	5.227****	5.301****	5.240****	4.795****	4.346***	4.833****
	(1.307)	(1.322)	(1.312)	(1.330)	(1.362)	(1.324)
State fixed effects	Y	Y	Y	Y	Y	Y
Year fixed effects	Y	Y	Y	Y	Y	Y
R-squared	0.354	0.357	0.356	0.361	0.362	0.362
N	322	322	322	322	322	322

NOTE: Robust standard errors clustered at the state level are reported in parentheses. * significant at the 0.10 level; ** significant at the 0.05 level; *** significant at the 0.01 level; **** significant at the 0.001 level.
SOURCE: Author's compilation of licensing statutes; ACS.

Appendix D
Statutory Right to an Occupation
Model Legislation

Table of Contents

100.01 PURPOSE

This chapter's purpose is to (a) ensure that an individual may pursue a lawful occupation free from unnecessary regulations and (b) protect against the misuse of occupational regulations to reduce competition and increase prices to consumers.

100.02 DEFINITIONS

Subdivision 1. **Scope.** For the purposes of this chapter, the words defined in this section have the following meanings.

Subd. 2. **Business license.** "Business license" means a permit, registration, certification, franchise, or other approval required by law for a sole proprietorship, partnership, or corporate entity to do business.

Subd. 3. **Certification.** "Certification" is a voluntary program in which the government grants nontransferable recognition to an individual who meets personal qualifications established by a legislative body. Upon approval, the individual may use "certified" as a designated title. A noncertified individual may also perform the lawful occupation for compensation but may not use the title "certified." "Certification" is not intended to be synonymous with an "occupational license" in this chapter or to prohibit the use of private certification.

Subd. 4. **Court.** "Court" means any court, administrative tribunal, or other government agency acting in a judicial or quasijudicial capacity.

Subd. 5. **Government.** "Government" means the government of this state or any of its political subdivisions.

Subd. 6. **Lawful occupation.** "Lawful occupation" means a course of conduct, pursuit, or profession that includes the sale of goods or services that are not themselves illegal to sell, irrespective of whether the individual selling them is subject to an occupational regulation.

Subd. 7. **Least restrictive occupational regulation.** "Least restrictive occupational regulation" means, from least to most restrictive, (a) a provision for private civil action to remedy consumer harm, (b) inspection, (c) bonding or insurance, (d) registration, (e) certification, or (f) occupational license.

Subd. 8. **Occupational license.** "Occupational license" is a nontransferable authorization in law for an individual to perform a lawful occupation for compensation based on meeting personal qualifications established by a legislative body. It is illegal for an individual who does not possess an occupational license to perform the occupation for compensation. Occupational licensing is the most restrictive form of occupational regulation.

Subd. 9. **Occupational regulation.** "Occupational regulation" means a statute, ordinance, rule, practice, policy, or other law requiring an individual to possess certain personal qualifications to work in a lawful occupation. It excludes a business license, facility license, building permit, land use regulation, or other commercial regulations except to the extent those laws regulate an individual's personal qualifications to perform a lawful occupation.

Subd. 10. **Personal qualifications.** "Personal qualifications" are criteria established by a legislative body related to an individual's personal background, including completion of an approved educational program, satisfactory performance on an examination, work experience, moral standing, and completion of continuing education.

Subd. 11. **Registration.** "Registration" means a requirement established by a legislative body in which an individual gives notice to the government that may include the individual's name and address, the individual's agent for service of process, the location of the activity to be performed, and a description of the service the individual provides. "Registration" does not include personal qualifications but may require a bond or insurance. Upon approval, the individual may use "registered" as a designated title. A nonregistered individual may not perform the occupation for compensation or use "registered" as a designated title. "Registration" is not transferable. It is not intended to be synonymous with an "occupational license" in this chapter or to prohibit the use of private registration.

Subd. 12. **Substantial burden.** "Substantial burden" means a legal or other regulatory obstacle that imposes significant difficulty or cost on an individual seeking to enter into or continue in a lawful occupation. A substantial burden is a burden that is more than incidental.

100.03 RIGHT TO ENGAGE IN A LAWFUL OCCUPATION

Subdivision 1. **Statutory right.** An individual has a right to engage in a lawful occupation free from any substantial burden unless the government demonstrates (a) it has a compelling interest in protecting against present and recognizable harm to the public health or safety, and (b) the occupational regulation is the least restrictive means of furthering that compelling interest.

Subd. 2. **Defense and relief.**

(a) An individual may assert as a defense the right to engage in a lawful occupation in any judicial or administrative proceeding to enforce an occupational regulation that violates subdivision 1.

(b) An individual may bring an action for declaratory judgment or injunctive or other equitable relief for a violation of subdivision 1.

(c) An individual may assert as a defense or bring an action against the enforceability of an occupational regulation, pursuant to subsections (a) and (b), which is:

(1) in law at the effective date of this chapter; or

(2) enacted, adopted, or amended after the effective date of this chapter and does not include in the state statute an explicit exemption from this chapter.

(d) An individual who asserts a defense or brings an action under this section has the initial burden of proof that an occupational regulation substantially burdens the individual's right to engage in a lawful occupation.

(e) If the individual meets the burden of proof under subsection (d), the government must demonstrate by clear and convincing evidence that the government has a compelling interest in protecting against present and recognizable harm to the public health or safety, and that the occupational regulation is the least restrictive means for furthering that compelling interest.

Subd. 3. **Judicial determination.** A court shall liberally construe this chapter to protect the right established in subdivision 1. A court shall make its own findings of fact and conclusions of law. It shall not grant any presumption to legislative or administrative determinations of harm to the public health or safety, or that the regulation is the least restrictive means of furthering a compelling governmental interest.

100.04   FEDERAL LAW'S USE OF STATE OCCUPATIONAL REGULATIONS

To the extent necessary to meet federal law, the statutory right established in section 100.03, subdivision 1, does not apply to an individual who is required by federal law to meet a state occupational regulation.

Note

I thank Lee McGrath, of the Minnesota chapter of the Institute for Justice, for providing this model legislation (McGrath 2012).

Appendix E

Data Sources Used in This Volume

The sources of many of the data used in this volume are given, along with the years of the surveys and their frequency. In addition, units of observation for the data are presented, along with the sources' unique characteristics that make them useful for analyzing the influence of various stages of occupational regulation in the United States.

American Community Survey (ACS)

Conducted by: U.S. Department of Commerce, Census Bureau, as provided by the Minnesota Population Center (Integrated Public Use Microdata Series), University of Minnesota.

Survey years: Every year.

Unit surveyed: Individuals, by household.

Number of units in survey: The full implementation of the ACS, which began in 2005, sampled approximately 2.9 million housing unit addresses annually. The 2011 ACS sampled approximately 3.3 million housing unit addresses. This corresponds to a 3.54 million annual level beginning in June 2011.

Unique characteristics: The survey provides broad social, economic, housing, and demographic profiles. For example, it includes age, gender, race, family relationships, income and benefits, health insurance, education, veteran status, disabilities, where you work and how you get there, and where you live and how much you pay for some essentials.

Census of Fatal Occupational Injuries (CFOI)

Conducted by: Bureau of Labor Statistics (BLS). CFOI is a federal-state co-operative program that has been implemented in all 50 states and the District of Columbia since 1992. To compile counts that are as complete as possible, the census uses multiple sources to identify, verify, and profile fatal worker injuries. Information about each workplace fatal injury—occupation and other worker characteristics, equipment involved, and circumstances of the event—

is obtained by cross-referencing the source records, such as death certificates, workers' compensation reports, and federal and state agency administrative reports. To ensure that fatal injuries are work-related, cases are substantiated with two or more independent source documents, or a source document and a follow-up questionnaire.

Survey years: 1992 through 2010.

Units surveyed: Firms and states. About 200,000 business establishments are surveyed annually.

Number of units in survey: A work relationship exists if an event or exposure results in the fatal injury or illness of a person under the following three circumstances: 1) on the employer's premises and the person was there to work, 2) off the employer's premises and the person was there to work, or 3) the event or exposure was related to the person's work or status as an employee. The employer's premises include buildings, grounds, parking lots, and other facilities and property used in the conduct of business. Work is defined as duties, activities, or tasks that produce a product or result; that are done in exchange for money, goods, services, profit, or benefit; and that are legal activities in the United States.

Unique characteristics: The database has contractor starts and ownership, and recently it added information by occupation and state. The data also have information on the age of the individual, birthplace, gender, day of the incident, and what happened during the incident.

Census of the Population

Conducted by: U.S. Department of Commerce, Census Bureau, as provided by the Minnesota Population Center (Integrated Public Use Microdata Series), University of Minnesota.

Survey years: Every 10 years, dating to the founding of the United States.

Unit surveyed: Individuals, by household.

Number of units in survey: Between 5 and 100 percent of the population, depending on the question.

Unique characteristics: Provides large samples of individuals' labor force status (employed, wages, earnings), demographic characteristics, industry and occupation, national origin, and area of residence.

Current Population Survey (CPS)

Conducted by: U.S. Department of Commerce, Census Bureau, for the U.S. Department of Labor, Bureau of Labor Statistics.

Survey years: Monthly since 1943.

Unit surveyed: Individuals 16 years or older, by household.

Number of units in survey: Currently approximately 120,000 individuals that make up 60,000 households.

Unique characteristics: Each CPS survey includes data on demographic characteristics, labor force status, industry, region, state, and occupation.

Department of Labor Listing of Licensed Occupations

Conducted by: Department of Labor's Employment and Training Administration in conjunction with state labor market information agencies.

Survey years: Various years, including 2000.

Units surveyed: State agencies responsible for occupational regulation.

Unique characteristics: Census of state-licensed occupations in the United States, as provided to the U.S. Department of Labor in 2000 by state agencies responsible for labor market information and licensing occupations.

Early Childhood Longitudinal Program from Birth, ECLS-B

Conducted by: National Center for Education Statistics. The Early Childhood Longitudinal Study Birth Cohort (ECLS-B) was designed to supply policymakers, researchers, child care providers, teachers, and parents with detailed information about children's early life experiences. Data collected for the ECLS-B focus on children's health, development, care, and education during the formative years from birth through kindergarten entry.

Survey years: Children were followed from birth through kindergarten entry. Information about these children was collected when they were approximately nine months old (2001–2002), two years old (2003–2004), and four years old/ preschool age (2005–2006).

Units surveyed: Children and their parents, and another module was gathered from teachers on the children's cognitive ability.

Unique characteristics: A nationally representative sample of approximately 14,000 children born in the United States in 2001. The children participating in the study came from diverse socioeconomic and racial/ethnic backgrounds, with oversamples of Chinese children, other Asian and Pacific Islander children, American Indian and Alaska Native children, twins, and children born with low and very low birth weight.

Early Childhood Longitudinal Program, Kindergarten Class of 1998–1999 (ECLS-K)

Conducted by: National Center for Education Statistics. It focuses on children's early school experiences, beginning with kindergarten and following children through middle school. The ECLS-K data provide descriptive information on children's status at entry to school, their transition into school, and their progression through eighth grade. The longitudinal nature of the ECLS-K data enables researchers to study how a wide variety of family, school, community, and individual factors are associated with school performance.

Survey years: 1998–1999, 1999–2000, 2002, 2004, and 2007.

Units surveyed: To collect information from children, trained assessors visited the children in their schools. The direct child assessment, which was untimed and conducted one-on-one with each child, collected information about children's reading and mathematics skills and knowledge in each round of data collection, their general knowledge (i.e., science and social studies) in kindergarten and first grade, and their science knowledge in third, fifth, and eighth grades. In addition, the assessment included measurements of height and weight and, in fall kindergarten only, children's psychomotor skills (e.g., ability to hop, skip, jump, manipulate blocks, and draw figures). In the third, fifth, and eighth grades, children completed questionnaires on various topics including their perceptions of their social and academic competence and skills, their school experiences and activities, and their diet.

To collect information from parents, a trained interviewer phoned the parent at his or her home and conducted a 45–50 minute interview. Computer-assisted interviewing methods were used to record the parent's answers. If the child's family did not have a telephone, the interview was conducted in person. The sample now includes 18,300 kindergartners and their families, teachers, school administrators, and before- and after-school care providers.

Unique characteristics: No large national study that was focused on education had followed a cohort of children from kindergarten entry to middle school until the ECLS-K. The ECLS-K was designed to provide comprehensive and reliable data that could be used to describe and to better understand children's development and experiences in the elementary and middle school grades, as well as how children's early experiences relate to their later development, learning, and experiences in school. The multifaceted data collected across the years allow researchers and policymakers to study how various child, home, classroom, school, and community factors at various points in children's lives relate to cognitive, social, emotional, and physical development.

National Longitudinal Surveys

Conducted by: The National Longitudinal Surveys (NLS) are a set of two surveys sponsored by the U.S. Department of Labor's Bureau of Labor Statistics and conducted by the National Opinion Research Center (NORC) at the University of Chicago, with assistance from the Center for Human Resource Research (CHRR) at Ohio State University, and the fieldwork is conducted by the census.

Survey years: Occasionally since 1965.

Units surveyed: The current survey consists of a nationally representative sample of approximately 9,000 participants and their households.

Unique characteristics: The NLS are a set of surveys designed to gather information at multiple points in time on the labor market activities and other significant life events of several groups of men and women. There are five cohorts that make up the National Longitudinal Surveys NLSY97 and NLSY79: 1) children, 2) mature women, 3) young women, 4) older men, and 5) young men. An extensive two-part questionnaire was administered to each respondent; this questionnaire listed and gathered demographic information on members of the household and on the respondent's immediate family members living elsewhere. Youths are interviewed on an annual basis. Questions are asked about current and former occupations.

Option One

Conducted by: Data come from Option One, a lending company that obtains almost all its loans from brokers.

Survey year: 2005.

Units surveyed: Broker-dependent mortgage originators of several million loans.

Unique characteristics: Detailed data on mortgage originators in the United States that includes borrower's income and racial/ethnic identity, the loan amount, and several economic and demographic properties of the census tract where the property is located (the distribution of credit scores, unemployment rate, median age of applicants, median age of housing stock, percentage of minority population, median income, and the percentage of owner-occupied and vacant housing units).

Princeton Data Improvement Initiative (PDII)

Conducted by: Westat conducted a national random-digit-dial (RDD) survey on behalf of Princeton University.

Survey year: 2008.

Units surveyed: In order to be eligible for the study, persons had to be adults in the labor force—for this project the labor force was defined as persons who are either a) currently working at a job for pay or profit or b) currently looking for work and have worked at a job in the past. Households in which no adults are currently in the labor force were not eligible for the study. If a household contained more than one adult in the labor force, one was randomly selected by the CATI program for participation in the extended interview. When the person chosen for the extended interview was someone other than the screener respondent, age and workforce status were confirmed with that person before continuing with the extended interview. There were 2,513 completed interviews.

Unique characteristics: Major topics covered in the survey included worker perceptions of occupational licensing, adult lifetime work experience, and the potential for their jobs to be offshored. On occupational licensing, there was a module to assess the accuracy of self-reported occupational licensing and certification. The key questions were as follows:

Q11. Do you have a license or certification that is required by a federal, state, or local government agency to do your job?

YES 1

NO .... 2 (Go to Q25)

IN PROCESS/WORKING ON IT.. 3

Q11a. Would someone who does not have a license or certificate be legally allowed to do your job?

YES 1

NO 2

Q12. Is everyone who does your job eventually required to have a license or certification by a federal, state, or local government agency?

YES 1

NO 2

Those who answered affirmatively to Q11 were asked additional questions about the agency (federal, state, or local) that required their license or certificate, and about the requirements they needed to satisfy, such as achieving a high school or college degree, passing a test, demonstrating certain skills, or completing an internship or apprenticeship.

Survey of Licensing Statutes

Conducted by: Center for Labor Policy, University of Minnesota, Jing Cai, Yaffa Epstein, Heidi Liu, and Cynthia Pahl.

Survey years: Various years between 1980 and 2010.

Units surveyed: State statutes for interior designers, mortgage brokers, preschool teachers and their assistants, plumbers and electricians, and dentists and dental hygienists.

Unique characteristics: Statutory data and changes in laws on age, citizenship, residency, good moral character, special education, graduate education requirements, experience, exam requirements, bachelor's degree requirement, and reciprocity requirements with other states or countries.

Survey of Occupational Injuries and Illnesses (SOII)

Conducted by: U.S. Department of Labor's Bureau of Labor Statistics for establishments with 10 or more workers.

Survey years: Data are provided annually on the rate and number of work-related injuries, illnesses, and fatal injuries, and how these statistics vary by incident, industry, geography, occupation, and other characteristics.

Units surveyed: These are surveys of establishments annually. This survey is made possible through the cooperation of participating state agencies and nearly 200,000 business establishments that provide information on workplace injuries and illnesses to the BLS. State agencies collect and verify most of the data provided. BLS field offices collect and verify data from nonparticipating states.

Unique characteristics: The SOII collects data on nonfatal injuries and illnesses for each calendar year from a sample of employers. Just before the start of the year, the BLS sends notification (and record-keeping information) to the sampled employers. In the following January, the BLS sends these employers requests for the injury and illness information for the year just ended, along with instructions on how to report it to the BLS. These reports form the basis of the annual estimates published in the following October and November, after the data are collected.

References

Adams, Tracey L. 2004. "Inter-Professional Conflict and Professionalization: Dentistry and Dental Hygiene in Ontario." *Social Science and Medicine* 58(11): 2243–2252.

Akerlof, George A. 1970. "The Market for 'Lemons': Quality Uncertainty and the Market Mechanism." *Quarterly Journal of Economics* 84(3): 488–500.

Alabama v. Lupo. 2007. 984 So.2d 395.

Alexander, Adrienne, Chris Henjum, Jeremy Jones, Meg Luger-Nikolai, Aaron Rosenberger, and Caro Smith. 2009. *Regulating Interior Designers: Overview and Analysis of Public Policy and Law*. Minneapolis, MN: University of Minnesota, Humphrey School of Public Affairs. http://conservancy.umn.edu/bitstream/61691/1/Regulating%20Interior%20Designers.pdf (accessed May 16, 2013).

Alexander, William P., Scott D. Grimshaw, Grant R. McQueen, and Barrett A. Slade. 2002. "Some Loans Are More Equal Than Others: Third-Party Originations and Defaults in the Subprime Mortgage Industry." *Real Estate Economics* 30(4): 667–697.

Ambrose, Brent W., and James N. Conklin. 2012. "Mortgage Brokers, Origination Fees, and Competition." Working paper. State College, PA: Pennsylvania State University.

American Dental Hygienists' Association (ADHA). 1994. *State Dental Board Composition*. Chicago: American Dental Hygienists' Association.

American Society of Interior Designers (ASID). 2005. *The History of ASID: 30 Years of Advancing the Interior Design Profession*. Washington, DC: American Society of Interior Designers.

Anderson, Michael L. 2008. "Multiple Inference and Gender Differences in the Effects of Early Intervention: A Reevaluation of the Abecedarian, Perry Preschool, and Early Training Projects." *Journal of the American Statistical Association* 103(484): 1481–1495.

Anderson v. Minnesota Board of Barber and Cosmetology Examiners. 2005. Case No. 05-5467, Hennepin Co. Dist. Ct.

Andrich, David. 1988. *Rasch Models for Measurement*. Quantitative Applications in the Social Sciences 68. Newbury Park, CA: Sage.

Angrist, Joshua D., and Jonathan Guryan. 2003. "Does Teacher Testing Raise Teacher Quality? Evidence from State Certification Requirements." NBER Working Paper No. 9545. Cambridge, MA: National Bureau of Economic Research.

Apgar, William, Amal Bendimerad, and Ren S. Essene. 2007. "Mortgage Market Channels and Fair Lending: An Analysis of HMDA Data." Working

Paper No. MM07-2. Cambridge, MA: Harvard University, Joint Center for Housing Studies.

Avery, Robert B., Kenneth P. Brevoort, and Glenn B. Canner. 2006. "Higher-Priced Home Lending and the 2005 HMDA Data." *Federal Reserve Bulletin* 92(September): A123–A166.

Barker, David. 2008. "Ethics and Lobbying: The Case of Real Estate Brokerage." *Journal of Business Ethics* 80(1): 23–35.

Bartik, Timothy J. 2011. *Investing in Kids: Early Childhood Programs and Local Economic Development*. Kalamazoo, MI: W.E. Upjohn Institute for Employment Research.

Beach, M. Miles, Jay D. Shulman, Glenna Johns, and Jeffrey C. Paas. 2007. "Assessing the Viability of the Independent Practice of Dental Hygiene—A Brief Communication." *Journal of Public Health Dentistry* 67(4): 250–254.

Becker, Gary S. 1991. *A Treatise on the Family*. Enlarged edition. Cambridge, MA: President and Fellows of Harvard College.

Berndt, Antje, Burton Hollifield, and Patrik Sandås. 2010. "The Role of Mortgage Brokers in the Subprime Crisis." NBER Working Paper No. 16175. Cambridge, MA: National Bureau of Economic Research.

Berry, Kate. 2010. "Licensing Snags Set Nonbanks Back More—Only Loan Officers." *American Banker* 175(F329): 6.

Bielick, Stacey, Stephanie Cronen, Celeste Stone, Jill M. Montaquila, and Shelley Brock Roth. 2013. *The Adult Training and Education Survey (ATES) Pilot Study*. NCES 2013-190 Technical Report. Washington, DC: U.S. Department of Education, National Center for Education Statistics. http://nces.ed.gov/pubsearch (accessed June 4, 2013).

Blau, David M. 2003. "Do Child Care Regulations Affect the Child Care and Labor Markets?" *Journal of Policy Analysis and Management* 22(3): 443–465.

Blau, David, and Janet Currie. 2006. "Preschool, Day Care, and After School Care: Who's Minding the Kids?" In *Handbook of the Economics of Education*, vol. 2, Eric Hanushek and Finis Welch, eds. Handbooks in Economics 26. New York: North Holland, pp. 1163–1275.

Boal, William M., and Michael R. Ransom. 1997. "Monopsony in the Labor Market." *Journal of Economic Literature* 35(1): 86–112.

Boivin, Sharon A. 2012. "Developing New Federal Survey Data on Credentials for Work." Paper presented at the annual conference of the Association of Public Data Users, held in Washington, DC, September 12–13.

Bond, Ronald S., John E. Kwoka Jr., John J. Phelan, and Ira Taylor Whitten. 1980. *Effects of Restrictions on Advertising and Commercial Practice in the Professions: The Case of Optometry*. Washington, DC: Federal Trade Commission, Bureau of Economics.

Boschee, Marlys Ann, and Geralyn M. Jacobs. 1997. *Child Care in the United States: Yesterday and Today*. Ames, IA: Iowa State University, National Network for Child Care. http://www.nncc.org/Choose.Quality.Care/ccyesterd.html (accessed April 24, 2013).

Bostic, Raphael W., Kathleen C. Engel, Patricia A. McCoy, Anthony Pennington-Cross, and Susan M. Wachter. 2007. "State and Local Anti-Predatory Lending Laws: The Effect of Legal Enforcement Mechanisms." Paper presented at the Federal Reserve System Community Affairs Research Conference, held in Washington, DC, March 29–30.

Brown, Charles, and James Medoff. 1989. "The Employer Size-Wage Effect." Working Paper No. 2870. Cambridge, MA: National Bureau of Economic Research.

Bryson, Alex, John Forth, Amy Humphris, Morris M. Kleiner, and Maria Koumenta. 2012. "The Incidence and Labor Market Outcomes of Occupational Regulation in the UK." Paper presented at the annual meeting of the Allied Social Science Associations, January 5–8, Chicago, IL.

Burchinal, Margaret, Carollee Howes, and Susan Kontos. 2002. "Structural Predictors of Child Care Quality in Child Care Homes." *Early Childhood Research Quarterly* 17(1) 87–105. http://www.sciencedirect.com/science/article/pii/S0885200602001321 (accessed July 11, 2013).

Bureau of Labor Statistics (BLS). 2011. *Census of Fatal Occupational Injuries*. Washington, DC: U.S. Department of Labor, Bureau of Labor Statistics. http://www.bls.gov/iif/oshwc/cfoi/cfch0008.pdf (accessed May 2, 2013).

———. 2012a. *Occupational Outlook Handbook: Dental Hygienists*. Washington, DC: U.S. Department of Labor, Bureau of Labor Statistics. http://www.bls.gov/oco/ocos097.htm (accessed April 24, 2013).

———. 2012b. *Occupational Outlook Handbook: Electricians*. Washington, DC: U.S. Department of Labor, Bureau of Labor Statistics. http://www.bls.gov/oco/ocos206.htm (accessed June 2, 2013).

———. 2012c. *Occupational Outlook Handbook: Home*. Washington, DC: U.S. Department of Labor, Bureau of Labor Statistics. http://www.bls.gov/ooh/ (accessed May 16, 2013).

———. 2012d. *Occupational Outlook Handbook: Interior Designers*. Washington, DC: U.S. Department of Labor, Bureau of Labor Statistics. http://www.bls.gov/oco/ocos293.htm (accessed February 11, 2013).

———. 2013a. *Injuries, Illnesses, and Fatalities*. Washington, DC: Bureau of Labor Statistics. http://www.bls.gov/iif/ (accessed June 1, 2013).

———. 2013b. *Occupational Employment Statistics*. Washington, DC: U.S. Department of Labor, Bureau of Labor Statistics. http://www.bls.gov/oes/ (accessed December 12, 2012).

Butler, Richard J., and John D. Worrall. 1983. "Workers' Compensation: Benefit and Injury Claims Rates in the Seventies." *Review of Economics and Statistics* 65(4): 580–589.

Callender, David. 1995. "Interior Designers Push for State Licensing." *Capital Times*, September 13, A:3.

Card, David, and John E. DiNardo. 2002. "Skill-Biased Technological Change and Rising Wage Inequality: Some Problems and Puzzles." *Journal of Labor Economics* 20(4): 733–783.

Carneiro, Pedro, James J. Heckman, and Edward J. Vytlacil. 2009. "Evaluating Marginal Policy Changes and the Average Effect of Treatment for Individuals at the Margin." NBER Working Paper No. 15211. Cambridge, MA: National Bureau of Economic Research.

Carpenter, Dick M. II. 2008. "Regulation through Titling Laws: A Case Study of Occupational Regulation." *Regulation and Governance* 2(3): 340–359.

———. 2011. "Testing the Utility of Licensing: Evidence from a Field Experiment on Occupational Regulation." Working paper. Colorado Springs, CO: University of Colorado–Colorado Springs.

Carroll, Sidney L., and Robert J. Gaston. 1981. "Occupational Restrictions and the Quality of Service Received: Some Evidence." *Southern Economic Journal* 47(4): 959–976.

Cathles, Alison, David E. Harrington, and Kathy Krynski. 2010. "The Gender Gap in Funeral Directors: Burying Women with Ready-to-Embalm Laws?" *British Journal of Industrial Relations* 48(4): 688–705.

Center for Construction Research and Training. 2009. *The Construction Chart Book*. Silver Spring, MD: Center for Construction Research and Training. http://www.cpwr.com/rp-chartbook.html (accessed April 25, 2013).

Centers for Medicare and Medicaid Services (CMS). 2008. *Historical Health Expenditure Data*. Baltimore, MD: Centers for Medicare and Medicaid Services. http://www.cms.gov/Research-Statistics-Data-and-Systems/Statistics-Trends-and-Reports/NationalHealthExpendData/NationalHealthAccounts Historical.html (accessed July 29, 2013).

Chi, Wei, Morris M. Kleiner, and Xiaoye Qian. 2013. "Do Occupational Regulations Increase Earnings? The Influence of Professional Certification and Licensing on Wage Determination in China." Paper presented at the Fifteenth NBER-CCER Conference on China and the World Economy," held in Beijing, June 27–29.

Chipty, Tasneem. 1995. "Economic Effects of Quality Regulations in the Day-Care Industry." *American Economic Review* 85(2): 419–424.

Clarke-Stewart, K. Alison, Deborah Lowe Vandell, Margaret Burchinal, Marion O'Brien, and Kathleen McCartney. 2002. "Do Regulable Features of

Child-Care Homes Affect Children's Development?" *Early Childhood Research Quarterly* 17(1): 52–86.

Coase, R. H. 1960. "The Problem of Social Cost." *Journal of Law and Economics* 3(October): 1–44.

Cohn, Jonathan B., and Malcolm Wardlaw. 2013. "The Effect of Financial Leverage on Workplace Safety." Working paper. Austin, TX: University of Texas.

Comer, Shirley K. 2007. *Nursing Licensure.* Adventure of the American Mind: Joining Educators of Students with Library of Congress Resources. University Park, IL: Governors State University, College of Education. http://aam .govst.edu/projects/scomer/student_page1.html (accessed April 25, 2013).

Cooney, Richard. 2013. "Occupational Licensing in Australia: An Institutional Approach." Paper presented at the annual meeting of the Labor and Employment Relations Association, held in St. Louis, June 6–9.

Council on Licensure, Enforcement, and Regulation (CLEAR). 2004. *About CLEAR.* Lexington, KY: Council on Licensure, Enforcement, and Regulation. http://www.clearhq.org (accessed September 9, 2013).

Council of State Governments. 1952. *Occupational Licensing Legislation in the States.* Chicago: Council of State Governments.

Cox, Carolyn, and Susan Foster. 1990. *The Costs and Benefits of Occupational Regulation.* Washington, DC: U.S. Federal Trade Commission, Bureau of Economics.

Crosby, Jackie. 2012. "Dental Therapists Bridge Gap." *Minneapolis Star Tribune,* July 15. http://www.startribune.com/printarticle/?id=162430866 (accessed April 16, 2013).

Cumming, John, and Larry J. Rankin. 1999. "150 Hours: A Look Back: What the Fifth Year of Education Did to Florida—And What It Will Do to You." *Journal of Accountancy* 187(4): 53–58.

Currie, Janet, and V. Joseph Hotz. 2004. "Accidents Will Happen? Unintentional Childhood Injuries and the Effects of Child Care Regulations." *Journal of Health Economics* 23(1): 25–59.

Dickens, William T., and Kevin Lang. 1992. "Labor Market Segmentation Theory: Reconsidering the Evidence." NBER Working Paper No. 4087. Cambridge, MA: National Bureau of Economic Research.

Dong, Xiuwen Sue, Xuanwen Wang, and Brett Herleikson. 2010. "Work-Related Fatal and Nonfatal Injuries among U.S. Construction Workers, 1992–2008." Silver Spring, MD: Center for Construction Research and Training.

Dunlop, John T. 1958. *Industrial Relations Systems.* New York: Henry Holt.

El Anshasy, Amany, Gregory Elliehausen, and Yoshiaki Shimazaki. 2005. "The Pricing of Subprime Mortgages by Mortgage Brokers and Lenders."

Paper presented at the 2005 Federal Reserve System Community Affairs Research Conference "Promises and Pitfalls: As Consumer Finance Options Multiply, Who Is Being Served and at What Cost?" held in Washington, DC, April 7–8.

Engel, Kathleen C., and Patricia A. McCoy. 2002. "A Tale of Three Markets: The Law and Economics of Predatory Lending." *Texas Law Review* 80(6): 1255–1367.

Essene, Ren S., and William Apgar. 2007. "Understanding Mortgage Market Behavior: Creating Good Mortgage Options for All Americans." Joint Center for Housing Studies Working Paper MM07-1. Cambridge, MA: Harvard University.

Federal Financial Institutions Examination Council (FFIEC). 2007. *Home Mortgage Disclosure Act: On-Line Reports*. Washington, DC: Federal Financial Institutions Examination Council. http://www.ffiec.gov/hmda/online_rpts.htm (accessed April 29, 2013).

FINRA Investor Education Foundation. 2013. *National Financial Capability Study*. Washington, DC: FINRA Investor Education Foundation. http://www.usfinancialcapability.org/downloads.php (accessed May 29, 2013).

Freeman, Richard B., and Morris M. Kleiner. 1990. "The Impact of New Unionization on Wages and Working Conditions." *Journal of Labor Economics* 8(1), pt. 2: S8–S25.

Freeman, Richard B., and James L. Medoff. 1985. *What Do Unions Do?* New York: Basic Books.

Frey, Julie. 2008. "Hygiene Clinics: Without Dentists, Hygienists Have No Profit." *The Wealthy Dentist* (blog), December 16. http://www.thewealthydentist.com/blog/654/dental-hygiene-clinics/ (accessed June 2, 2013).

Friedman, Milton. 1962. *Capitalism and Freedom*. Chicago: University of Chicago Press.

Gittleman, Maury, and Morris M. Kleiner. 2013. "Wage Effects of Unionization and Occupational Licensing Coverage in the United States." NBER Working Paper No. 19061. Cambridge, MA: National Bureau of Economic Research.

Goldhaber, Dan D., and Dominic J. Brewer. 2000. "Does Teacher Certification Matter? High School Teacher Certification Status and Student Achievement." *Educational Evaluation and Policy Analysis* 22(2): 129–145.

Goldstein, Jacob. 2012. "So You Think You Can Be a Hair Braider?" *New York Times*, June 12. http://www.nytimes.com/2012/06/17/magazine/so-you-think-you-can-be-a-hair-braider.html?pagewanted=all&_r=0 (accessed April 29, 2013).

Gooch, Barbara F., Susan O. Griffin, Shellie Kolavic Gray, William G. Kohn, R. Gary Rozier, Mark Siegal, Margherita Fontana, Diane Brunson, Nancy

Carter, David K. Curtis, Kevin J. Donly, Harold Haering, Lawrence F. Hill, H. Pitts Hinson, Jayanth Kumar, Lewis Lampiris, Mark Mallatt, Daniel M. Meyer, Wanda R. Miller, Susan M. Sanzi-Schaedel, Richard Simonsen, Benedict I. Truman, and Domenick T. Zero. 2009. "Preventing Dental Caries through School-Based Sealant Programs: Updated Recommendations and Reviews of Evidence." *Journal of the American Dental Association* 140(11): 1356–1365. http://jada.ada.org/content/140/11/1356.full .pdf+html?sid=a5c27984-cad9-4cf4-a26a-11bc07701204 (accessed April 29, 2013).

Gormley, William T. Jr. 2007. "Early Childhood Care and Education: Lessons and Puzzles." *Journal of Policy Analysis and Management* 26(3): 633–671.

Gray, Wayne B., and John M. Mendeloff. 2005. "The Declining Effects of OSHA Inspections on Manufacturing Injuries, 1979 to 1998." *Industrial and Labor Relations Review* 58(4): 571–587.

Groshen, Erica L. 1991. "Five Reasons Why Wages Vary among Employers." *Industrial Relations* 30(3): 350–381.

Grunewald, Rob, and Arthur Rolnick. 2006. "A Proposal for Achieving High Returns on Early Childhood Development." Working paper. Minneapolis, MN: Federal Reserve Bank of Minneapolis.

Guttentag, Jack. 2000. "Another View of Predatory Lending." Financial Institutions Center Working Paper 01-23-B. Philadelphia: University of Pennsylvania, Wharton School.

Hamermesh, Daniel S. 1993. *Labor Demand.* Princeton, NJ: Princeton University Press.

Harrington, David E., and Jaret Treber. 2009. *Designed to Exclude: How Interior Design Insiders Use Government Power to Exclude Minorities and Burden Consumers.* Arlington, VA: Institute for Justice.

Harrison, Will, Clark Koenigs, Ryan Merz, Sakawdin Mohamed, Sebastian Monroy-Taborda, Alison Piumbroeck Groebner, and Erik White. 2012. "Unique Institutions in Unique Places: A Look at the Effects of Occupational Licensing in Indian Country." Master of Public Policy Professional Paper. Minneapolis, MN: University of Minnesota, Hubert H. Humphrey School of Public Affairs.

Heeb, Randal, and M. Rebecca Kilburn. 2004. "The Effects of State Regulations on Childcare Prices and Choices." Working paper. Santa Monica, CA: RAND.

Helburn, Suzanne W., ed. 1995. *Cost, Quality, and Child Outcomes in Child Care Centers.* Technical report. Denver, CO: University of Colorado at Denver, Department of Economics, Center for Research in Economic and Social Policy.

Helburn, Suzanne W., and Carollee Howes. 1996. "Child Care Cost and Quality." *Future of Children* 6(2): 62–82.

Helm, Maria R. 1993. "Survival of the Fittest: Dental Hygiene's Future Evolves from Its Past." *Access* 1993(September–October): 25–32.

Hirsch, Barry T. 2012. "Unions, Dynamism, and Economic Performance." In *Research Handbook on the Economics of Labor and Employment Law*, Cynthia L. Estlund and Michael L. Wachter, eds. Northampton, MA: Edward Elgar, pp. 107–145.

Hirsch, Barry T., and David A. Macpherson. 2011. *Union Membership and Coverage Database from the Current Population Survey.* Washington, DC: Bureau of Labor Statistics, Current Population Survey. http://www.unionstats.com (accessed April 29, 2013).

Hofferth, Sandra L., and Duncan D. Chaplin. 1998. "State Regulations and Child Care Choice." *Population Research and Policy Review* 17(2): 111–140.

Holmes, Thomas J. 1998. "The Effect of State Policies on the Location of Manufacturing: Evidence from State Borders." *Journal of Political Economy* 106(4): 667–705.

Hotz, V. Joseph, and M. Rebecca Kilburn. 1994. "Regulating Child Care: The Effects of State Regulations on Child Care Demand and Its Cost." Working paper. Santa Monica, CA: RAND.

Hotz, V. Joseph, and Mo Xiao. 2005. "The Impact of Minimum Quality Standards on Firm Entry, Exit, and Product Quality: The Case of the Child Care Market." Working paper. Los Angeles: University of California, Los Angeles; California Center for Population Research.

———. 2011. "The Impact of Regulations on the Supply and Quality of Care in Child Care Markets." *American Economic Review* 101(5): 1775–1805. http://www.aeaweb.org/articles.php?doi=10.1257/aer.101.5.1775 (accessed April 29, 2013).

Humphris, Amy, Morris M. Kleiner, and Maria Koumenta. 2011. "How Does Government Regulate Occupations in the United Kingdom and the United States? Issues and Policy Implications." In *Employment in the Lean Years: Policy and Prospects for the Next Decade*, David Marsden, ed. Oxford: Oxford University Press, pp. 87–101.

Hur, Yoon Sun, Morris M. Kleiner, and Yingchun Wang. 2013. "The Influence of Licensing Engineers on their Labor Market." Updated version of a paper presented at the National Bureau of Economic Research Conference, held in Cambridge, MA, September 26, 2011.

Jackson, Howell E., and Laurie Burlingame. 2007. "Kickbacks or Compensation: The Case of Yield Spread Premiums." *Stanford Journal of Law, Business, and Finance* 12(2): 289–361.

Jacobides, Michael G. 2005. "Industry Change through Vertical Disintegration: How and Why Markets Emerged in Mortgage Banking." *Academy of Management Journal* 48(3): 465–498.

Kahn, Lawrence M. 2000. "The Sports Business as a Labor Market Laboratory." *Journal of Economic Perspectives* 14(3): 75–94.

Kahneman, Daniel, and Amos Tversky. 1979. "Prospect Theory: An Analysis of Decision under Risk." *Econometrica* 47(2): 263–292.

Kessler, Daniel P. 2011. "Introduction." In *Regulation vs. Litigation: Perspectives from Economics and Law*, Daniel P. Kessler, ed. Cambridge, MA: National Bureau of Economic Research, pp. 1–9.

Ketel, Nadine, Edwin Leuven, Hessel Oosterbeek, and Bas van der Klaauw. 2012. "The Returns to Medical School in a Regulated Labor Market: Evidence from Admission Lotteries." Working paper. Amsterdam: University of Amsterdam, Research Institute in Economics and Econometrics.

Klee, Mark A. 2010. "Reassessing Aggregate Welfare under Professional Licensing and Certification." Working paper. New Haven, CT: Yale University.

Kleiner, Morris M. 1990. "Are There Economic Rents for More Restrictive Occupational Licensing Practices?" Industrial Relations Research Association *Proceedings* 1990(1): 177–185.

———. 2006. *Licensing Occupations: Ensuring Quality or Restricting Competition?* Kalamazoo, MI: W. E. Upjohn Institute for Employment Research.

———. 2011. "Enhancing Quality or Restricting Competition: The Case of Licensing Public School Teachers." *Journal of Policy and Law* 5(2): 1–16.

Kleiner, Morris M., Robert S. Gay, and Karen Greene. 1982. "Barriers to Labor Migration: The Case of Occupational Licensing." *Industrial Relations* 21(3): 383–391.

Kleiner, Morris M., and Alan B. Krueger. 2010. "The Prevalence and Effects of Occupational Licensing." *British Journal of Industrial Relations* 48(4): 676–687.

———. 2013. "Analyzing the Extent and Influence of Occupational Licensing on the Labor Market." *Journal of Labor Economics* 31(2, Part 2): S173–S202.

Kleiner, Morris M., and Robert T. Kudrle. 2000. "Does Regulation Affect Economic Outcomes? The Case of Dentistry." *Journal of Law and Economics* 43(2): 547–582.

Kleiner, Morris M., Allison Marier, Kyoung Won Park, and Coady Wing. 2012. "Relaxing Occupational Licensing Requirements: Analyzing Wages and Prices for a Medical Service." Paper presented at the annual meeting of the Allied Social Science Associations, held in Chicago, January 5–8.

Kleiner, Morris M., and Kyoung Won Park. 2010a. "Battles among Licensed Occupations: Analyzing Government Regulations on Labor Market Outcomes for Dentists and Hygienists." NBER Working Paper No. 16560. Cambridge, MA: National Bureau of Economic Research.

———. 2010b. *Occupational Licensing and Injuries and Death in Construction: An Analysis of Electricians and Plumbers.* CPWR Technical Report. Washington, DC: Center for Construction Research and Training.

Kleiner, Morris M., and Daniel L. Petree. 1988. "Unionism and Licensing of Public School Teachers: Impact on Wages and Educational Output." In *When Public Sector Workers Unionize*, Richard B. Freeman and Casey Ichniowski, eds. Chicago: University of Chicago Press, pp. 305–322.

Kleiner, Morris M., and Richard M. Todd. 2007. "Mortgage Broker Regulations That Matter: Analyzing Earnings, Employment, and Outcomes for Consumers." NBER Working Paper No. 13684. Cambridge, MA: National Bureau of Economic Research. http://www.nber.org/papers/w13684 (accessed May 29, 2013).

Kleiner, Morris M., and Evgeny S. Vorotnikov. 2012. "Complementarities and Substitutions between a Licensed and a Certified Occupation: An Analysis of Architects and Interior Designers." Presented at the Society for the Advancement of Socio-Economics (SASE) Annual Conference, held in Cambridge, MA, June 28–30.

Kontos, Susan, Carollee Howes, Marybeth Shinn, and Ellen Galinsky. 1995. *Quality in Family Child Care and Relative Care.* New York: Teachers College Press.

Koumenta, Maria, Amy Humphris, and Morris M. Kleiner. 2011. "Occupational Licensing versus Unionisation: A Comparison of Two Labour Market Institutions in the UK." Paper presented at the SASE Annual Conference, held in Madrid, Spain, June 23, 2011.

Kugler, Adriana D., and Robert M. Sauer. 2005. "Doctors without Borders? Relicensing Requirements and Negative Selection in the Market for Physicians." *Journal of Labor Economics* 23(3): 437–465.

LaCour-Little, Michael. 2007a. "The Home Purchase Mortgage Preferences of Low- and Moderate-Income Households." *Real Estate Economics* 35(3): 265–290.

———. 2007b. "The Pricing of Mortgages by Brokers: An Agency Problem?" Working paper. Fullerton, CA: California State University, Fullerton; College of Business and Economics; Department of Finance.

———. 2007c. "Economic Factors Affecting Home Mortgage Disclosure Act Reporting." Working paper. Fullerton, CA: California State University, Fullerton; College of Business and Economics; Department of Finance.

LaCour-Little, Michael, and Gregory H. Chun. 1999. "Third-Party Originators and Mortgage Prepayment Risk: An Agency Problem?" *Journal of Real Estate Research* 17(1–2): 55–70.

Larsen, Bradley. 2012. "Occupational Licensing and Quality: Distributional and Heterogeneous Effects in the Teaching Profession." Working paper. Cambridge, MA: Massachusetts Institute of Technology.

Law, Marc T., and Sukkoo Kim. 2005. "Specialization and Regulation: The Rise of Professionals and the Emergence of Occupational Licensing Regulation." *Journal of Economic History* 65(3): 723–756.

Lazear, Edward P., and Kathryn L. Shaw. 2007. "Personnel Economics: The Economist's View of Human Resources." *Journal of Economic Perspectives* 21(4): 91–114.

Lee, David, and Alexandre Mas. 2009. "Long-Run Impacts of Unions on Firms: New Evidence from Financial Markets, 1961–1999." NBER Working Paper No. 14709. Cambridge, MA: National Bureau of Economic Research.

Lewis, H. Gregg. 1986. *Union Relative Wage Effects: A Survey*. Chicago: University of Chicago Press.

Lipscomb, Joseph, and Chester W. Douglass. 1982. "A Political Economic Theory of the Dental Care Market." *American Journal of Public Health* 72(7): 665–675.

Lowenberg, Anton D., and Thomas D. Tinnin. 1992. "Professional versus Consumer Interests in Regulation: The Case of the U.S. Child Care Industry." *Applied Economics* 24(6): 571–580.

Manning, Alan. 2003. *Monopsony in Motion: Imperfect Competition in Labor Markets*. Princeton, NJ: Princeton University Press.

Marks, Mindy S., and Marc T. Law. 2012. "Certification vs. Licensure: Evidence from Registered and Practical Nurses in the United States, 1950–1970." Working paper. Riverside, CA: University of California, Riverside.

Martin, Caren S. 2008. "Rebuttal of the Report by the Institute for Justice Entitled *Designing Cartels: How Industry Insiders Cut Out Competition*." *Journal of Interior Design* 33(3): 1–49.

Matsudaira, Jordan D. 2010. "Monopsony in the Low-Wage Labor Market? Evidence from Minimum Nurse Staffing Regulations." Working paper. Ithaca, NY: Cornell University, Department of Policy Analysis and Management.

Maurizi, Alex. 1974. "Occupational Licensing and the Public Interest." *Journal of Political Economy* 82(2): 399–413.

McGarity, Mary. 2001. "A Broker's Market." *Mortgage Banking* 61(6): 32.

McGrath, Lee. 2012. "Model Economic Liberty Law: Occupational Licensing Relief and Job Creation Act." Working paper. Arlington, VA: Institute for Justice. http://ij.org/statutory-right-to-an-occupation (accessed May 17, 2013).

Miller, John W. 2004. "Europe's 'Outdated' Job Rules: Some Say Certification Requirements Hinder EU Productivity." *Wall Street Journal*, August 16, A:11.

Minnesota State Legislature. 2012. *HF 2002, as Introduced.* St. Paul, MN: Minnesota State Legislature. https://www.revisor.mn.gov/bills/text.php ?number=HF2002&session=ls87&version=list&session_number=0 &session_year=2012 (accessed July 22, 2013).

Mocan, H. Naci. 2001. "Can Consumers Detect Lemons? Information Asymmetry in the Market for Child Care." NBER Working Paper No. 8291. Cambridge, MA: National Bureau of Economic Research.

Moore, Michael J., and W. Kip Viscusi. 1990. *Compensation Mechanisms for Job Risks: Wages, Workers' Compensation, and Product Liability.* Princeton, NJ: Princeton University Press.

Mortgage Bankers Association. *National Delinquency Survey, 1979–2005.* Washington, DC: Mortgage Bankers Association. http://www.mortgage bankers.org/ResearchandForecasts/ProductsandSurveys/National DelinquencySurvey.htm (accessed May 17, 2013).

Motley, Wilma. 1988. "The Movement for Independent Practice of Dental Hygienists: From Evolution to Revolution." *Bulletin of the History of Dentistry* 36(2): 108–119.

National Association of Mortgage Brokers. 2013. *Frequently Asked Questions.* Plano, TX: National Association of Mortgage Brokers. http://www.namb .org/namb/FAQs1.asp?SnID=1916912282 (accessed May 29, 2013).

National Association for Regulatory Administration (NARA) and National Child Care Information and Technical Assistance Center (NCCIC). 2006. *The 2005 Child Care Licensing Study: Final Report.* Lexington, KY: National Association for Regulatory Administration. http://www.naralicensing .drivehq.com/2005_Licensing_Study/2005_Licensing_Study_Final _Report_Web.pdf (accessed May 1, 2013).

———. 2010. *The 2008 Child Care Licensing Study.* http://www.naralicensing .drivehq.com/2008_Licensing_Study/1005_2008_Child%20Care%20 Licensing%20Study_Full_Report.pdf (accessed May 1, 2013). Lexington, KY: National Association for Regulatory Administration.

National Center for Health Workforce Analysis. 2004. *The Professional Practice Environment of Dental Hygienists in the Fifty States and the District of Columbia, 2001.* Rockville, MD: National Center for Health Workforce Analysis. http://bhpr.hrsa.gov/healthworkforce/reports/dentalhygiene50statesdc .pdf (accessed April 25, 2013).

National Institute of Child Health and Human Development (NICHD) Early Child Care Research Network. 2002. "Child Care Structure → Process → Outcome: Direct and Indirect Effects of Child-Care Quality on Young Children's Development." *Psychological Science* 13(3): 199–206.

Nationwide Mortgage Licensing System and Registry. 2012. *A Nationwide View on State-Licensed Mortgage Entities: 2011 Quarters I, II, III, and IV.* Washington, DC: Conference of State Bank Supervisors. http://mortgage.nationwidelicensingsystem.org/about/Reports/2011%20Nationwide%20View%20of%20State-Licensed%20Mortgage%20Entities.pdf (accessed May 17, 2013).

Olson, David. 2007. *FHA: An Alternative to Nonprime.* Bothell, WA: Scotsman Guide Media. http://www.scotsmanguide.com/default.asp?ID=2194 (accessed May 1, 2013).

Olson, Mancur. 1965. *The Logic of Collective Action: Public Goods and the Theory of Groups.* Cambridge, MA: President and Fellows of Harvard College.

Pagliero, Mario. 2010. "Licensing Exam Difficulty and Entry Salaries in the U.S. Market for Lawyers." *British Journal of Industrial Relations* 48(4): 726–739.

Pagliero, Mario, and Edward Timmons. 2012. "Occupational Regulation in the European Legal Market." Working Paper No. 2844. Turin, Italy: Collegio Carlo Alberto. http://www.carloalberto.org/assets/working-papers/no.284.pdf (accessed May 1, 2013).

Pahl, Cynthia J. 2007. "A Compilation of State Mortgage Broker Laws and Regulations, 1996–2006." Community Affairs Report No. 2007-2. Minneapolis, MN: Federal Reserve Bank of Minneapolis. http://www.minneapolisfed.org/publications_papers/pub_display.cfm?id=4983 (accessed May 1, 2013).

Pappalardo, Janis K., and James M. Lacko. 2007. "Improving Consumer Mortgage Disclosures: An Empirical Assessment of Current and Prototype Disclosure Forms." Federal Trade Commission, Bureau of Economics Staff Report. Washington, DC: Federal Trade Commission. http://www.ftc.gov/be/workshops/mortgage/articles/lackopappalardo2007.pdf (accessed May 1, 2013).

Perlman, Selig. 1928. *A Theory of the Labor Movement.* New York: A. M. Kelley.

Perloff, Jeffrey M. 1980. "The Impact of Licensing Laws on Wage Changes in the Construction Industry." *Journal of Law and Economics* 23(2): 409–428.

Phillips, Deborah, and Edward Zigler. 1987. "The Checkered History of Federal Child Care Regulation." *Review of Research in Education* 14(1): 3–41.

Powell, Benjamin W., and Evgeny S. Vorotnikov. 2012. "Real Estate Continuing Education: Rent Seeking or Improvement in Service Quality?" *Eastern Economic Journal* 38(1): 57–73.

Princeton Data Improvement Initiative (PDII). 2008. *Princeton Data Improvement Initiative (PDII).* Princeton, NJ: Princeton University, Industrial Re-

lations Section. http://krueger.princeton.edu/akrueger/pages/princeton-data
-improvement-initiative-pdii (accessed May 17, 2013).

Raikes, H. Abigail, Helen Raikes, and Brian Wilcox. 2005. "Regulation, Subsidy Receipt, and Provider Characteristics: What Predicts Quality in Child
Care Homes?" *Early Childhood Research Quarterly* 20(2): 164–184.

Ramey, Alice. 2010. "Licensing Occupations." *Monthly Labor Review* 133(6):
56.

Reinhardt, Uwe E. 1972. "A Production Function for Physician Services." *Review of Economics and Statistics* 54(1): 55–66.

Rigby, Elizabeth, Rebecca M. Ryan, and Jeanne Brooks-Gunn. 2007. "Child
Care Quality in Different State Policy Contexts." *Journal of Policy Analysis
and Management* 26(4): 887–907.

Robertson, Colin. 2009. "Mortgage Broker Firms to Fall 72 Percent from
Peak." thetruthaboutmortgage.com, September 30. http://www.thetruth
aboutmortgage.com/mortgage-broker-firms-to-fall-72-percent-from-peak/
(accessed July 11, 2013).

Rostow, W. W. 1960. *The Stages of Economic Growth: A Non-Communist
Manifesto*. Cambridge: Cambridge University Press.

Rottenberg, Simon. 1980. "Introduction." In *Occupational Licensure and Regulation*, Simon Rottenberg, ed. Washington, DC: American Enterprise Institute, pp. 1–10.

Scarr, Sandra, and Richard A. Weinberg. 1986. "The Early Childhood Enterprise: Care and Education of the Young." *American Psychologist* 41(10):
1140–1146.

Schloemer, Ellen, Wei Li, Keith Ernst, and Kathleen Keest. 2006. *Losing
Ground: Foreclosures in the Subprime Market and Their Cost to Homeowners*. Durham, NC: Center for Responsible Lending.

Schmidt, James A. Jr. 2012. *New and Larger Costs of Monopoly and Tariffs*.
Economic Policy Paper 12-5. Minneapolis, MN: Federal Reserve Bank of
Minneapolis.

Schwieters, Jill, and David Harper. 2007. "Seven Steps toward Gaining Control of Your Labor Costs." *Healthcare Financial Management* 61(4): 76–
80. http://www.hfma.org/Content.aspx?id=2110 (accessed May 1, 2013).

Scully, Gerald W. 1974. "Pay and Performance in Major League Baseball."
American Economic Review 64(6): 915–930.

Sendrowicz, Bartosz. 2012. "Gowin Otwiera Zawody." Gazeta Wyborcza,
March 5. http://wyborcza.pl/1,75478,11282066,Gowin_otwiera_zawody
.html (accessed May 16, 2013).

Shapiro, Carl. 1986. "Investment, Moral Hazard, and Occupational Licensing." *Review of Economic Studies* 53(5): 843–862.

Shepard, Lawrence. 1978. "Licensing Restrictions and the Cost of Dental Care." *Journal of Law and Economics* 21(1): 187–201.

Shi, Lan. 2012. "The Effect of Mortgage Broker Licensing on Loan Origination Standards and Defaults: Evidence from the U.S. Mortgage Market 2000–2007." Working paper. Seattle, WA: University of Washington, Department of Economics.

Shimberg, Benjamin, Barbara F. Esser, and Daniel H. Kruger. 1973. *Occupational Licensing: Practices and Policies*. Washington, DC: Public Affairs Press.

Shleifer, Andrei. 2011. "Efficient Regulation." In *Regulation vs. Litigation: Perspectives from Economics and Law*, Daniel P. Kessler, ed. Chicago: University of Chicago Press for the National Bureau of Economic Research, pp. 27–43.

Shonkoff, Jack P., and Deborah A. Phillips, eds. 2000. *From Neurons to Neighborhoods: The Science of Early Childhood Development*. Washington, DC: National Academies Press.

Shultz, George P. 1995. "Economics in Action: Ideas, Institutions, Policies." *American Economic Review* 85(2): 1–8.

Sichelman, Lew. 2003. "Brokers Dominate Lending." *Realty Times*, July 2. http://realtytimes.com/rtpages/20030702_lending.htm (accessed May 2, 2013).

Simonsen, Richard J. 1991. "New Materials on the Horizon." *Journal of the American Dental Association* 122(7): 24–31.

Smith, Adam. 1937. *The Wealth of Nations*. First Modern Library Edition. New York: Random House. First published 1776 by W. Strahan and T. Cadeli.

Smith, Robert. 1976. *The Occupational Safety and Health Act: Its Goals and Its Achievements*. Evaluative Study Series. Washington, DC: American Enterprise Institute for Public Policy Research.

Smolensky, Eugene, and Jennifer Appleton Gootman, eds. 2003. *Working Families and Growing Kids: Caring for Children and Adolescents*. Washington, DC: National Academies Press.

Tanta. 2007. "Mortgage Origination Channels for UberNerds." *Calculated Risk* (blog), September 7. http://calculatedrisk.blogspot.com/2007/09/mortgage-origination-channels-for.html (accessed May 29, 2013).

Tenn, Steven Aaron. 2001. "Three Essays on the Relationship between Migration and Occupational Licensing." Unpublished dissertation. Department of Economics, University of Chicago.

Thaler, Richard H., and Cass R. Sunstein. 2008. *Nudge: Improving Decisions about Health, Wealth, and Happiness*. New Haven, CT: Yale University Press.

Thornton, Robert J., and Edward J. Timmons. 2013. "Licensing One of the

World's Oldest Professions: Massage." *Journal of Law and Economics* 56(2): 371–388.

Timmons, Edward J., and Robert J. Thornton. 2008. "The Effects of Licensing on the Wages of Radiologic Technologists." *Journal of Labor Research* 29(4): 333–346.

———. 2010. "The Licensing of Barbers in the USA." *British Journal of Industrial Relations* 48(4): 740–757.

U.S. Census Bureau. 2008. *Who's Minding the Kids? Child Care Arrangements: Spring 2005—Detailed Tables.* Washington, DC: U.S. Department of Commerce, Census Bureau. http://www.census.gov/hhes/childcare/data/sipp/2005/tables.html (accessed May 2, 2013).

———. 2013. *American Community Survey—Data and Documentation.* Washington, DC: U.S. Department of Commerce, Census Bureau. http://www.census.gov/acs/www/data_documentation/data_main/ (accessed June 3, 2013).

U.S. Department of Housing and Urban Development. 2002. *Economic Analysis and Initial Regulatory Flexibility Analysis for RESPA Proposed Rule to Simplify and Improve the Process of Obtaining Mortgages to Reduce Settlement Costs to Consumers.* Washington, DC: U.S. Department of Housing and Urban Development, Office of Policy Development and Research. http://www.compliancetimes.org/pdfs/ea-chapters.pdf (accessed May 17, 2013).

U.S. Department of the Treasury and U.S. Department of Defense. 2012. *Supporting our Military Families: Best Practices for Streamlining Occupational Licensing across State Lines.* Washington, DC: U.S. Department of the Treasury and U.S. Department of Defense.

Vandell, Deborah Lowe, and Barbara Wolfe. 2002. "Child Care Quality: Does It Matter and Does It Need to Be Improved?" In *Early Childhood Care and Education: What Are States Doing?*, Karen Bogenschneider, Bettina Friese, Karla Balling, and Jessica Mills, eds. Wisconsin Family Impact Seminar Briefing Report No. 17. Madison, WI: University of Wisconsin, Center for Excellence in Family Studies, pp. 1–11.

Viscusi, W. Kip, Joseph E. Harrington Jr., and John M. Vernon. 2005. *Economics of Regulation and Antitrust.* 4th ed. Cambridge, MA: MIT Press.

Wanchek, Tanya. 2010. "Dental Hygiene Regulation and Access to Oral Healthcare: Assessing the Variation across the U.S. States." *British Journal of Industrial Relations* 48(4): 706–725.

Weil, David. 2001. "Assessing OSHA Performance: New Evidence from the Construction Industry." *Journal of Policy Analysis and Management* 20(4): 651–674.

Wetterhall, Scott, James D. Bader, Barri B. Burrus, Jessica Y. Yee, and Daniel A. Shugars. 2010. *Evaluation of the Dental Health Aide Therapist Workforce Model in Alaska: Final Report.* Research Triangle Park, NC: RTI International.

Wholesale Access. 2005. "New Research about Mortgage Brokers Published." Press release, July 28. Columbia, MD: Access Mortgage Research and Consulting (formerly Wholesale Access).

———. 2007. "New Broker Research Published." Press release, August 17. Columbia, MD: Access Mortgage Research and Consulting.

Woodward, Susan E. 2003. "Consumer Confusion in the Mortgage Market." Working paper. Sonoma, CA: Sand Hill Econometrics. www.sandhillecon .com/pdf/consumer_confusion.pdf (accessed May 2, 2013).

Zimbalist, Andrew. 1992. *Baseball and Billions: A Probing Look inside the Big Business of Our National Pastime.* New York: Basic Books.

Author

Morris M. Kleiner is a professor at the Humphrey School of Public Affairs, and he teaches at the Center for Human Resources and Labor Studies, both at the University of Minnesota–Twin Cities. He has received many teaching awards including university- and school-wide ones for classes in public affairs, business, and economics. He is a research associate in labor studies with the National Bureau of Economic Research in Cambridge, Massachusetts. He is currently also serving as a visiting scholar in the economic research department at the Federal Reserve Bank of Minneapolis. He has been a professor at the University of Kansas, an associate in employment policy with the Brookings Institution, a visiting scholar in the Harvard University economics department, a visiting researcher in the Industrial Relations Section at Princeton University, a visiting scholar at the W.E. Upjohn Institute for Employment Research, and a research fellow at the London School of Economics. He received a doctorate in economics from the University of Illinois. He began his research on occupational licensing at the U.S. Department of Labor in 1976, while working for the Brookings Institution. His work has been supported by the National Science Foundation, the Department of Labor, the Department of Health and Human Services, the United Kingdom Commission for Employment and Skills, and the Upjohn Institute for Employment Research. In the United States, Professor Kleiner has provided advice on occupational regulation policy to the Federal Trade Commission, the Council of Economic Advisers, the Department of the Treasury, the Department of Justice, the Board of Governors of the Federal Reserve System, federal interagency statistical panels, state legislatures, and occupational licensing associations. Internationally, he has provided testimony on occupational regulation to United Kingdom cabinet officers and their parliamentary committees, to cabinet officials responsible for regulation in Australia, and to officials of the European Union. This is his second book for the Upjohn Institute on occupational regulation; the first, titled *Licensing Occupations: Ensuring Quality or Restricting Competition?,* was published in 2006.

Index

The italic letters *b*, *f*, *n*, or *t* following a page number indicate a box, figure, note, or table on that page. Double italic letters mean more than one such item on a single page.

Arizona, 186*t*
   electrician regulation in, 144*t*, 236*t*
   regulation changes in, 100*t*, 226–227
   type of labor market regulation in, 26,
      27*t*
Arkansas, 186*t*
   regulated occupations in, 100*t*, 236*t*
   type of labor market regulation in, 26,
      27*t*
ARMs (Adjustable Rate Mortgages), 47
Asian Americans, 30*t*, 105*t*
   mortgage refinancing and, 75–77, 76*t*
ASID. *See* American Society of Interior
      Designers
Attorneys. *See* Lawyers
Australia, occupational licensing in, 224

Baby-sitting. *See* Child care services
Barbers, as universally regulated, 210,
      214, 218
Bethel Community Services Foundation,
      report funded by, 176–177
Better Business Bureau, consumer
      complaints and, 39
Black Americans. *See* African Americans
BLS. *See* Bureau of Labor Statistics
Branstad, Gov. Terry, of Iowa, regulatory
      legislation and, 222–223,
      227*nn*2–3
Britain. *See* United Kingdom (UK)
BSL Inc., Simoneaux v., as health and
      safety lawsuit, 24, 41*nn*16–17
Bureau of Labor Statistics (BLS), 13*n*1,
      17
   employment data from, 26, 36*f*
   industrial safety data from, 129, 144
   wage data from, 26, 33, 33*f*

California, 78, 136, 186*t*
   regulated occupations in, 100*t*, 171,
      175, 236*t*
   type of labor market regulation in, 26,
      27*t*
Census of Fatal Occupational Injuries
      (CFOI), 249–250
   data from, 134*f*, 144, 146, 147*t*, 169*n*7

Center-based care, 102, 208
   family-based *vs.,* 89, 96, 230*t*–231*t*,
      232*t*–233*t*
Center for Construction Research and
      Training, 132, 133–134, 169*n*1
Certification
   governmental role in, 3, 145*t*, 213,
      219–220, 221
   interprofessional agreements on,
      18–19, 51
   requirements for, 3, 29*f*
   titling act and, 19–20, 39, 41*nn*4–8
   wages with, 40, 207, 213
   workforce with, 8*t*, 13*n*3, 224
CFOI. *See* Census of Fatal Occupational
      Injuries
Child care services
   characteristics of personnel for, 99,
      103*t*
   enrollment in, 94, 109–110, 112–117,
      116*t*, 124
   provision of, and family structure, 86,
      90, 104, 105*t*
   quality of, with regulation, 90–92,
      118–122, 208
   types of, 89, 94, 102, 104, 105*t*, 115,
      116*t*
      (*see also* Center-based care)
Child care services, regulation of,
      85–125
   data sources for, 94, 95
   effects of, 87–88, 95, 99, 123–124,
      208
      (*see also under* Wages; Child care
      services, enrollment in;
      Educational attainment)
   evolution of, 85, 89–90
   influence on economic factors, 92–94,
      124
   states and, 88–89, 96–99, 98*f*,
      100*t*–101*t*
China, licensed *vs.* unlicensed workers
      and wages in, 7
Closed shops, 215, 221
Coal Mine Safety Act, 129
Collective bargaining, 2–3, 5, 215

Missouri, *cont.*
  type of labor market regulation in, 26,
    27*t*
Monopsony markets
  regulation and consistent conditions
    with, 180–183, 182*f*
  skill levels and wage relationship in,
    178, 180, 200, 201, 201*b*–202*b*
Montana, 79, 186*t*
  regulated occupations in, 100*t*, 175,
    237*t*
  statutory provisions for mortgage
    brokers in, 44, 56, 57*t*
  type of labor market regulation in, 26,
    27*t*
Mortgage brokers, 43–53, 78–84
  evaluation criteria for, 12, 45, 49–51
  home loans by, 48–49, 66–78,
    83*nn*15–16
  as independents in service industry,
    43–46, 82*n*3
  occupational evolution of, 43–44,
    46–49, 80, 82*nn*6–7
  regulatory rationale for, 51–53, 53*t*
Mortgage brokers, regulatory influence
    on, 54–78
  bonding of, 44, 57–59, 62–64, 63*t*,
    65*t*, 78–80, 82*n*4, 83*nn*10–11,
    207–208
    (*see also* Surety bonds)
  consumer market outcomes of, 43,
    66–78
  labor market outcomes of, 59–65, 61*t*,
    63*t*, 65*t*, 83*nn*13–14
    (*see also* Employment; Wages)
  licenses for, required by states, 11*f*, 12
  MSAs *vs.* state by state and, 77–78,
    84*nn*22–23
  state by state level of, over time, 44,
    54–59, 82*n*8, 83*n*9
Mortgage foreclosures
  licensing and, 66, 68–69
  rates of, 81, 208
Mortgage lenders
  banks with, 47, 82*n*7

roles of, *vs.* mortgage brokers, 46–47,
    49, 82*nn*6–7
Mortgages, originators of, 73–74, 78,
    83*n*17, 253–254

NAMB. *See* National Association of
    Mortgage Brokers
National Association of Child Care
    Resource and Referral Agencies,
    licensing goals of, 90
National Association of Mortgage
    Brokers (NAMB)
  broker wages from, as check on ACS,
    60–62, 61*t*, 83*n*12
  roles in industry distinguished by,
    46–47
National Center for Health Workforce
    Analysis, DHPPI from, 177*f*–178*f*,
    184–185, 186*t*
National Kitchen and Bath Association,
    licensing of interior designers and,
    23
National Labor Relations Act,
    amendment to, 215
National Longitudinal Survey of Youth
    (NLSY), 253
  early childhood services data from,
    94, 95, 106–108, 115–117, 116*t*,
    117*t*, 119–122, 122*t*–123*t*, 208
Native Americans, licensing in tribal
    lands of, 224
Nebraska, 186*t*
  regulated occupations in, 100*t*, 143,
    145*t*, 175, 237*t*
  type of labor market regulation in, 26,
    27*t*
Neil v. City of New York, as health and
    safety lawsuit, 24, 41*nn*10–13
Netherlands, occupational licensing
    in, 218, 224
Nevada
  regulated occupations in, 56, 57*t*,
    100*t*, 237*t*
  type of labor market regulation in, 16,
    26, 27*t*, 31, 32*t*

U.S. Department of Labor, 13*n*3, 251
BLS within (*see* Bureau of Labor
Statistics)
U.S. law and legislation
banking, 69, 73–78, 84*nn*20–21
employment, 51, 215
health and safety, 129, 139
Utah
regulated occupations in, 56, 57*t*,
101*t*, 238*t*
regulatory legislation in, 222, 226–
227
type of labor market regulation in, 26,
28*t*

Vermont
regulated occupations in, 101*t*, 238*t*
type of labor market regulation in, 26,
28*t*
Virginia, 186*t*
plumber regulation in, 142–143, 145*t*
some other regulated occupations in,
101*t*, 238*t*
type of labor market regulation in, 26,
28*t*

Wages
hourly, of various service providers,
30, 30*t*, 188*t*
licensed *vs.* unlicensed workers and,
7, 216
Wages, influence of regulation on, 2, 5,
6, 12, 13*n*4, 211*t*, 214, 215
child care providers and, 108–109,
111–112, 113*t*, 114*t*, 123, 125*n*2
construction industry, 127–128, 149–
151, 167, 169*nn*8–9
dental services and, 180–183, 182*f*,
201*b*–202*b*
interior designers and, 17, 25, 26,
30–34, 30*t*, 32*t*, 33*f*, 40, 207
mortgage brokers and, 60–62, 61*t*, 64,
65*t*, 81, 83*nn*12–14
theories on effects of, 137–138
Washington, DC. *See* District of
Columbia

Washington (State), 186*t*
regulated occupations in, 101*t*, 174,
175, 238*t*
type of labor market regulation in, 26,
28*t*
Wealth of nations, The (Smith),
craftsmen's restricted liberty in, 2
West Virginia, 186*t*
regulated occupations in, 101*t*, 145*t*,
238*t*
type of labor market regulation in, 26,
28*t*
Westat (firm), as survey provider, 7, 8*f*,
13*n*3
White Americans, 105*t*
occupations of, 103*t*, 150*t*
Wisconsin, 39
regulated occupations in, 101*t*, 238*t*
type of labor market regulation in, 26,
28*t*
Women in the workforce, 30*t*, 103*t*, 150*t*,
188*t*
mortgage refinancing and, 75–77, 76*t*
mothers as, 86, 89–90, 105*t*
Work slowdown, as trade union action, 5
Worker compensation laws, 139, 157,
167
Workforce
health and safety of, 2, 129, 139, 167
(*see also* Workplaces)
licensed, in U.S., 1, 8*f*, 8*t*, 13*n*1,
13*n*3, 210
nonunion workers in, 5, 7, 8*t*
occupational mobility of, 12, 210,
212, 223
See also Women in the workforce
Workplaces, conditions in, 128, 144, 146
Wyoming
mortgage brokers and statutory
regulations in, 44, 56, 57*t*
other regulated occupations in, 101*t*,
144*t*, 145*t*, 238*t*
type of labor market regulation in, 26,
28*t*

About the Institute

The W.E. Upjohn Institute for Employment Research is a nonprofit research organization devoted to finding and promoting solutions to employment-related problems at the national, state, and local levels. It is an activity of the W.E. Upjohn Unemployment Trustee Corporation, which was established in 1932 to administer a fund set aside by Dr. W.E. Upjohn, founder of The Upjohn Company, to seek ways to counteract the loss of employment income during economic downturns.

The Institute is funded largely by income from the W.E. Upjohn Unemployment Trust, supplemented by outside grants, contracts, and sales of publications. Activities of the Institute comprise the following elements: 1) a research program conducted by a resident staff of professional social scientists; 2) a competitive grant program, which expands and complements the internal research program by providing financial support to researchers outside the Institute; 3) a publications program, which provides the major vehicle for disseminating the research of staff and grantees, as well as other selected works in the field; and 4) an Employment Management Services division, which manages most of the publicly funded employment and training programs in the local area.

The broad objectives of the Institute's research, grant, and publication programs are to 1) promote scholarship and experimentation on issues of public and private employment and unemployment policy, and 2) make knowledge and scholarship relevant and useful to policymakers in their pursuit of solutions to employment and unemployment problems.

Current areas of concentration for these programs include causes, consequences, and measures to alleviate unemployment; social insurance and income maintenance programs; compensation; workforce quality; work arrangements; family labor issues; labor-management relations; and regional economic development and local labor markets.